Information Sources in

Environmental Protection

Guides to Information Sources

A series under the General Editorship of
Ia C. McIlwaine,
M.W. Hill and
Nancy J. Williamson

*This series was known previously as 'Butterworths Guides to Information
Sources'.*

Other titles available include:

Information Sources in Architecture and Construction (Second edition)
  edited by Valerie J. Nurcombe
Information Sources in Chemistry (Fourth edition)
  edited by R.T. Bottle and J. F. B. Rowland
Information Sources in Physics (Third edition)
  edited by Dennis F. Shaw
Information Sources in Engineering
  edited by Ken Mildren and Peter Hicks
Information Sources in Finance and Banking
  by Ray Lester
Information Sources in Grey Literature (Third edition)
  by C.P. Auger
Information Sources in Music
  edited by Lewis Foreman
Information Sources in the Life Sciences (Fourth edition)
  edited by H.V. Wyatt
Information Sources in Sport and Leisure
  edited by Michele Shoebridge
Information Sources in Patents
  edited by C.P. Auger
Information Sources for the Press and Broadcast Media
  edited by Selwyn Eagle
Information Sources in Information Technology
  edited by David Haynes
Information Sources in Pharmaceuticals
  edited by W.R. Pickering
Information Sources in Metallic Materials
  edited by M.N. Patten
Information Sources in the Earth Sciences (Second edition)
  edited by David N. Wood, Joan E. Hardy and Anthony P. Harvey
Information Sources in Cartography
  edited by C.R. Perkins and R.B. Barry
Information Sources in Polymers and Plastics
  edited by R.T. Adkins
Information Sources in Economics (Second edition)
  edited by John Fletcher

Information Sources in
Environmental Protection

Edited by
Selwyn Eagle
and
Judith Deschamps

London · Melbourne · Munich · New Providence, N.J.

British Library Cataloguing in Publication Data
A catalogue record for this title is available from the British Library

Library of Congress Cataloging-in-Publication Data
A catalog record for this book is available from the Library of Congress

Published by Bowker-Saur, Maypole House, Maypole Road,
East Grinstead, West Sussex RH19 1HU, UK
Tel: +44(0)1342 330100 Fax: +44(0)1342 330191
E-mail: lis@bowker-saur.co.uk
Internet Website: http://www.bowker-saur.co.uk/service/

ISBN 1-85739-062-8

Cover design by Calverts Press
Typesetting by GCS
Printed on acid-free paper
Printed and bound in Great Britain by Antony Rowe Ltd, Chippenham

Series editors' foreword

The second half of the 20th century has been characterized by the recognition that our style of life depends on acquiring and using information effectively. It has always been so, but only in the information society has the extent of the dependence been recognized and the development of technologies for handling information become a priority. These modern technologies enable us to store more information, to select and process parts of the store more skilfully and transmit the product more rapidly than we would have dreamt possible only 40 years ago. Yet the irony still exists that, while we are able to do all this and are assailed from all sides by great masses of information, ensuring that one has what one needs just when one wants it is frequently just as difficult as ever. Knowledge may, as Johnson said in the well known quotation, be of two kinds, but information, in contrast, is of many kinds and most of it is, for each individual, knowable only after much patient searching.

The aim of each Guide in this series is simple. It is to reduce the time which needs to be spent on that patient searching; to recommend the best standing point and sources mostly likely to yield the desired information. Like all subject guides, the sources discussed have had to be selected, and the criteria for selection will be given by the individual editors and will differ from subject to subject. However, the overall objective is constant; that of providing a way into a subject to those new to the field or to identify major new or possibly unexplored sources to those already familiar with it.

The great increase in new sources of information and the overwhelming input of new information from the media, advertising, meetings and conferences, letters, internal reports, office memoranda, magazines, junk mail, electronic mail, fax, bulletin boards etc. inevitably tend to make one reluctant to add to the load on the mind and memory by consulting books and journals. Yet they, and the other traditional types of printed material, remain for many purposes the most reliable sources of information. Despite all the information that is instantly accessible via the new technologies one still has to look things up in databooks, monographs, journals, patent specifications, standards, reports both official and commercial, and on maps and in atlases. Permanent recording of facts, theories and opinions is still carried out primarily by publishing in printed form. Musicians still work from printed scores even though they are helped by sound recordings. Sailors still use printed charts and tide tables even though they have radar and sonar equipment.

However, thanks to computerized indexes, online and CD-ROM, searching the huge bulk of technical literature to draw up a list of references can be undertaken reasonably quickly. The result, all too often, can still be a formidably long list, of which a knowledge of the nature and structure of information sources in that field can be used to put in order of likely value.

It is rarely necessary to consult everything that has been published on the topic of a search. When attempting to prove that an invention is genuinely novel, a complete search may seem necessary, but even then it is common to search only obvious sources and leave it to anyone wishing to oppose the grant of a patent to bear the cost of hunting for a prior disclosure in some obscure journal. Usually, much proves to be irrelevant to the particular aspect of our interest and whatever is relevant may be unsound. Some publications are sadly lacking in important detail and present broad generalizations flimsily bridged with arches of waffle. In any academic field there is a 'pecking order' of journals so that articles in one journal may be assumed to be of a higher or lower calibre than those in another. Those experienced in the field know these things. The research scientist soon learns, as it is part of his training, the degree of reliance he can place on information from co-workers elsewhere, on reports of research by new and (to him) unknown researchers, on data compilations and on manufacturers of equipment. The information worker, particularly when working in a field other than his own, faces very serious problems as he tries to compile, probably from several sources, a report on which his client may base important actions. Even the librarian, faced only with recommending two or three books or journal articles, meets the same problem though less acutely.

In the Bowker-Saur Guides to Information Sources we aim to bring you the knowledge and experience of specialists in the field. Each author regularly uses the information sources and services described and any tricks of the trade that the author has learnt are passed on.

Nowadays, two major problems face those who are embarking upon research or who are in charge of collections of information of every kind. One is the increasingly specialized knowledge of the user and the concomitant ignorance of other potentially useful disciplines. The second problem is the trend towards cross-disciplinary studies. This has led to a great mixing of academic programmes – and a number of imprecisely defined fields of study. Courses are offered in Environmental Studies, Women's Studies, Communication Studies or Area Studies, and these are the forcing ground for research. The editors are only too aware of the difficulties raised by those requiring information from such hybrid subject fields and this approach, too, is being handled in the series alongside the traditional 'hard disciplines'.

Guides to the literature have a long and honoured history. Marion Spicer of SRIS recently drew to our attention a guide written in 1891 for engineers. No doubt there are even earlier ones. Nowadays, with the information and even the publishing fields changing quite frequently, it is necessary to update guides every few years and this we do in this present Series.

Michael Hill
Ia McIlwaine
Nancy Williamson

About the contributors

Monica Barlow worked in publishing before completing a PhD at the University of Bristol. She specializes in environmental information research and consultancy, and now acts as Projects Manager for ECO Environmental Information Trust, a UK charity working to improve the provision of environmental information.

Mary Frances Campana is the Technical Librarian at Intel Corp. in New Mexico: she is the former Director of the Desert Research Institute Library.

Judith Deschamps began her career in the analytical library of a pharmaceutical company and has recently retired from her post in the HQ Library of the Department of the Environment. Her special interests are international information exchange and grey literature in environmental protection.

Selwyn Eagle was Chief Librarian, BBC Data, from 1983–89, responsible for the print based library and news information services provided for the TV, Radio, and World Services as well as the Pronunciation Unit. He had previously served on the library staffs of two Government departments and two Polytechnics, and had worked in a public library service.

Ian H. Flindell is a member of the academic staff at the institute of Sound and Vibration Research at the University of Southampton. He has been active in the field of subjective acoustics for 20 years, with wide experience of fundamental research questions, applied consultancy tasks, and both national and international standards committee work.

John Goodier has worked for over 20 years in information management and reference librarianship in several central government departments. His work has covered aspects of agriculture, environment protection, and occupational and environmental health. He now works as an information consultant and broker.

Jan McHarry has been working as an independent environmental consultant since leaving Friends of the Earth (UK) in 1990. Since 1992 she has been working as Development Consultant for the National Recycling Forum and is also Convenor of the Information Resources Taskforce. Amongst her many varied contributions to books, reports and guides, she is the author of *Waste and Recycling* (1993).

Graham McKenna has been Principal Librarian with the Natural Environment Research Council (NERC) since 1984 and is responsible for the management of the library service of the British Geological Survey (BGS) at Keyworth. After joining NERC he oversaw the building of the new BGS Library and the transfer of the Library's collections. Previously, he worked with Leeds City Libraries where he was Librarian of the Library of Commerce, Science and Technology for 10 years.

Diana Maslin was formerly Manager of the Waste Management Information Bureau at AEA Technology, Harwell. She is a qualified Librarian and has been working with waste management information since 1986. In addition to answering enquiries from all over the world, she has been responsible for the development of the Waste Info database.

Linda Noble is Deputy Head of Library and Information Services of the Plymouth Marine laboratory and Marine Biological Association, and head of its marine Pollution Information Centre. During the past 15 years she has been closely concerned with European Commission and United Nations Environment Programme environmental data banks, and with the development of computerized information services in Plymouth. She is Editor of *Marine Pollution Research Titles* and *Estuaries and Coastal Waters of the British Isles*, an annual bibliography.

John O'Hara graduated in Physics from Leeds University followed by an Msc in Radiation and Environmental Protection at the University of Surrey. He worked in environmental consultancy for a number of years before joining the Institution of Chemical Engineers as its first Environmental Officer. Since 1991 he has been Information Officer for the Environmental Law Group at London based solicitors Denton Hall. He has contributed to the British Library Publication *Environmental Information: A Guide to Sources*.

Ian Pettman is Head of Library and Information Services for both the Freshwater Biological Association and the Institute of Freshwater Ecology. He has been active in the field of freshwater information for over 22 years and is Chairman of the Britain and Ireland Association of Aquatic Sciences Libraries and Information Centres (BIASLIC) as well as the European equivalent (EURASLIC).

John Smith was County Librarian of Cumbria from 1974 to 1994. He was awarded Entrepreneur of the Year in 1993 for work on environmental information. He was responsible for establishing the Cumbria Environmental Information Network (CEIN) in 1990 and has been Chairman from that date. He has published numerous articles on management and librarianship.

Shirley M. Smith was formerly the Director of the Desert Research Institute Library and has been with the DRI library from its inception.

Tim Treuherz is a qualified librarian and a researcher with an interest in freedom of information. He is currently training to be a barrister.

Alan Varley was Head of Library and Information Services at the Plymouth Marine laboratory and Marine Biological Association until his retirement in 1992. Since the 1970s he has collaborated with United Nations and other agencies in international and regional marine information programmes, and is the founder member of the British and European associations of aquatic sciences libraries and information centres. His publications include *Marine Information Centre Development: An Introductory Manual* (1991).

Katherine Wesenberg is the librarian at the national Wildlife Health Centre in Madison, Wisconsin. Previously, she was the librarian at Anaquest, a division of the British Oxygen Corporation. She received her Master's of Library Science degree from the University of Wisconsin.

Dorothy Williams is a reader and researcher in the School of Information and Media, The Robert Gordon University. Previously, she was involved in research into public access to environmental information, and her experience as a researcher in the natural sciences, combined with her later research into the development of information skills, has helped form her more recent interest in the management of environmental information and its impact on decision making.

Heather Wiseman obtained an MSc in Information Science in 1977 and since then has worked in poisons information at the National Poisons Unit. After working for many years in the National Poisons Information Service, she now provides administrative and information support to the Unit's research programme. She is an active participant in the Poisons Centre Working Group for the Project to develop a Poisons Information Package for Developing Countries.

Helen Woolston is Environmental Information Specialist for the BOC Group. Previously she was responsible for the day-to-day running of the British Libraries Environmental information service. She was a joint author of *Environmental Information: A Guide to Sources and how to Find Information – Environment,* and has edited *Environmental Auditing: An Introduction and Tactical Guide and Business* and *Environmental Accountability.*

Contents

Part III Practicalities

Part IV Controls and public awareness

Introduction

SELWYN EAGLE

Definitions

This book attempts to provide a narrative introduction to the principal sources of information on the subject of environmental protection and such relevant information about the natural environment as is necessary for understanding the problems raised. The principal sources are a selected, rather than a comprehensive, group. These may be printed books and journals, available in online or other electronic form or, in some cases, be societies or institutions. Although a few lists are included in the work, the main aim has been to give some evaluative description of the position and usefulness of the individual sources cited, within the considerable array of information available on this vast and amorphous subject.

Pervasiveness

The environment is eternal, ubiquitous and pervasive. If it were an enemy, there would be no hiding place. For the purposes of this book, some kind of 'defence' was needed in order to contain the subject in a manageable form. It therefore surveys the relatively limited area of the natural environment, as opposed to one which is sometimes known as the built environment. Edging towards more specific matters, consideration is given to exploitation of naturally occurring resources; the disposal of wastes and pollutants arising from manufacturing and other processes; and the effects of these, in turn, on such basic requirements for life as atmosphere and water.

Areas of disagreement/agreement

The assumption, so far, has been that we are dealing with an environment which is beneficial not only to mankind, but which will support all life. There are those such as James Lovelock who has argued through his Gaia theories that whatever mankind does, the earth itself will continue as a live and evolving geological planet, but may not always produce the conditions which support all kinds of life. Environmental protectionists hope to avoid this situation. Towards this end they gather information of the kind discussed here, to measure and describe the extent to which mankind is actively destroying its own environment.

Whose environment is it?

To adapt a cliché, one nation's march towards industrialization may mean the rape of another's natural resources. Uncontrolled emissions into the atmosphere will not necessarily subsequently rain down upon those who caused them, but possibly upon others, who may be defenceless against them. One might hope that sensible, caring humans would see the problems being caused for others in these situations and take alleviating action. Political considerations might well allow some alleviation, but may exclude any more complete or permanent action.

Priorities

In a developing economy, the bicycle may be seen as a symbol of poverty and degradation. The political aim might be for everyone to own their own motor car. In a developed economy, at the same time, all motor vehicles may be seen as transports of death and the bicycle as a potent weapon in a war against the pollution of vehicle exhausts.

Decisions

If the political system allows argument and discussion, then information may be of some help in deciding what is necessary, what is tolerable, what is sustainable and what is allowable, while simultaneously preserving all forms of life. There are few absolutes or clear-cut alternatives. There is usually scope for research and room for moderation and compromise. Such activities feed on the kind of information illustrated in this book.

Content of the work

The pervasive nature of the subject, alluded to above, has resulted in marginal overlaps between different chapters. For example, Chapter 14, by Tim Treuherz, mentions the following matters which are referred to in earlier chapters: pressure groups (Chapter 2), water (Chapter 5), contaminated land (Chapter 12) and law (Chapter 13).

There are also links from the chapters on poisons and pollutants to those on the atmosphere and water. Waste management, besides being covered in Chapter 7 by Diana Maslin is also touched upon by Helen Woolston in Chapter 11.

Historical aspects of the subject are included in Chapter 2 by Jan MacHarry and Chapter 17 by Dorothy Williams; touched upon by John Goodier in Chapters 10 and 12 and, initially and very briefly, by John O'Hara in Chapter 13.

Towards the end of the work Monica Barlow (Chapter 15), John Smith (Chapter 16) and Dorothy Williams (Chapter 17) address questions relating to dissemination of environmental information. They also cover some of the points about the spread and availability of information, raised in the opening paragraphs of this Introduction. Though these chapters form the later part of the book, those new to the subject may prefer to read one or more of them prior to reading the earlier and more specific chapters.

Organization contact details are listed in the Appendix. Where appropriate some addresses may also appear in specific chapters.

The index will lead readers to other multiple references to topics of interest.

Other works in the series

Obviously the references given throughout the work are intended to guide readers to more detailed and substantial treatment of the topics covered. Graham McKenna (Chapter 9) and John Goodier (Chapters 10 and 12) have both cited other works from the Guides to Information Sources series of which this book forms a part. In addition to cited references, readers may refer to p. ii where the series is listed. The title on *Architecture and Construction* covers the built environment. Other titles which cover areas such as the sciences, technology, engineering, energy and education may contain references to further relevant and detailed information.

The Internet

Several chapter authors have referred to online databases and to CD-

ROM versions of these (or of printed sources). Katherine Wesenberg (Chapter 4) and Monica Barlow (Chapter 15) have given references to addresses on the World Wide web.

There is a large number of Web pages displaying 'green' and environmental information, which might justify a Guide to Information Sources of its own. The Internet is not a static information field and, with hypertext and browsing software, aims to allow users instant access to up-to-date information across a wide range of related topics, in one place and at one time. In spite of 'websurfing' being a preferred access method, many addresses or web springboards are still distributed to would-be users in printed form.

For example, at the time of going to press it has been announced, (*ENDS Report* (1995), 249, October 8), that Friends of the Earth has extended a 'right to know' campaign by making data from the Chemical Release Inventory available at: http://www.foe.co.uk/cri. The aim is to call for more comprehensive data similar to those provided in the US Toxic Release Inventory. Publication of the CRI in a conventional fashion would not have been possible. The Alternative Technology Association provided readers of its journal, *Clean Slate* (1995), 18, autumn, 12), with a list of 10 web springboards for sites dealing with renewables technology. Readers were given thumbnail sketches of the sites located all over the globe and told that the links provided by each one would lead them to hundreds more on related topics.

An attitude which I have often adopted towards reference books is one which urges the reader to use index, contents page, running headlines, etc., and not to read the work from cover to cover. Due again to the pervasive element, I hope readers of this work may be tempted to read more than just the apparently most relevant chapter. However, the fact that each is written by a separate author does enable chapters to be read in relative isolation.

PART ONE

The Official and the Unofficial

CHAPTER ONE

Government policies, national and international

JUDITH DESCHAMPS

UK government sources

Introduction

Recent changes in the way government is organized have had a profound effect on the methods that have to be used to obtain official information. Also, as the extent of informal publishing increases, there is a growing number of publications issued in a less than controlled fashion by government which can be thought of as 'official grey literature'. In addition to the printed word, the rapidly increasing use of information superhighways (notably the Internet) means that information may not even exist other than electronically. The wide subject scope of 'environment' leads to the production of a vast range of documentation from a large number of government departments and agencies.

As an example of change, it used to be true that British government publications fitted neatly into two groups, parliamentary and non-parliamentary, and that most were published by HMSO. Now neat and tidy distinctions are being eroded and it is less certain that HMSO will be the publisher, although it has the first option on a department's publications.

Changes in the administrative structure of the public sector, particularly the continuing creation of agencies and the transfer of bodies from the public to the private sector are leading to a diversity of sources and hence problems in, for example, tracking down items produced in the past by organizations that no longer exist in the same form or indeed have been abolished. Legislation enacted during 1995 has led to the formation of the Environment Agency in April 1996 which comprises

Her Majesty's Inspectorate of Pollution, the National Rivers Authority and the Waste Regulatory Authorities, together with some other Department of the Environment functions. This major shake-up has the potential for exacerbating the problems outlined above.

Departmental publications

In this ever-changing world, the Department of the Environment (DoE) endeavours to maintain control over how its publications are made available, especially those not published by HMSO. It has a Publications Sales and Distribution Unit (see Addresses) which sells all priced non-HMSO departmental publications. Its Library produces for sale monthly and annual lists which give details of where publications can be obtained. Free publications are available from the DoE Publications Despatch Centre (see Addresses).

To return to the parliamentary/non-parliamentary divide, parliamentary publications are those needed for, or which are produced directly as a result of the work of, parliament. Their details are usually included in guides to government publications (1, 2). Many deal with environmental topics, as do many·non-parliamentary publications which are produced by various departments and agencies. The range of environmental and related topics includes agriculture, environmental health, and health and safety, for example, so many bodies issue relevant publications.

Many departments produce their own lists of publications which supplement HMSO's daily or monthly lists. In addition to the DoE list, the Health and Safety Executive produces a publications list (3). HMSO produces a free list of publications on the environment (4). No listing can ever be guaranteed to be complete. You will therefore need to get to know the 'green' responsibilities of government departments. Their libraries are the best starting-points for further information. Several departments, including the DoE, have public enquiry units which can help with general information about publications and refer users to specialist contacts where appropriate. The Department of Trade and Industry (DTI) operates a free environmental helpline (0800 585794). The *Civil Service Yearbook* (5) is a good introduction and information about the libraries themselves can be found in *Guide to libraries and information units in government departments and other organisations* (6), which is published by the British Library. The commercial publisher, Chadwyck-Healey produces a very useful catalogue of non-HMSO government publications (7).

A useful guide to government departments concerned with environmental matters is *Environmental contacts: a guide for business* (8) which is updated periodically and is available without charge from the DTI. The guide gives contacts for a wide range of environmental issues and sets out the roles of the individual departments. A companion publication, *The DTI guide for business* (9) gives contacts for queries on environmental topics within the department.

The DoE has joint units with DTI and MAFF respectively, and many committees and working groups have cross-departmental representation.

Examples of the roles of government departments

Department of the Environment (DoE)	To improve the standard of the environment by promoting responsible attitudes and disseminating ideas of good practice. To increase scientific knowledge and public awareness of the state of the environment, and create a framework for environmental control systems. To promote efficiency in the supply and use of energy.
Department of Trade and Industry (DTI)	To help firms to respond to environmental challenges and market opportunities. To provide practical advice to business on issues such as waste management and recycling. To ensure that UK environmental policy takes full account of the interests of business.
Department of Health (DH)	To advise the government on environmental influences on health. To promote good environmental practice throughout the NHS.
Health and Safety Commission and Executive (HSE)	To be responsible for protecting the health and safety of workers and the public. To have specific responsibility for major accident hazards, pesticides, genetically modified organisms and hazardous chemicals.
Ministry of Agriculture, Fisheries and Food (MAFF)	To encourage action to reduce water pollution and take positive environmental measures. To make the countryside more attractive and protect the rural economy.

Parliament

Apart from *Hansard* (Commons and Lords) or, more correctly, *Parliamentary debates (Hansard)*, and the online/CD-ROM database POLIS, which cover the proceedings of parliament, there are a number of distinct types of publications.

House of Lords and House of Commons Papers are usually responses from government departments to requests from parliament for information. Other Papers include reports or accounts which have to be laid before parliament and reports of Select Committees such as the Select Committee on the Environment.

Command Papers are so called because they are presented to parliament by royal command, examples are White Papers and reports of Royal Commissions. Recent key titles are the White Paper on the environment, better known as *This common inheritance*, and its follow-up reports (10). These documents give an insight into the government's policy, promises and their delivery. Other important publications are *Managing waste: the duty of care* (11) and *Best practicable environmental options* (12).

Statistics

Many government and non-government bodies are concerned with research and monitoring in the environmental protection area. Much information is contained in technical reports and it can be difficult to track them down and, having done so, to obtain them. Additionally, because the 'environment' covers so many aspects of our world, environmental statistics are still in their infancy and there are no universally accepted simple indicators of the health of the environment.

The key publication is the Department of the Environment's annual *Digest of environmental protection and water statistics* (13) which has been produced for some 17 years in an attempt to overcome the problems of access. The Digest takes figures from a wide range of sources and brings them together to make national statistics easily available, sources of the original data and the availability of further information are always given. Topics covered have varied from issue to issue with the current edition containing sections on the global atmosphere, air quality, land use and land cover, inland water quality and use, coastal and marine waters, radioactivity, noise, waste and recycling, land, and wildlife.

The previous issue of the Digest included a chapter on public attitudes which gave the results from a 1993 survey carried out on behalf of the DoE. A Statistical bulletin (14) giving more information, including comparisons with previous surveys, was published in 1994. It covers concerns relating to the environment, environmental action, knowledge and awareness, personal actions, and environmental policy options.

Changes have been made recently to the Digest following the publication of *The UK environment* (15) in 1992 to avoid duplication with the latter which aims to bring together environmental information in an easily accessible form. It is intended to be an aid to public discussion and to act as a reference source. In addition to the expected range of topics, it includes sections on pressures on the environment, and public attitudes and expenditure on the environment. Each section is followed by an extensive reading list and names of contacts.

A companion volume is produced for Scotland. The most recent edition is *The Scottish environment – statistics no. 4* (16). Major sections are population, land, land cover, atmosphere, water, conservation, radioactivity, recreation and attitudes to the environment in Scotland.

With the current emphasis on open government, a number of public registers have been set up by the DoE. A general guide to what exists has been produced and can be obtained without charge (17).

Examples of useful publications in more specialized areas are: *Drinking water 1994* (18) which, among other items, includes water quality data in sections covering technical audit of individual water companies, and a general overview of the topic; *HMIP Monitoring programme radioactive substances report for 1993* (19). This report contains further references and very extensive tables. *Chemical release inventory, annual report 1994* (20). This is the second UK report in the series. The data it contains are selected from the database maintained by Her Majesty's Inspectorate of Pollution (HMIP). It is intended to give a clear picture of the scale and nature of releases from the major industrial sources of pollution. It forms part of a wider public information service offered by HMIP and subsequently by the Environment Agency.

General guides to sources of statistical information include *Government statistics – a brief guide to sources* (21) which is published annually and is available without charge from the Central Statistical Office. More detailed information can be found in *Guide to official statistics* (22) which is published every few years.

Research

This is one of the most difficult areas to track down information, despite government having participated in this area since the 17th century. Papers arising from specific research projects are not generally identifiable in 'regular' abstracting journals. Progress during the 20th century has been rapid, especially during the period 1916 to 1964, the lifetime of the Department of Scientific and Industrial Research (DSIR).

During the 1960s, government responsibilities for research became more widely dispersed and some departments became responsible for

R&D related to their executive duties. Some appointed chief scientists to coordinate the work. In 1972 a White Paper, *Framework for government R&D*, was published which set out the 'customer–contractor' relationship, that is government departments (the customers) set out their requirements for work to be done by 'contractors' who can be from the public or private sector.

The research councils were reorganized during 1994 and now comprise councils dealing with biotechnology and biological sciences, engineering and physical sciences, economic and social sciences, medical research, the natural environment, and particle physics and astronomy.

The DoE produces an annual account of the areas of research in which it will be commissioning work (23). Parts of DoE also issue reports on their research activities. The Building Research Establishment and the Transport Research Laboratory are agencies of DoE and the Department of Transport respectively (although they may move to the private sector). Both organizations produce useful reports which can be purchased.

The DTI is responsible for a number of research establishments. The Laboratory of the Government Chemist which offers analytical and advisory services is relevant to the environmental area and the National Environmental Technology Centre at Culham which has adsorbed much of the work formerly carried out by the Warren Spring Laboratory is a key player.

The Department of the Environment's Library collects information concerning environmental research from DoE and DoT, and from local authorities and academic bodies for inclusion in an online database, RESLINE, which is made available to the general public by the London Research Centre.

International information sources

The services included in this section are operated by the United Nations (particularly the UN Environment Programme), the Organization for Economic Co-operation and Development (OECD) and the Commission of the European Communities.

United Nations Environment Programme (UNEP)

UNEP came into being after the Stockholm Conference of 1972 which represented the first worldwide attempt to deal with environmental problems. It was given a catalytic role since other agencies, such as the Food and Agriculture Organization (FAO) existed already. Its role was confirmed and enhanced at the Rio Conference in 1992.

THE INTERNATIONAL REGISTER OF POTENTIALLY TOXIC CHEMICALS (IRPTC)

This service has a central databank at Geneva which contains information on a large number of environmentally significant chemical substances in such areas as toxicity and ecotoxicity, biodegradation, and waste management. A key aspect of the databank is its emphasis on details of the regulation of chemicals. The *Legal file* which is available in both hard copy (24) and machine-readable form has recently been updated and contains regulatory information from 12 countries, including the UK, and a number of international organizations. It can also be accessed online via ECDIN (see p. 11).

IRPTC works through a network of national correspondents. It also co-operates with the Soviet State Committee for Science and Technology and its predecessor in the production of a series of monographs reviewing the Russian literature on the toxicity and hazards of chemicals. Well over one hundred titles have been produced so far; many deal with pesticides.

INTERNATIONAL PROGRAMME ON CHEMICAL SAFETY (IPCS)

IPCS is a joint programme of UNEP, the International Labour Office and the World Health Organization. It evaluates the effects of chemicals on human health and on the environment, develops guidelines on exposure limits and methodology for toxicity testing and related studies, and develops information needed for dealing with chemical accidents. It publishes an extensive series of monographs, Environmental Health Criteria. Individual titles in this series deal both with chemical substances and with other agents. Recent titles include phenol, chloroform and ultraviolet radiation. A companion series of Health and Safety Guides is produced. IPCS also issues, in cooperation with the Commission of the European Communities, a number of series of International Chemical Safety Cards which summarize the collective views of a peer review committee on the health and safety information on many commonly used chemicals.

Additionally, IPCS produces, in co-operation with IRPTC, the computerized listing of *Chemicals currently being tested for toxic effects (CCTTE)* (25), which is updated periodically. *CCTTE* lists, by chemical name, work currently being done, and gives the name and organization of the research worker. It also lists reviews that have recently been completed. Data are exchanged with OECD's EXICHEM database (see p. 11). CCTTE will shortly be replaced by a joint publication of IRPTC and the European Centre for Ecotoxicology and Toxicology of Chemicals (ECETOC) which will have the title, *Inventory of critical reviews on chemicals*.

IRPTC also co-operates in the production of a key publication, *Consolidated list of products whose consumption and/or sale have been banned, withdrawn, severely restricted or not approved by govern-ments.* The 5th edition was issued by the United Nations Department for Policy Coordination and Sustainable Development in 1994 (26).

INDUSTRY AND ENVIRONMENT PROGRAMME ACTIVITY CENTRE (IE)

The IE, which is located in Paris, was set up in 1975 to bring govern-ment and industry together to co-operate in reducing the adverse effects of industries on the environment. It has a central computerized data-bank, the *Industry and environment file*, which contains, for example, information on pollution and abatement control technologies and their costs. It produces a Technical Report series and other publications which provide practical information to readers worldwide. Recent titles include *Cleaner production worldwide, Audit and reduction manual for individual emissions and wastes*, and *Public communication on en-vironmental issues*. IE does not offer an online service, but its staff will answer enquiries using the wide range of resources available to them.

IE publishes a quarterly newsletter, *Industry and Environment*, which is available on subscription. Each issue focuses on a specific topic, such as low-waste and non-waste technology, and recycling and recovery in the metals industry. It also produces the newsletters, *Cleaner Produc-tion, Ozonaction* and *EnTA* which reports on technology assessment as a tool to develop environmentally–sound technologies and to discourage the export of those that pose potential environmental hazards. IE issues guidelines for emergency awareness and preparedness; it is a partner in UNEP's APELL (Awareness and Preparedness at Local Level) Programme in which it co-operates with OECD, ILO, CEC and others.

Finally, it operates a number of outreach activities which address a broad range of issues concerning industry as a whole. UNEP IE de-velops partnerships with industry, government and NGOs; organizes consultative meetings; and publishes supporting documents aimed at spreading advances in the field of sustainable development.

THE INTERNATIONAL ENVIRONMENTAL INFORMATION SYSTEM (INFOTERRA)

INFOTERRA differs from IRPTC and IE because it covers the whole environmental subject area and operates on the referral principle; it refers enquirers to sources of information or expertise. However, factual information is frequently supplied, including much grey literature. INFOTERRA is of particular value for multi-disciplinary topics.

It has two components: the *International Directory* containing descriptions of around 7000 information sources worldwide from a wide range of organizations, including government bodies, research groups, academic institutions, and private consultants; and a network of National Focal Points (NFPs) each NFP having knowledge of information sources in its own country. Requests to INFOTERRA are usually made through NFPs, although the availability of the Directory on the Internet is changing this pattern. In many areas of the world there is a supporting network of Regional Service Centres.

INFOTERRA also has a number of Special Sectoral (subject) Sources which provide substantive information, particularly to developing countries. Examples of these, in addition to IRPTC and IE, are the Waste Management Information Unit at Culham, CAB International, and the Environmental Law Information Service of the International Union for the Conservation of Nature and Natural Resources.

TRACING UN PUBLICATIONS

UNEP issues a list of its publications which is updated periodically (27). A general catalogue of UN publications is also produced (28) and Chadwyck-Healey produces a CD-ROM database, UNBIS PLUS, which assists in the tracing of UN publications in general from 1992 to date. It is updated quarterly.

Organization for Economic Co-operation and Development (OECD)

EXICHEM

OECD has a special programme for the control of chemicals. As part of this activity, it co-ordinates a database, EXICHEM, which contains details of work being carried out on existing chemicals. This database is available as a printed version and on diskette. EXICHEM, in common with other records of work in progress, can be used to avoid duplication and to identify possibilities for co-operation. Data held on EXICHEM are available from IRPTC.

WORK ON HIGH PRODUCTION VOLUME CHEMICALS

OECD is carrying out work on filling gaps in data on high production volume chemicals that are considered likely to have any adverse effects. The results lead to the preparation of Screening Information Data Sheets (SIDS). The information obtained will be supplied to IRPTC. OECD's risk reduction programme includes the appointment of lead countries for specific substances (29, 30).

European Union (EU)

ENVIRONMENTAL CHEMICALS DATA AND INFORMATION NETWORK (ECDIN)

ECDIN was initially designed as a network-based system. However, for a number of reasons, it is at present the online equivalent of a chemical handbook. The main categories of 'official' data included in the commercial version, which can be accessed via DIMDI, are legislation and rules (supplied by IRPTC), occupational health and safety, and waste management. Basic information is included on around 65000 substances, although the numbers covered by individual files vary considerably. ECDIN also operates the online version of EINECS, the *European inventory of existing commercial chemical substances.*

COMMUNITY R&D INFORMATION SERVICE (CORDIS)

CORDIS is a relatively new multi-database service which was launched in 1990; it is available on ECHO, the Commission of the European Communities Host. It is also available on CD-ROM and the Internet. It contains information on Community Research and Technological Development (RTD) activities, particularly those included in the EU's R&D Framework Programme. Other information in areas such as energy, agriculture and environment is also included. The details of project reports listed in European Abstracts (EABS) form part of CORDIS. A key component database is RTD-Partners which enables a user to find contacts for co-operative work.

SYSTEM FOR INFORMATION ON GREY LITERATURE IN EUROPE (SIGLE)

SIGLE is an EU-wide database on grey literature and contains records from 1981 onwards. Although it covers all subject areas, much information relevant to the environment is included. The UK input is provided by the British Library and is the online equivalent of *British Reports, Translations and Theses* (BRTT).

USA

The US government, notably the Environmental Protection Agency (EPA), is responsible for very many publications in the environmental area. The chief way in which details of US government publications are made known is through the US National Technical Information Service (NTIS) which publishes *Government Reports Announcements and Index* (GRA&I) twice monthly with an annual index. Other NTIS publications are a series of weekly *Abstracts Newsletters* including one on environmental pollution and control, and an extensive series of Published Searches for which individual titles are updated periodically. NTIS also makes available a computer-readable database on US government-funded research, FEDRIP (Federal research in progress) (31). FEDRIP contains summaries of around 150 000 projects that are either current or recently funded. The EPA issues a number of guides to its publications, notably *Access* (32).

The following report series are also of value: Toxicological profiles

(Agency for Toxic Substances and Disease Registry, and EPA); Pesticide fact sheets (EPA); Ambient water quality criteria (EPA); Drinking water health advisories (EPA). More detailed information concerning NTIS publications and services is given by Auger (33).

Japan

The US National Technical Information Service has produced a *Directory of Japanese technical resources* which lists US sources giving access to Japanese technical information. The directory includes a list of technical reports that have been translated into English.

Japan Chemical Industry Ecology – Toxicology and Information Centre (JETOC) publishes a continuing series of Information sheets which include regular reviews of Japanese laws, regulations and related matters.

It is also worth noting that the British Library's Science Reference and Information Service (SRIS) offers a special Japanese information service.

Other non-British government publications

The following sources should be able to provide assistance in tracking down official information from most countries. The major nations maintain counsellors and attachés, some dealing specifically with scientific and environmental concerns. Their addresses can be found in the *London diplomatic list* (HMSO), the *London telephone directory, Kelly's Post Office London business directory, Whitaker's almanack,* etc.

Other useful sources are *HM diplomatic service overseas reference list,* issued by the Foreign and Commonwealth Office, and the *Diplomatic service list* (HMSO). These give details of staff and their responsibilities in British Embassies abroad who can be approached for help.

INFOTERRA and other international networks which have been mentioned can be used to identify overseas contact points.

Some final comments

In addition to the vast range of conventionally published literature that has been described in this chapter, a considerable number of references have been made to the 'grey literature' and where to go for information and advice. Non-conventional sources fall into several, not necessarily exclusive categories. Each information channel has its strengths and weaknesses, particularly concerning currency, comprehensiveness, reliability and ease of access.

Databanks such as IRPTC, CCTTE and ECDIN are of the greatest value in giving an overview. They are strong in their coverage of information contained in the key works of international agencies. Their scope is, however, limited.

Referral services, for example IRPTC and INFOTERRA, give access to a wide range of services through their national and international networks. Their most obvious drawback is that they suffer from an inbuilt delay. Their ability to provide information about publications and data that are not generally available, and to specialist advice is a very real strength.

Bibliographic records such as those included in CORDIS and GRA&I do not usually contain data. The original documentation will have to be obtained or the research worker contacted. Coverage can be patchy, depending on the resources available to contributors. On the plus side, the records are a valuable source of information on the 'grey literature'.

To sum up, many official sources of information in the environmental protection area are available. Most can be accessed without too much trouble once you know where to look. Resources range from personal contact via the printed word to data accessible using the Internet. The use of less obvious sources is recommended when a comprehensive overview is needed.

Organizations

Department of the Environment
Publications Sales and Distribution Unit
Room 1, Spur 2
Block 3
Government Buildings
Lime Grove
Eastcote HA4 8SE
Tel: 0181 429 5186
Fax: 0181 429 5195

Department of the Environment
Publications Despatch Centre
Blackhorse Road
London SE99 6TT
Tel: 0181 691 9191
Fax: 0181 694 0099
(for supply of free publications)

Environment Agency
Head Office
Rivers House
Waterside Drive
Aztec West
Almondsbury
Bristol BS12 4UD
Tel: 01454 624400
Fax: 01454 624409

Environment Directorate
Organization for Economic Cooperation and Development
2 rue André Pascal
75775 Paris Cedex 16
France
Tel: 00 331 4524 7903
Fax: 00 331 4524 7876

European Centre for Ecotoxicology and Toxicology of Chemicals
Av. E Van Nieuwenhuyse 4, bte 6
B-1160 Brussels
Belgium
Tel: 00 32 2 675 3600
Fax: 00 32 2 675 3625

European Commission
DG XII-D-2
JMO B4-082
L-2920 Luxembourg
(for details of CORDIS)
Tel: 00 352 3498 1240
Fax: 00 352 3498 1248

HSE Books
PO Box 1999
Sudbury
Suffolk CO10 6FS
Tel: 01787 88 1165
Fax: 01787 31 3995

Industry and Environment
United Nations Environment Programme
39–43 Quai André Citroën
73739 Paris Cédex 15
France
Tel: 00 331 40 588850
Fax: 00 331 40 5888 74

INFOTERRA
United Nations Environment Programme
PO Box 30552
Nairobi
Kenya
Tel: 00 2542 23 08 00
Fax: 00 2542 22 69 49

International Programme on Chemical Safety
World Health Organization
1211 Geneva 27
Switzerland
Tel: 00 41 22 791 3589
Fax: 00 41 22 791 4848

International Register of Potentially Toxic Chemicals
United Nations Environment Programme
Case Postale 356
1219 Chatelaine
Geneva
Switzerland
Tel: 00 41 22 979 9111
Fax: 00 41 22 797 3460

Japan Chemical Industry Ecology – Toxicology and Information Centre
(JETOC)
Nanba Building 2F
19-4, 1-Chome
Nishishinbashi
Minato-ku
Tokyo 105
Japan
Tel: 00 813 3593 1190
Fax: 00 813 3593 1166

The Research Library
London Research Centre
81 Black Prince Road
London SE1 7SZ
Tel: 0171 627 9660
Fax: 0171 627 9674

US Environmental Protection Agency Public Information Center
Office of Administration and Resources Management
401 M Street, 3404
Washington DC 20460
USA
Tel: 001 202 260 2080
Fax: 001 202 260 6257

References

1. Butcher D. (1991). *Official publications in Britain* 2nd edn. London: Library Association Publishing.
2. *Catalogue of United Kingdom official publications.* London: HMSO/Chadwyck-Healey. CD-ROM (updated quarterly).
2. HSE (1994). *Price list of current HSE publications (Catalogue 27).* London: HMSO.
4. *The environment catalogue* (1995). London: HMSO (free).
5. Cabinet Office (1995). *Civil Service Yearbook.* London: HMSO.
6. The British Library (1994). *Guide to libraries and information units in government departments and other organisations.* London: The British Library.
7. *Catalogue of British official publications not published by HMSO.* Cambridge: Chadwyck-Healey (bi-monthly).
8. Department of Trade and Industry, *Environmental contacts a guide for business (who does what in government departments).* London: DTI. (updated periodically).
9. Department of Trade and Industry, *Guide for business.* London: DTI (updated periodically).
10. Department of the Environment, (1990). *This common inheritance, Britain's environmental strategy* (Cm 1200). London: HMSO.
11. Royal Commission on Environmental Pollution (1985). *Managing waste: the duty of care.* Report No. 11 (Cmnd 9675). London: HMSO.
12. Royal Commission on Environmental Pollution (1988). *Best practicable environmental option.* Report No. 12 (Cm 310). London: HMSO.
13. Department of the Environment/Government Statistical Service (1995). *Digest of environmental statistics No. 17 1995.* London: HMSO.
14. Department of the Environment Environmental Protection Statistics Division (1994). *1993 Survey of public attitudes to the environment England and Wales.* London: HMSO.
15. Department of the Environment/Government Statistical Service (1992). *The UK environment.* London: HMSO.
16. Scottish Office (1993). *The Scottish environment – statistics no. 4.* London: HMSO.
17. Department of the Environment (1995). *Environmental facts: A guide to using public registers of environmental information.* London: HMSO.
18. Drinking Water Inspectorate (1995). *Drinking water 1994: A report by the Chief Inspector.* London: HMSO.
19. Her Majesty's Inspectorate of Pollution (1994). *HMIP monitoring programme radioactive substances report for 1993.* London: HMSO.
20. Her Majesty's Inspectorate of Pollution (1996). *Chemical release inventory: CRI annual report 1994.* London: HMSO.
21. Central Statistical Office (1994). *Government statistics – a brief guide to sources 1994.* London: HMSO.
22. Central Statistical Office (1990). *Guide to official statistics.* London: HMSO.
23. Department of the Environment, Chief Scientist's Group (1995). *DoE research market: 1995 (Science and Technology Information Note No. 1/95).* London: HMSO.

24. International Register of Potentially Toxic Chemicals (1992–3). *IRPTC legal file 1992–93 regulations and guidelines on chemicals: an extract from the IRPTC databank.* Geneva: United Nations. (3 volumes plus user's guide).
25. International Programme on Chemical Safety/International Register of Potentially Toxic Chemicals. *Chemicals currently being tested for toxic effects.* (CCTTE) 6th edn. Geneva: United Nations.
26. United Nations Department for Policy Coordination and Sustainable Development (1994). *Consolidated list of products whose consumption and/or sale have been banned, withdrawn, severely restricted or not approved by governments.* Geneva: United Nations.
27. United Nations Environment Programme (1995). *Environment in print 1995.* Geneva: United Nations.
28. United Nations (1995). *United Nations publications catalogue 1994/95.* Geneva: United Nations.
29. Brydon, J.E., Chemical risk reduction activities in the OECD. *International Environment Reporter* (1993) 600–604.
30. *International Environment Reporter* (1995). 18 (17), 638–639.
31. *Federal research in progress (FEDRIP) database.* 1995 release on magnetic tape. Available for lease through US National Technical Information Service. Washington: EPA.
32. United States Environmental Protection Agency (1993). *Access EPA.* 3rd rev. edn. Washington: EPA.
33. Auger, C.P. (1993). *Information sources in grey literature*, 3rd edn. East Grinstead: Bowker-Saur.

CHAPTER TWO

Pressure groups and recent history

JAN MCHARRY

Inaction on the part of the individual, is often simply not knowing what to do.

(Ward, 1972)

The quest for knowledge has to be somewhat opportunistic, we must take it when and where we can.

(Sears, 1962)

Introduction

The changing perceptions in the environmental movement and the broadening of many environmental debates to encompass economic and social issues has led to increased visibility for the work of non-governmental organizations, including the pressure groups. Their role in raising public awareness should not be underestimated. In terms of information provision, combined with local authority departments, they provide the bulk of environmental information to the public. For many information seekers pressure groups are the first point of call.

The high standard of information released by groups and the resources (not necessarily financial) which they can now command to produce exacting scientific research has enhanced their reputation and status. No longer can they be referred to as an 'occasionally irritating minority' (*Sunday Times*, 1989 February). They have become significant opinion-shapers and a force to be reckoned with.

Information from pressure groups often falls into the category of 'grey literature' which libraries have tended to overlook in the past. Belatedly the value of this detailed research literature, which is published more quickly than equivalent research papers, is being recognized in library acquisition systems. The British Library acknowledges that their experience of compiling user guides on environmental information matters was considerably enhanced by such material. They are working to expand the comprehensiveness of this type of literature in their collections and are encouraging organizations to deposit copies of research and practice reports with them. *The System for Information on Grey Literature in Europe (SIGLE)* is available for consultation at the British Library's Science Reference and Information Service in London.

This chapter reviews the broad shifts in attitude that have taken place in recent history relating to pressure groups, the information they produce and how they use information to promote their viewpoints. The diversity of groups makes it impossible to specify a particular 'good practice' approach for obtaining information but with the help of information signposting services and the groups themselves it should be possible for the information professional to build a comprehensive picture of what is obtainable. Many professional journals across a range of disciplines now report on the availability of new information arising from these sources. Management of the environment, natural or built, is a multi-disciplinary activity and this is reflected in the growing breadth of coverage.

The changing environmental agenda

Edgar Mitchell, aboard Apollo 14 on its 1971 moon mission, captured the public's imagination with his description of the earth from space as a 'sparkling blue-and-white jewel . . . laced with slowly swirling veils of white . . . like a small pearl in a thick sea of black mystery'. This description provided the inspiration for a new world view which perceives humanity as just one small part of a much larger living entity. These ideas place the focus on environmental stewardship rather than mankind's domination over nature.

Throughout the 1970s public awareness was mobilized by headline stories of environmental destruction and pollution. Publications such as Rachel Carson's *Silent spring* (1962) documented the devastating effects of pesticide use and *The Ecologist* magazine's *Blueprint for Survival* and the Club of Rome's *Limits to Growth*, acted as catalysts for this new viewpoint. *Small is beautiful* (Schumacher, 1974) became the 'bible' for many environmentalists and today the book's arguments about how we use resources and the need to integrate environmental and economics have dated little.

The burgeoning environmental movement seized upon these milestone publications to promote their case. Hard-hitting information combined with peaceful direct action became the fundamental cornerstones of pressure groups such as Friends of the Earth (FoE) and Greenpeace. The growth of the environmental movement and its underlying ideologies are well documented in O'Riordan (1981) and Lowe and Goyder (1983). More up-to-date reviews are provided by McCormick (1989) and Pearce (1990), which study the changes in the Green movement over the last twenty years and reflect on current thinking and conflicts.

Perceptions about the major pressure groups have shifted dramatically over the last decade. The environmental lobby has become a major force to be reckoned with and although increased dialogue with governments and involvement in political processes might not have borne the fruit groups would wish, many groups today operate within a climate where the door is ajar, if not wide open, compared to the past where the door was firmly shut and groups had to argue passionately the case for their credibility. Porritt and Winner (1988) examine how green thinking started to permeate and influence all aspects of society in the late 1980s.

Further changes to pressure groups' credibility have occurred in the last few years. The limitations of political systems in promoting change, combined with the new agenda of sustainable development, have led major groups to switch tactics from working solely on means of influencing the government by highlighting problems to a more flexible approach with an emphasis on demonstrating the viability of practical solutions.

One such approach is Greenpeace's promotion of the Greenfreeze refrigerator which does not use ozone destroying chemicals. No longer is it enough to oppose; groups have to join in the debate and propose solutions. While it may be argued that this aspect has always been part of the function of pressure groups in their role of influencing policy-making through dialogue and debate, what we are seeing today is a greater focus on solution seeking rather than 'doom and gloom' predictions.

Sustainable development – a new emphasis

What quickly becomes evident to anyone now seeking environmental information is the tremendous diversity of groups. These range from international and national broad-based campaigning groups (e.g. FoE, Greenpeace, WWF), to specific single-issue groups, sectorally-based initiatives, lobbying groups, environmental networks, local environmental fora and a strong environment and development network of groups (e.g. Oxfam, World Development Movement, Christian Aid), all tackling the environmental agenda in different ways. This diversity now presents an enormous challenge for the information seeker in relation to questions of objectivity, accuracy, availability and target audiences.

The diversity has arisen partly as a response to the complexity of environmental issues, with many different stakeholders proposing viewpoints on how to mitigate problems. In the 1980s a further expansion occurred with the introduction of the concept of sustainable development into the public arena.

The publication of *Our common future*, commonly known as the Brundtland Report (World Commission on Environment and Development, 1987) was lauded for its strong message that environment and development issues were closely interlinked and therefore needed tackling together in policy-making processes. Today the Bruntland Report remains an authoritative publication for its breadth of ideas and for its often quoted definition of sustainable development as 'development which meets the needs of the present without compromising the ability of future generations to meet their own needs'.

This wording was refined in the United Nations Environment Programme/International Union for the Conservation of Nature and Natural Resources publication *Caring for the Earth* (1991) which added quality of life dimensions. Thus sustainable development is explained as 'development which improves people's quality of life, within the carrying capacity of the earth's life support system'. Both publications remain important texts for background information on the emergence of the sustainable development concept. Non-governmental organizations played a key role in supplying documentation and comments for both publications.

Since the Brundtland Report there have been many attempts by organizations to further define what is meant by the term 'sustainable development'. It has spawned its own literature with numerous periodicals which carry features on what the concept might mean. Generally it is now recognized that the term has a variety of meanings for different sectors of the community. As a result some groups argue that the definition is now almost worthless, and further energies should be directed towards ensuring that actions stem from the words.

So while the sustainable development terminology is criticized by some as being a contradiction in terms, the underlying principles have been embraced by environmental and development groups and the new strands of thought are emerging in their literature. Much closer working relationships and partnerships between traditional environment groups and development movement are being forged, bringing with them a whole new range of challenges and campaigning opportunities.

One of the recent watersheds was the 1992 United Nations Conference on Environment and Development (UNCED), commonly known as the Earth Summit, held in Rio de Janeiro. The major document under discussion – Agenda 21, the international plan for action –

reiterated the call to integrate environment and development into future policy making at all levels, including the local level. It highlights the provision of sound information as an urgent and necessary requirement for action. In particular it identifies two programme areas requiring better implementation, first, the need to bridge the data gap, and second the need to improve information availability.

Despite their limited financial resources many pressure groups have taken on board Agenda 21's message about initiating a concerted and consistent effort to explain, educate, and train the next generation of decision-makers. The strong links between environmental protection, economic security and social equity are increasingly reflected in published literature, in debates, and in the work of groups themselves. *Policies for a small planet* (1992), written by a small team from an authoritative non-profit think tank, the International Institute for Environment and Development, promoted the need for an integrated approach.

Agenda 21 is an ambitious document identifying a broad raft of changes that must occur if the world is to move onto the path of sustainable development. It is this diversity of ideas, encompassing issues of poverty, environment, consumption patterns, technology, population, health, human settlements, waste, trade and a myriad other issues that makes it hard for the information professional to categorize the environment into one section in a library or documentation system.

Environment and development groups: agents of change

'To describe all these groups as members of the same movement is to underplay the deep differences in goals and values, in perceptions of what constitutes threats to the environment, and in what are considered to be the appropriate strategies of environmental protection' (McCormick, 1989). Environment and development groups are increasingly forming strategic alliances and partnerships with other sectors while continuing to command considerable public backing on high profile issues. In 1995 the widespread public opposition to the UK government's road-building programmes and veal shipments again spotlighted the changing nature of the politics of protest, with pressure groups being supported by large numbers of people from all walks of life defending their right to voice their opinions.

Although the tag of 'green fundamentalist' is frequently pinned on pressure groups opposing controversial projects, as witnessed in media reports quoting nuclear industry spokespeople at the time of the start-up of the Thermal Oxide Reprocessing Plant (THORP) in Cumbria March 1994), the reputation of environmental groups has grown in stature. They have become increasingly professional, backing arguments with well-honed, hard-hitting literature.

The development of extensive internal documentation systems within pressure groups has assisted not only their own campaigning and research work but also their ability to operate public information services. For example, Friends of the Earth has long been recognized as an independent information provider to the media and to the wider public. The provision of grant aid to voluntary groups under various schemes operated by the Department of the Environment has encouraged this type of work.

With many surveys revealing a widespread public distrust of information supplied by governments (including local government) the role of the environmental pressure group as a source of information becomes elevated. This leads to the question of whether information from pressure groups can ever be objective. Groups at the cutting edge will always be open to criticism and accusations of bias. Greenpeace has often in the past been accused of producing distorted, subjective and misleading information, yet at the 1994 review of THORP their scientific reports and evidence won specific praise from the judge for their high standards. The objectivity issue re-emerged in the summer of 1995 with the debate on the disposal of Shell's Brent Spar oil platform.

One tactic now employed by groups to overcome questions of objectivity is to incorporate specific information supplied by others, for example, manufacturers about their products, within a group's campaigning work. Publicizing the facts in a straightforward manner and leaving consumers, empowered or not, to choose their subsequent course of action has been at the forefront of campaigns from the major groups.

Friends of the Earth produced a very successful consumer booklet, *The aerosol connection* (1989), at the height of the debate about the potentially damaging effects of CFCs, propellants used in aerosols, upon the ozone layer. As a result of the spotlight being placed upon manufacturers, those still using CFCs were forced to act swiftly to retain their competitive edge in the marketplace. The issue was not new – the USA had banned the use of CFCs as propellants in aerosols in 1978 – but emerging scientific evidence about the extent of ozone depletion, combined with an effective consumer information campaign, acted in a pincer movement to highlight the inadequacy of the UK government's voluntary approach.

Objectivity can become distorted by external pressures. The green consumer movement was founded on a bedrock of information provision designed to empower the user, but became hijacked by some manufacturers and retailers who made misleading claims about the 'environmental friendliness' of their products. Difficulties arose due to a mixture of false green marketing ploys, misleading terminology (there is no such thing as an 'environment-friendly product) and misrepresentation in the media.

The well-respected and accessible information tools produced by the independent US-based World Watch Institute prove beyond a doubt that it is possible to produce influential material which is objective. Their annual *State of the world reports* are highly rated, as well as often quoted, by pressure groups and decision-makers alike. Another acclaimed annual guide, *Vital signs*, from the same organization, published in association with the Worldwide Fund for Nature (Earthscan), sets out the underlying trends that are shaping our future. Data from these publications, plus other information distilled from national/international databases and periodicals are also available in disk form: the *World watch database disk 1995* (Earthscan).

Information and pressure groups

Information and pressure groups use information in many different ways including:

- lobbying governments and the European Union;
- monitoring world/country/specific sector trends in terms of the environmental impact of certain activities by institutions or industry;
- achieving legislative compliance;
- building in-house reference/research bases for policy-making;
- providing information to promote awareness and action;
- campaigning for external representation;
- building new alliances and coalitions (e.g. health and environment).

The supply of environmental information occurs in many different formats ranging from standard research reports, through newsletters and populist campaigning literature, to innovative outreach tools, videos and electronic mail. The information professional should also be aware that while many groups do not produce a wealth of literature they still remain an invaluable source of primary information. A glance through any of the growing number of environmental directories usually indicates the nature of a group's work and what can be provided. A series of publications with a reputation for concise, up-to-date information is the Environment Council's *Who's Who in the environment*, with separate volumes for England, Wales, Northern Ireland and Scotland.

Some environmental organizations such as The Wildlife Trusts Partnership have expanded their work to include a consultancy wing. Indeed environmental consultancies, large and small, remain a source of much leading-edge information, often in the form of 'grey literature'.

A comprehensive guide to major environmental consultancies is produced by the London-based Environmental Data Services, which also produces the well-respected *ENDS Journal.*

When assessing the impact of pressure groups, it is evident from information in the public domain that the environmental awareness-raising exercises run by many pressure groups have succeeded in creating greater understanding of environmental threats. As a result the public are now bored with the rhetoric arising from many different sectors in society and want to see action.

The call for solutions is an important factor underlying the greater availability of information, but there are other important drivers such as the growing legislative pressure and influence of Europe. Recourse to the European Parliament over the UK government's non-compliance with drinking water quality standards was highly successful for Friends of the Earth in the early 1990s. The thoroughness of their research, backed by detailed analysis and populist information for the consumer on how to request information from the water companies, revealed just how effective pressure groups can be in independent gathering and reporting of data (FoE, 1992, 1993).

Barriers remain to a group's effectiveness. Lack of freedom of information has in the past been a major stumbling block to any group trying to influence policy-making procedures and organizations. Indeed it was once the subject of its own campaign by a coalition of environmental groups. Secrecy has often forced groups to gather required research material from the USA or Europe. *The environmental information regulations 1992* gave new legal rights of access to environmental information held by many public authorities and other bodies in Great Britain. These regulations make a massive amount of information potentially available to the public on request from a wide range of official bodies with environmental responsibilities, including government departments, their executive agencies and local authorities. Several research institutions are now investigating the actual experiences and practices of voluntary environmental groups in trying to access local environmental information (see Chapter 14).

Examples of groups and their information provision

The idea of local state-of-the-environment reporting was introduced to the UK by Friends of the Earth in 1987. Targeted primarily at local authorities, the information gathered helps to assess and quantify environmental capacity and targets for future development plans and policies. The concept was successfully piloted by Kirklees Council. Although still in its infancy, state-of-the-environment reporting is becoming widely accepted as good practice in local authority decision-making.

Friends of the Earth subsequently produced a *Charter for local government* which has influenced many authorities to initiate some form of environmental reporting. FoE remains a point of information although better resourced organizations such as the Local Government Management Board have adopted much of the advisory work through the production of guidance material.

Awareness raising through action

Many smaller groups, often tackling a single issue, can be equally if not more effective than larger groups in highlighting specific issues. One of the UK's fastest growing pressure groups, Surfers Against Sewage, has deliberately targeted key issues such as the link between people's health and the environment. This has proved to be a powerful motivator for action.

Surfers Against Sewage (SAS) are lobbying for tighter standards and compliance with EC Directives for bathing water quality. Growing concern over the inadequacies of sewage treatment, the impact upon people's health and the visual evidence of pollution in bathing water and on beaches have led to a highly vocal and visual campaign. Rather than building up a collection of glossy literature to promote the case, the organization focuses on specific approaches. For example, it has become increasingly involved in helping people to pursue legal actions against water companies and in applying pressure on statutory bodies to carry out their legal responsibilities. Recognizing that groups have to have a 'strong case when making a lot of noise about the health risk', they have built up a database of over 250 incidents of illness believed to be caused by sewage-contaminated water. This medical response information, combined with the results of blood tests carried out by doctors, gives SAS excellent material with which to promote the case.

Consumer information

Spending power can be a potent agent of social change, but only if the information provision leads to empowered consumers taking action and voting with their purses. The Fair Trade movement, promoted by development groups such as Oxfam and Traidcraft, is a practical example. Fair Trade products are rated both on social impact and on environmental grounds. Small-scale producers and co-operatives, often based in the Third World, are paid a fair price for their products, thus avoiding the often exploitative situations that occur in mainstream trading.

One of the fundamental points made by the more substantial literature of the green consumer boom of the late 1980s and early 1990s is that such consumerism should not only be about consuming in a more environmentally benign manner but also about challenging the basic assumption that the product is necessary in the first place. Public acceptance is often quoted as a reason for manufacturers not changing to more environmentally benign materials. The CFC aerosol debate clearly demonstrated that resistance to change is not so entrenched as manufacturers and retailers make it out to be. The lack of information about product availability plus misleading product information are serious obstacles to progress.

Information provision was a key tool of FoE's campaign against the importation and use of tropical hardwoods. Together with WWF, FoE remains a focal point for information on sustainable forestry practices and hardwoods.

Overcoming political inertia

Pressure groups frequently develop public information resources on issues which have slipped from government attention or where expectations have been raised through consultation papers but little concrete action has followed. Additionally, they often exploit identified information niches. A lack of guidance for local authorities on planning for sustainable development was one reason why FoE produced *Planning for the planet* (1994). This well-received document provides draft wordings on environmental policies for development plans, as well as supporting materials, reasoning and references.

Information and research

The voluntary sector has access to data and information not easily available from other sources, but the limited resources and the unsure financial status of many of the groups hamper its collection and analysis. This is one of the serious challenges faced by many voluntary sector groups in trying to respond to information requests.

Non-governmental organizations have been working to expose another particular problem which affects many seeking information on the environment and pollution. The lack of reliable official data on issues such as waste 'continues to impair the formulation of appropriate waste management strategies and the assessment of their effectiveness' (United Nations Environment Programme, *Environmental Data Report*, 1993/4). Even the Department of the Environment acknowledges such inadequacies:

> Unless an authority has information about current waste arisings and recycling levels and likely future trends, it lacks the most basic tools for preparing and monitoring its recycling strategy. Statistics are the foundation on which the plan is built. If they are inaccurate or unreliable, the authority will to an extent be taking decisions in the dark.
>
> (Department of the Environment, 1991).

But it is not just the lack of data which causes problems. Using the example of waste again, the changing definitions and different criteria of what actually constitutes 'waste' and how they are measured compound the problem of data collection over varying timescales. Thus the accuracy of official published data becomes questionable. Agenda 21 states that all figures on industrial waste generation are suspect, if not open to scepticism.

Use of computer technology

Computer databases are just another tool to the information professional, but are respected as an enormous potential resource by NGOs. The growing interest in computer networking through the Internet or electronic mail is recognized by non-governmental organizations as a powerful vehicle for change. FoE has established a Home Page on the Internet where copies of leaflets, press releases, details of local groups and international FoE contacts can be downloaded. It also provides a sign-posting service to many other information systems.

With online systems and CD-ROM becoming key sources of information for many professionals, non-governmental organizations are seeking to ensure that their work is reflected in the growing number of databases carrying environmental information or 'information of relevance to environmental problems'. Another computer tool beginning to be used by environmental groups for assessing environmental impacts is Geographical Information Systems (GIS) (Haines-Young *et al.*, 1993).

However, there are limitations to the current technologies. Information gives people knowledge and knowledge provides power, but here the inequities begin. The power to ask questions does not necessarily mean that the answers come back or, if they do, they may be in an unsuitable form. The technology is open to manipulation by informed individuals. Much more awareness and training has to occur before a greater majority of potential information users feel comfortable about using electronic systems to gather information.

The results from a pilot project undertaken in 1994 to explore the feasibility of establishing a common database for groups to use reported that: 'All too often the databases and the information they contain remain inaccessible to the people actively involved in environmental improvement'.

Links with the media

The information revolution, bringing global news to people's homes through the mediums of TV and radio, has been extremely powerful in raising awareness. Non-governmental organizations (NGOs) have reinforced this message by taking on a powerful advocacy role on many issues. As well as directly supplying information to TV and radio programme researchers, NGOs frequently supply information for programme back-up materials run by organizations such as Broadcasting Support Services.

Others supply videos to the Television Trust For the Environment – a non-profit-making and non-governmental organization set up in 1984 by Central Independent TV, with co-sponsorship from the UN Environment Programme. The Trust was established to support worldwide production and distribution of environmental programmes, particularly to Third World countries.

The key role of TV in supplying environmental information is demonstrated by many opinion polls. One survey conducted by Harris in 1989 found that 84 per cent of British adults gave TV as their main source of information about 'developing' countries and their problems. But the media can distort, trivialize or sensationalize issues – leaving pressure groups to correct the picture – and can instil a sense of powerlessness to act in the face of massive global problems. For example, in February 1989 the *Sunday Times Magazine* ran a provocative feature about the destruction of many natural resources: 'The world is dying: what are you going to do about it?'. Such a message is strong and guilt-provoking for the individual but awareness and collective action by all sectors of society can only ever be the true way forward.

These elements are glimpsed in authoritative journals such as Environmental Data Services (ENDS) monthly *ENDs Bulletin*. Respected by pressure groups, this has become a major source of up-to-date information about industry's environmental performance, environmental groups and government action/inaction on all environmental issues, particularly pollution control.

Stemming the tide of enquiries

Before participation comes the need for information provision. Market research undertaken for the government-backed 'Going for Green' initiative (reported at a launch in February 1995) showed that when people were asked how they would like to gain advice on helping the environment, 59 per cent specified they would like leaflets through the post, 23 per cent would like to borrow a free loan video or audio cassette, 22 per cent would visit a local environmental advice centre, 22 per cent wanted a local environmental watch group, 19 per cent would call a Freephone helpline, 11 per cent would join an environmental organization, and just 8 per cent would invite an environmental adviser to visit for free.

The rising demand for environmental information on already overstretched enquiry services in voluntary environmental organizations is causing problems. It is worth highlighting some of these issues since library professionals might be a major source of referral. Difficulties include inappropriate enquiries, duplication of effort, confusion over what is and what is not readily available, and the need to streamline referral procedures between organizations.

These problems are being tackled by the Environmental Information Forum, set up to facilitate co-operation between organizations which provide environmental information, with the aim of promoting improvements in provision. Forum participants include researchers, information officers, policy developers, librarians, editors from a range of environmental organizations, across all sectors.

In addition, a range of sign-posting services to other sources of environmental information is being developed by the various groups. For example, '*Who's who in the environment*' is a series of guides compiled by the Environment Council, listing UK organizations concerned with both the built and natural environment and the advice or support offered. The Environment Council's Information Programme aims to make the environment sector as accessible as possible at the lowest cost.

Information providers

Some major information providers in the environment/development movement include:

Earthscan Publications Ltd, 120 Pentonville Road, London N1 9JN. Earthscan is a leading publisher on environmental and developmental issues, plus a distributor for the US Island Press and the World Resources Institute.

Friends of the Earth Ltd (FoE), 26–28 Underwood Street, London N1 7JQ. FoE is one of the leading pressure groups in the UK. It believes in informing and empowering the public by providing authoritative information on a wide range of environmental issues and campaigning at the local, national and international level. With an emphasis on solution seeking, FoE creates pressure for change through mobilizing public opinion and lobbying politicians and industry. FoE has gained an impressive reputation for giving 'early warnings' of environmental hazards.

Greenpeace, Canonbury Villas, London N1 2PN. Greenpeace is an international, independent environmental pressure group which acts against abuse to the natural world and provides public briefings and information material. The direct actions of Greenpeace are backed by impartial scientific research commissioned from independent consultants.

Intermediate Technology Development Group 103–105 Southampton Row, London WC1B 4HH. This is a mail order book service which lists a selection of about 500 recommended titles on development and appropriate technology from publishers around the world.

The National Society for Clean Air and Environmental Protection, 136 North Street, Brighton, BN1 1RG. The annual *Pollution Handbook* is widely regarded as the best 'one-stop shop' guide to pollution law.

It covers UK and European legislation on air, water, waste and noise. **Oxfam**, 274 Banbury Road, Oxford OX2 7DZ. Publications such as *No time to waste* (Davidson and Myers, 1992) draw from Oxfam's experiences of working with people in the Third World and highlight the fact that the poor are often the first to feel the effects of a deteriorating environment. Oxfam's work focuses on the many innovative ways that are being devised to protect and conserve natural resources for the future with a major theme of 'Only a fairer world can save the earth'.

The Wildlife Trusts Partnership, The Green, Witham Park, Waterside South, Lincoln LN5 7JR. Wildlife Trusts Partnership is the largest voluntary organization in the UK concerned with all aspects of wildlife protection. With its network of groups and ability to muster grassroots support for national initiatives, it manages over 2,000 nature reserves or sites of wildlife interest and produces a range of educational materials.

World Development Movement, 25 Beehive Place, London SW9 7QR. The World Development Movement works to raise awareness and promote action about the gross inequalities and poverty issues experienced by many in developing countries. It calls for a redirection of spending away from the military and helps to promote Fair Trade issues.

World Directory of Environmental Organisations. Compiled by the Californian Institute of Public Affairs and the World Conservation Union (IUCN), this directory includes descriptions of over 2,600 organizations in more than 200 countries, including government and intergovernmental agencies and national and international NGOs. In addition there are guides to 'who's doing what' in over 50 key areas, full addresses and fax numbers and a bibliography of database and directories.

World Wide Fund for Nature (WWF), Panda House, Wayside Park, Godalming Surrey GI7 1XR. WWF is the largest international voluntary organization entirely devoted to the care and protection of the natural living world. WWF finances conservation projects wherever the need is greatest and produces a wide range of literature and educational resources.

References

Carson, R. (1962) *Silent spring*. Harmondsworth: Penguin.
Club of Rome (1972) *Limits to growth*. London: Earth Island.
Department of the Environment (DoE) (1991) *Waste Management Paper No. 28*. London: HMSO.
Deziran, M. and Bailey, L. (1993) *A directory of European environmental organisations* 2nd ed. Oxford: Blackwell.
Haines-Young, R. *et al.* (1993) Landscape, ecology and geographical information systems. London: Taylor and Francis.

International Institute for Environment and Development (IIED) (1992) *Policies for a small planet*. London: IIED.

Lees, N. and Woolston, H. (1992) *Environmental information – a guide to sources* London: The British Library.

Lowe, P. and Goyder, J. (1983) *Environmental groups in politics*. London: George Allen & Unwin.

McCormick, J. (1989) *The global environment movement*. London: Bellhaven Press.

O'Riordan, T. (1981) *Environmentalism* 2nd edn. London: Pioneer.

Pearce, F. (1990) *Green warriors: the people and the politics behind the environmental revolution*. London: Bodley Head.

Porritt, J. and Winner, D. (1988) *The coming of the greens*. London: Fontana Collins.

Ruttner, D. (1992) *Ecolinking: everyone's guide to online environmental information*. Berkeley: Peachpit Press.

Schumacher, E.F. (1974) *Small is beautiful*. London: Abacus.

Sears, P.B. (1962) *An introduction to ecology*.

Ward, B. (1972) *Only one earth*.

World Commission on Environment and Development (1987) *Our common future* (the Bruntland Report) Oxford: Oxford University Press.

PART TWO

Effects and the Affected

CHAPTER THREE

The effects of hazardous chemicals on human health

HEATHER WISEMAN

Introduction

Information on the effects of hazardous chemicals on human health is needed by medical and health professionals, research scientists and people working in national and local government, emergency services, community agencies responsible for responding to chemical emergencies, industry, trade unions and the public. The responsibilities or interests of the different groups may include:

- assessment of the risk to a population from an existing or proposed hazard and planning for control measures for hazardous sites;
- planning resources and strategies to deal with exposures;
- emergency treatment of casualties and management of resources to cope with human effects of an incident;
- medical management of patients affected by exposure to hazardous chemicals;
- investigation of the association between a particular health effect and exposure to an environmental chemical;
- investigation of the possible environmental causes of adverse health effects;
- assessment and monitoring of the health of workers exposed to chemicals in the workplace environment;
- planning strategies, codes of practice, regulations or legislation to prevent exposure.

Toxicological information can be used to evaluate the hazards from chemicals, to estimate the likelihood and potential severity of an effect, to describe the nature of the effect and to identify potentially hazardous situations. Data generated by laboratory tests and clinical observation of unplanned or occupational exposures to a particular chemical may include:

- acute, chronic and subchronic toxicity by ingestion, skin absorption, inhalation or injection;
- skin/eye irritancy;
- specific organ effects;
- carcinogenicity;
- teratogenicity;
- mutagenicity;
- sensitization/allergic conditions;
- pharmacology;
- pharmacokinetics;
- toxicokinetics.

Epidemiological and statistical information may be available to show when, how frequently and where exposure to chemicals has occurred, and whether chemicals have been implicated as a cause of ill-health or death. Sources that record information about chemical exposures and incidents involving hazardous materials may describe the health effects, numbers of people affected, admitted to hospital or who died, the circumstances of exposure, the resources that were needed to limit and treat health effects and manage the incident, and the magnitude of the risk associated with the incident. Some sources may record analytical data confirming the presence of the chemical in the environment or in the body, and possibly an estimate of the quantity present.

Advice on first aid and decontamination procedures for casualties exposed to hazardous chemicals and on medical management is needed both by emergency responders and health care personnel and by people planning the resources needed to provide the response. These groups may also need guidance on occupational exposure limits, safety measures and protective clothing, and on methods and indications for biological monitoring and assessment, and laboratory diagnosis.

Where possible, information should be obtained from sources which have been reviewed and evaluated by experts and data from different sources should be compared, since different experts may base their evaluations on different criteria. Non-specialists may find it useful to make a direct approach to experts before, or instead of, using information directly from primary journals or databanks. Poisons information services, teratology information services and chemical emergency centres have an important function as providers of evaluated information appropriate to specific situations.

Relevant information is found in sources covering fields of toxicology and clinical toxicology, occupational health and safety, environmental health, and public health. For more detail on aspects of these disciplines not covered in this chapter, the reader is referred to Chapter 9 on public health in *Information sources in the medical sciences* (4th edn, L. Morton and S. Godbolt, eds, Bowker Saur, 1994); *Health and safety: a guide to sources of information* (3rd edn, S. Pantry, Capital Planning Information, 1992); and Chapter 10 on information resources for toxicology, by J. Deschamps and D. Morgan, in *General and applied toxicology* (B. Ballantyne, T. Marrs and P. Turner, eds, Macmillan, 1993).

It is important to understand that the use of toxicological information, the evaluation of its significance and its application to different situations require specialist knowledge and skills. For example, the extrapolation of animal data to estimate risks for humans is often controversial and uncertain. Also, much of the data about health hazards of chemicals are derived from acute occupational, accidental or intentional exposures and have limited application to environmental exposures, which are typically long term and of a much lower order. Associations between adverse effects and chemical exposure may be based on case reports that do not stand up to critical examination (Kimbrough *et al.*, 1989). For many thousands of chemicals little is known about their effects in man, but the absence of information does not imply absence of hazard.

Textbooks, manuals, monographs

Monographs and textbooks are good starting-points for a search, presenting an introduction to the literature and to the nature and limitations of toxicological information. Their coverage may be less up-to-date than computer information sources.

The social issues related to health effects of environmental chemicals are briefly presented in *Our planet, our health, the report of the WHO commission on health and environment* (World Health Organization, 1992) and in *Health and the environment* (F. Godlee and A. Walker, *British Medical Journal*, 1992). A detailed discussion of the risks and benefits of pesticides and their health effects is presented in the British Medical Association's *Pesticides, chemicals and health* (Edward Arnold, 1992).

Introduction to toxicology (2nd edn, J.A. Timbrell, Taylor & Francis, 1995) provides a concise overview of toxicology for students and non-specialist scientists, including reviews of environmental pollutants, pesticides and other chemicals. Another text aimed at this audience is *Toxic substances in the environment* (B.M. Frances, John Wiley & Sons, 1994), with chapters on neurotoxicity, developmental toxicology, genetic toxicology and carcinogenesis. Basic concepts of toxicology, detection of hazard and prediction of risk are explained for non-scientists in *Calculated risks: the toxicity and human health risks of chemicals in our environment* (J. Rodricks, Cambridge University Press, 1992).

For a more advanced overview of toxicology and the effects of chemicals on the body, the standard text is *Casarett and Doull's toxicology* (5th edn., C.D. Klaassen, ed., McGraw-Hill, 1995). It covers general principles of toxicology, the toxic response of different organ systems and the action of toxic agents. There are chapters on environmental toxicology, clinical toxicology, occupational toxicology and regulatory toxicology. *General and applied toxicology* (Ballantyne *et al.*) also provides a broad review and covers special aspects such as air pollution, combustion toxicology, toxicology of pesticides, major disasters and ethical and professional issues. *Principles and methods of toxicology* (A.W. Hayes, ed. Raven Press, 1994) covers principles of metabolism, kinetics, statistical techniques, extrapolation of results from animal experiments to man and descriptions of procedures for most types of toxicological investigation.

Useful guidance on retrieval and selection from the literature of appropriate data on chemical toxicity and their interpretation is given in *Toxic hazard assessment of chemicals* (M.L. Richardson, ed., Royal Society of Chemistry, 1986). The extrapolation of experimental results to the human is discussed in *Long-term animal studies. Their predictive value for man* (S.R. Walker and A.D. Dayan, MTP Press, 1986) and in *Development and ethical considerations in toxicology* (M.I. Weitzner, ed., Royal Society of Chemistry, 1993), which also includes chapters on cancer and environmental chemicals.

There are numerous texts on the toxicology of specific substances with varying coverage of their role as environmental hazards. *Ethel Browning's toxicity and metabolism of industrial solvents* (R. Snyder, ed., Elsevier, 1987) is a classic text, as is *Handbook on the toxicology of metals* (2nd edn, L. Friberg, G.F. Nordberg and V.B. Vouk, eds,). The latter covers general aspects of toxicology, risk assessment, prevention, diagnosis and treatment in one volume, and 28 reviews on specific metals in a second volume. Another standard text is *Handbook of pesticide toxicology* (W.J. Hayes and E.R. Laws, Academic Press, 1991) which includes chapters on the general toxicology of pesticides and their effects on humans, followed by detailed accounts of the toxicology of different classes of pesticides. More recent texts on pesticides include *Paraquat poisoning – mechanisms, prevention and treatment* (C. Bismuth and A.H. Hall, eds, Marcel Dekker, 1995), a useful review of mechanisms of tissue damage, general toxicity and circumstances of poisoning based on an extensive literature review, and *Clinical and experimental toxicology of organophosphates and carbamates* (B. Ballantyne and T.C. Marrs, eds, Butterworth and

Heinemann, 1992). The same authors have edited *Clinical and experimental toxicology of cyanides* (B. Ballantyne and T. Marrs, eds, IOP Publishing, 1987). Both texts cover basic science, exposure patterns, and diagnosis and management of poisoning. *Carbon monoxide poisoning* (K.K. Jain, Warren H. Green, 1990) discusses clinical effects, treatment and prevention and includes chapters on environmental and epidemiological aspects.

The effect of environmental chemicals on specific target organs is discussed in the series by Raven Press covering toxicology of specific target organs including cardiovascular toxicology, neurotoxicology, toxicology of the liver, toxicology of the kidney and several others. For example, *Toxicology of the lung* (2nd edn, D.E. Gardner, *et al.*, Raven Press, 1993), covers chemically induced pulmonary hypersensitivity and the use of inhalation toxicity data in the risk assessment of exposure to airborne materials. *Clinical immunotoxicology* (D.S. Newcombe, N.R. Rose and J.C. Bloom, eds, Raven Press, 1992) covers the immunotoxicity of environmental chemicals. *Dermatotoxicology* (5th edn, F.N. Marzulli and H.I. Maibach, Taylor & Francis, 1996) includes the effects of environmental chemicals on the skin, such as allergic irritancy, toxic reactions, light induced responses and carcinogenesis. *The vulnerable brain and environmental risks. Volume 3: Toxins in air and water* (R.L. Isaacson and K.F. Lenson, Plenum Press, 1994) discusses how environmental factors, including solvents and metals, can alter the brain and nervous system.

For most chemicals there is only limited information on their effects on foetal and neonatal development in man. *Chemically induced birth defects* (2nd edn, J.L. Schardein, Marcel Dekker, 1993) is a standard work that provides a catalogue of data, from laboratory and clinical studies, on the potential teratogenicity of drugs and chemicals in animals and humans. It includes extensive lists of references providing an introduction to the literature. *Developmental toxicology* (2nd edn, C.A. Kimmel and J. Buelke-Sam, eds., Raven Press, 1994), another book in the Target Organ Toxicology Series, is a comprehensive text including an overview of epidemiological problems, clinical care and genetics, risk assessment and a discussion of different approaches to testing of environmental chemicals.

Clinical texts provide descriptive information on the health effects of chemicals, criteria for diagnosis and advice on treatment of poisoning and often include some comment on the circumstances and occurrence of poisoning. *Principles and practice of environmental medicine* (A.B. Tarcher, ed., Plenum, 1992) discusses the basic principles behind environmental and occupationally induced disorders and the effects of toxic agents in the environment, their assessment and treatment. *Hazardous materials toxicology, clinical principles of environmental health* (J.B. Sullivan and G.R. Krieger, eds, Williams and Wilkins,

1992) covers basic science as well as clinical principles, emergency medical response and hazards of specific toxins, industries and sites. *Clinical effects of environmental chemicals* (R.D. Kimbrough *et al.*, Hemisphere Publishing, 1989) lists signs and symptoms by organ system and shows the chemicals that could be the cause for each one. The book also includes a computer disk with a program that allows the user to select major signs and symptoms and then obtain suggestions for the possible chemical cause.

Clinical toxicology texts generally deal mainly with acute poisoning. An introductory text suitable for a wide range of people, particularly non-medical toxicologists and students of health sciences, is provided by *Principles of clinical toxicology* (3rd edn., T.A. Gossel and J.D. Bricker, Raven Press, 1994). The book includes concise summaries of presentation and management of acute human poisoning with chemicals such as carbon monoxide, cyanide, hydrocarbons and pesticides, together with case histories and review questions.

For clinicians concerned with treatment of poisoned patients, there are three comprehensive English language texts, all originating from the USA: *Medical toxicology, diagnosis and treatment of human poisoning* (M.J. Ellenhorn and D.G. Barceloux, Elsevier, 1988); *Clinical management of poisoning and drug overdose* (L.M. Haddad and J.F. Winchester, eds, W.B. Saunders, 1990); and *Goldfrank's toxicologic emergencies* (5th edn., L.R. Goldfrank *et al.*, Appleton & Lange, 4th edn. 1994). The effects of chemicals on the eye are dealt with in *Toxicology of the eye* (4th edn. W.M. Grant and J.S. Schuman, Charles C. Thomas, 1993), which includes brief information on the effects and treatment of 1600 substances.

More concise information on effects and treatment of hazardous chemicals is found in pocket books intended as quick reference tools for professionals concerned with medical management of patients. *Poisoning and drug overdose* (2nd edn, K.R. Olsen, Appleton and Lange, 1994) includes information on diagnosis and treatment of approximately 150 common drugs and other chemicals, followed by sections on use of antidotes, emergency response to hazardous materials incidents, health hazard summaries for industrial and occupational chemicals, plus occupational exposure standards and guidelines. *Handbook of medical toxicology* (P. Viccellio, ed., Little Brown, 1993) has a similar format, but with more general information on treatment of poisoned patients and less on industrial and occupational poisoning. *Acute poisoning: diagnosis and management* (2nd edn, A.T. Proudfoot, Butterworth-Heinemann, 1993) is more selective, covering a smaller number of chemicals commonly implicated in acute poisoning in the UK.

Perhaps the most comprehensive reference book providing quantitative data for evaluating toxic hazards from industrial chemicals is

Dangerous properties of industrial materials (7th edn, N.I. Sax and R.J. Lewis, Van Nostrand Reinhold, 1989). This lists some 18,000 chemicals, with clinical toxicological data on skin and eye irritation, mutation, tumorigenesis, teratogenesis, carcinogenesis, neoplastigenesis, toxicity data and reproduction effects data, including the route of administration, the species tested and exposure data. Entries include clinical data on experimental animals and man and occupational exposure standards applicable in the USA, with brief descriptive information on toxicity and symptomatology.

Handbook of toxic and hazardous chemicals and carcinogens (3rd edn, M. Sittig, Noyes Publications, 1992), presents health and safety information on nearly 800 chemicals, with details of medical surveillance, first aid, harmful effects and symptoms. *Patty's industrial hygiene and toxicology. Volume 2: Toxicology* (4th edn, G.D. Clayton and F.E. Clayton, eds, John Wiley & Sons, 1994) is a useful, well-referenced text in six parts, reviewing acute and chronic adverse health effects and hygiene standards of a large number of chemicals encountered in industry. Proctor and Hughes' *Chemical hazards of the workplace* (3rd edn, G.J. Hathaway, Reinhold, Van Nostrand, 1993) covers fewer chemicals but includes useful descriptions of the main signs and symptoms caused by overexposure to the chemical, relating these, where data are available, to exposure levels. Odour threshold and other warning properties and brief information on treatment, diagnostic features and special tests are also included.

Disposition of toxic drugs and chemicals in man (4th edn, R.C. Baselt and R.H. Cravey, Year Book Medical Publishers, 1994) is a series of one-to-three-page monographs with information on the fate of chemicals in the body, the kinetics, metabolism, excretion, toxicity and methods of analysis.

Major series and special monographs from governmental, international and research organizations

Among the most important sources of information on health effects of hazardous chemicals are those produced by government bodies, international organizations and organizations working in the field. Their objective is usually to help groups such as decision-making bodies, national authorities, employers, workers and health professionals to understand the nature of chemical hazards and how to protect the health of workers and the public and prevent accidents. At their best such publications provide reliable evaluated information on health effects of environmental chemicals, based on critical reviews of the literature and expert assessments. The same agencies may also produce guidelines for exposure to chemicals, codes of practice and national or regional regulations related to chemical exposure.

Reference information for environmental health training and research (World Health Organization, 1992) lists the most significant current literature within the United Nations system and related institutions, including series from the European Regional Office of WHO, the EURO Environmental Health Series, EURO Health Aspects of Chemical Safety and EURO reports and studies.

Environmental Health Criteria published by The World Health Organization and the International Programme on Chemical Safety are monographs on nearly 200 selected chemicals, groups of chemicals or environmental pollutants, prepared by international groups of experts for national authorities. They present accurate, comprehensive information, based on a comprehensive literature review, about specific hazards posed by a chemical to the health of workers, the safety of the general public or the survival of the environment, and make recommendations about human and environmental risks. The series also includes guides to data interpretation, risk assessment and carcinogenicity and toxicity testing.

Health and Safety Guides, derived from the Environmental Health Criteria, are more concise and designed to alert workers to different forms and symptoms of exposure, short- and long-term risks to health, appropriate protective measures and emergency actions to be followed when accidents occur. For the physician there is an outline of emergency medical treatment and a description of the symptoms to look for during periodical medical examination of employees. Current regulations, guidelines and standards governing exposure limit values are summarized.

The International Agency for Research on Cancer (IARC) publishes Monographs on the Evaluation of the Carcinogenic Risk of Chemicals to Humans.

The Commission of the European Communities publishes two series: Toxicology of Chemicals, Series 1, Carcinogenicity; Toxicology of Chemicals, Series 2. Reproductive Toxicity; a third series on immunotoxicity is being planned. These are concise authoritative reviews of the scientific evidence with references to provide access to wider literature.

The US Agency for Toxic Substances and Disease Registry produces Toxicological Profiles, which are a succinct summary of the toxicological and adverse health effects, for health professionals and members of the public. The National Academy of Sciences publishes Medical and Biological Effects of Environmental Pollutants.

A series of reviews of the atmospheric concentrations of air pollutants in the UK and their effects on health have been published by the UK Government Department of Health Advisory Group on Medical Aspects of Air Pollution Episodes, on *Ozone* (HMSO, 1991), *Sulphur dioxide* (HMSO, 1992), *Oxides of nitrogen* (HMSO, 1993) and *Benzene* (HMSO, 1994). The UK Health and Safety Executive (HSE) publishes *Toxicology of substances in relation to major hazards*, reviewing available toxicological data for specific chemicals in order to establish appropriate toxicity values for land-use planning. HSE also publishes Environmental Hygiene Guidance Notes giving concise information about health hazards from specific chemicals to enable employers to assess the possible health risks to their workers and the measures which need to be taken to deal with them. Some of the Medical Series Guidance Notes, aimed at occupational physicians, deal with health effects of chemicals. HSE also produce leaflets for workers and the public giving information about industrial sources of exposure to hazardous chemicals and their health effects and what workers should do to protect themselves.

In Europe, the German Chemical Society (Gesellschaft Deutscher Chemiker) Advisory Committee on existing chemicals of environmental relevance has published over 80 reports, most with English and German language versions, including consideration of toxicity. The National Institute of Public Health and Environmental Protection in the Netherlands publishes Integrated Criteria Documents on chemicals. The European Chemical Industry Ecology and Toxicology Centre (ECETOC) produces three series: critical reviews of the toxicology and ecotoxicology of selected industrial chemicals chemical hazards; ECETOC monographs on aspects of toxicology including titles such as *Evaluation of the neurotoxic potential of chemicals* and *Risk assessment of occupational chemical carcinogens*; and Technical Reports including toxicity assessments of specific substances, methods of hazard assessment and an annual report of *Existing literature reviews and evaluations* on commodity chemicals. The British Industrial Biological Research Association BIBRA publishes Toxicity Profiles.

Other monographs produced by these organizations include expert evaluations of health risks and advice on measures to reduce them, such as *Acute effects on health of smog episodes* (WHO, 1992) and *Public health impact of pesticides used in agriculture* (WHO, 1990).

Reviews of data on health effects of contaminants are included in *Guidelines for drinking water quality, second revised edition. Vol. 2: Health criteria and other supporting information* (WHO, 1985), *Air quality guidelines for Europe* (WHO, 1988), and *Indoor air quality: organic pollutants* (WHO, 1989). *Safety in the use of chemicals at work: an ILO code of practice* (International Labour Organization, 1993) includes advice on personal protection and medical surveillance.

The Agency for Toxic Substances and Disease Registry has produced *Medical management guidelines for acute chemical exposures* (US Department of Health and Human Services, Public Health Service, 1994). In the UK, *Pesticide poisoning: notes for the guidance of medical practitioners* provides a brief summary of effects of pesticide poisoning. (2nd edn., A. Proudfoot, ed., Department of Health, 1996).

Journals

Relevant English language journals include:

- *Adverse Drug Reaction and Toxicological Reviews*
- *American Journal of Industrial Medicine*
- *Annals of Occupational Hygiene*
- *Archives of Environmental Health*
- *Archives of Environmental Contamination and Toxicology*
- *Archives of Toxicology*
- *Bulletin of Environmental Contamination and Toxicology*
- *Critical Reviews in Toxicology*
- *Dangerous Properties of Industrial Materials Report*
- *Environmental Health Perspectives*
- *Environmental Research*
- *Environmental Toxicology and Chemistry*
- *Human and Experimental Toxicology*
- *Journal of the American Industrial Hygiene Association*
- *Journal of Chemical Ecology*
- *Journal of Environmental Pathology, Toxicology and Oncology*
- *Journal of Exposure Analysis and Environmental Epidemiology*
- *Journal of Toxicology – Clinical Toxicology*
- *Journal of Toxicology and Environmental Health*
- *Occupational and Environmental Medicine* (formerly *British Journal of Industrial Medicine*)
- *Pharmacology and Toxicology*
- *Polish Journal of Occupational Medicine and Environmental Health*
- *Regulatory Toxicology and Pharmacology*
- *Reviews of Environmental Contamination and Toxicology*
- *Reviews on Environmental Health*
- *Scandinavian Journal of Work, Environment and Health*
- *Toxicology and Industrial Health*
- *Toxicology Letters*
- *Toxic Substances Journal*
- *Veterinary and Human Toxicology*

Relevant papers may also be found in general medical journals such as the *British Medical Journal*, the *Lancet*, the *Journal of the American Medical Association*, etc., and in journals covering other medical specialities such as emergency medicine, epidemiology, forensic science, intensive care, pharmacology, paediatrics, public health and psychiatry.

Analytical chemistry and biochemistry journals publish methods for detecting and measuring chemicals in biological fluids for biological monitoring and assessment.

Safety cards and data sheets

Safety data sheets and transport emergency cards provide basic information on first aid and sometimes indicate the need for specific treatment, but the quality and usefulness of health information varies widely. IPCS Safety Cards, produced by the International Programme on Chemical Safety, summarize essential health and safety information on chemicals for use by employees in factories and other workplaces. A collection of some 80 000 Chemical Safety Sheets is available from the ILO's Occupational Safety and Health Information Centre (CIS). *Chemical safety data sheets*, published in five volumes by the Royal Society of Chemistry between 1989–92, includes information on biological hazards, carcinogenicity, mutagenicity, reproductive hazards and first aid, with references. *The Sigma-Aldrich library of chemical safety data* (R. Lenga, 1988) includes toxicity data taken from the RTECS database (see below) and a brief summary of acute health hazards for over 24 000 chemicals. It is published in printed form and on CD-ROM.

Databanks and databases

Databanks often provide more up-to-date information than printed sources and are able to cover a very much greater number of chemicals.

The *Users guide to hazardous substance databanks available in OECD member countries*, OECD/GD(91) 102 (OECD, 1991), describes 28 databases. OECD Environment monograph No. 25, *A survey of information systems in OECD member countries covering accidents involving hazardous substances* (OECD, 1989), describes some 54 information systems, listing the contents of the databanks in detail so that the nature of the health information available in each is readily apparent.

Some publicly available sources of computerized information on environmental health and toxicology (US Department of Health and Human Services, Public Health Service, CDC, 1991) includes brief information about databases, bulletin boards and environmental networks, CD-ROM databases, microcomputer databases and instructional software packages.

The following are major hazardous substances databanks with information about toxicity and health effects:

RTECS (Registry of Toxic Effects of Chemical Substances) from the US National Institute of Occupational Safety and Health (NIOSH) contains information extracted from scientific literature on over 130 000 potentially toxic chemicals, including health hazard data and workplace limits and bibliographic references to the source of the data. The toxicity data are not evaluated.

CHEMINFO occupational health and safety information on chemicals, from the Canadian Centre for Occupational Health and Safety (CCOHS), includes detailed evaluated information of health hazards with recommendations on first aid and personal protection. It is available in English and French.

HSDB (Hazardous Substances Databank) from the US National Library of Medicine (NLM) contains scientifically reviewed, fully referenced profiles for over 4000 chemicals, including data items on toxicity, biomedical effects, exposure standards and regulations and monitoring methods. Data are derived from standard texts and monographs, government documents, technical reports and primary journal literature.

CHRIS (Chemical Hazard Response Information System) is produced by the US Coast Guard for emergency response personnel. Chemical handling information for over 2000 chemical substances includes information on health hazards and first aid information.

IRIS (Integrated Risk Information System) developed by the US Environmental Protection Agency (EPA) contains summary information related to human health risk assessment, particularly chronic health hazards, obtained from literature and EPA data resources and reviewed by the EPA. It is aimed at toxicologists, health risk assessors and environmental health professionals.

ECDIN (Environmental Chemical Data Information Network) is produced by the Commission of the European Communities Joint Research Centre and contains data on over 65 000 substances, including data on occupational health and safety and toxicity and hazard information.

TOXNET (produced by NLM, combines files from Chemical Carcinogenesis Research Information System (CCRIS), DART Developmental and Reproductive Toxicology database, ETICBACK Environmental Teratology Information Centre Backfile and EMICBACK, the Environmental Mutagen Information Center Backfile, HSDB and RTECS.

POISINDEX is a clinical toxicology database, primarily for use by poisons information centres, which contains descriptive textual information on effects in man and management of exposure to both toxic and non-toxic chemical substances and products. As with printed clinical toxicology sources, the emphasis is on effects and treatment of acute poisoning. Brand name products are mostly those on the US market. It is compiled by an editorial board of physicians and pharmacists with experience of work in US poisons centres and is regularly reviewed and updated. It is avavailable on CD-ROM from Micromedex. REPRORISK, also available on CD-ROM from MICROMEDEX, includes information about health effects and potential risks of chemicals with treatment.

Information on the human consequences of major chemical incidents can be obtained from MHIDAS (Major Hazard Incident Data Service). This provides historical information on the number of people killed, injured or evacuated as a result of incidents involving hazardous materials that resulted in, or had the potential to produce, a significant impact on the public at large. The database includes incidents which have occurred during the last 25 years in 95 countries. It is developed by the UK Atomic Energy Authority on behalf of the Major Hazards Assessment Unit of the UK Health and Safety Executive and is available on CD-ROM (OSH-ROM from SilverPlatter).

HSDB IRIS, RTECS and ECDIN are available online and on CD-ROM. MHIDAS, CCINFO, POISINDEX and REPRORISK are only available on CD-ROM. CHRIS is available on CD-ROM and in a micro-computer version.

Bibliographic databases

Toxicology is covered by the major online bibliographic databases in science and medicine: MEDLINE, from the NLM, EMBASE from Excerpta Medica, Chemical Abstracts and Biological Abstracts. The toxicology references from these databases have been extracted and combined on TOXLINE and POLTOX toxicological databases.

TOXLINE covers toxicological effects of drugs, pesticides and other chemicals and clinical research, including occupational health, poisoning and health and safety issues. Subfiles from 17 separate sources include Toxicity Bibliography from MEDLINE, Chemical–Biological Activities from Chemical Abstracts, Toxicological Aspects of Environmental Health from Biological Abstracts, Pesticides Abstracts, NIOSHTIC, Environmental Mutagen and Environment Environmental Teratology Information Centres and International Labour Office CIS abstracts. It is available online and on CD-ROM.

POLTOX combines subfiles from other databases to cover the detrimental effects of pollution and toxic substances on humans, plants, animals, and the environment. POLTOX I includes air, water, land, radiation and noise pollution, environmental risks, food additives, agrochemicals and industrial chemicals. It combines the TOXLINE bibliography from the NLM, the complete toxicology subset from Food Science and Technology Abstracts and the toxicology databases from Cambridge Scientific Abstracts including Toxicology Abstracts and

Health and Safety Science Abstracts. POLTOX II provides ten years of coverage from Excerpta Medica's EMBASE and includes chemical pollution and its effects on man, animals, plants and microorganisms, pharmaceutical toxicology and chemical teratogens, mutagens and carcinogens. They are available on CD-ROM.

CANCERLIT is compiled by the US National Cancer Institute from the cancer-related citations from MEDLINE.

Medical toxicology and environmental health is a database produced by the Medical Toxicology and Environmental Health Division of the UK Department of Health, indexing over 2000 journals, conference proceedings, reports, books, pamphlets and official publications in the areas of chemicals in food and consumer products, pesticides, industrial chemicals, health consequences of smoking, radiation and noise, air and water pollution, radiation biology, cosmetics and general toxicology. It is available online.

There are three major bibliographic databases which include information on health effects of hazardous chemicals as part of their coverage of health and safety information. They are available online and on CD-ROM:

CISDOC indexes worldwide literature on occupational safety and health, including chemical and physical hazard information sheets, toxicology and epidemiology. It is produced by International Occupational Safety and Health Information Centre (CIS) of the International Labour Organization in Geneva. Selected parts are included in HSELINE, TOXLINE and NIOSHTIC.

HSELINE produced by the Health and Safety Executive (HSE) in the UK, indexes its own publications and those of the Health and Safety Commission, also journal articles, conference proceedings and legislation.

NIOSHTIC, compiled by National Institute of Occupational Safety and Health (NIOSH) in the USA, references English language journals in occupational health and safety and related fields, NIOSH reports and abstracts from CIS Abstracts. It emphasizes research activities.

Organizations

Specialized information centres

Poisons information centres and chemical emergency centres are essential information sources in emergencies involving hazardous chemicals, when those responding to the emergency have no time to access information on their own account and may lack the training to evaluate it. Staff working in such centres are familiar with the relevant information sources and trained to evaluate the information quickly, taking account of all relevant factors related to the circumstances, the people exposed, etc.

POISONS INFORMATION CENTRES

These centres have been established in most developed and many developing countries to provide information on the diagnosis, management and prevention of exposure to chemicals. They are usually part of the health service and situated in a hospital, but some are situated in academic institutions. Information is usually available on a 24-hour basis every day of the year to health professionals and, in most countries, to the public as well. The majority of their work is concerned with acute poisoning, either accidental childhood poisoning or deliberate self poisoning, and only a relatively small proportion with exposures to environmental chemicals and/or chemical hazards in the workplace. As public concern about long-term exposure to environmental chemicals increases, so most poisons centres have improved their capability to provide information in this area. In Quebec the Toxicology Centre dealing with information about environmental issues is separate from the poisons information service dealing with acute poisoning.

An international list of poisons centres can be obtained from the Belgian Poison Centre (Box 15, 1 rue Joseph Stallaert, 1060 Brussels, Belgium) or from the International Programme on Chemical Safety.

Poisons centres are important sources of epidemiological and statistical data on exposure to chemicals, some of which are usually published in the centres' annual reports. Most centres keep files of case reports of exposure to chemicals, with information on clinical effects and efficacy of treatment, and sometimes qualitative or quantitative analytical data. Case reports can be a useful contribution to the evaluation of toxicity of individual chemicals. Some centres also carry out surveys and epidemiological studies to investigate the toxicity of a chemical or circumstances of exposure.

TERATOLOGY INFORMATION SERVICES

In many countries teratology information centres have recently established a network for collection and evaluation of data on effects on foetal and neonatal development of exposures to drugs and other chemicals occurring in the workplace or at home during pregnancy. The primary function of such services is to provide information to physicians and health care personnel and they may be situated in hospitals, research institutions or medical schools. In the UK the teratology information service is linked to the National Poisons Information Service.

CHEMICAL EMERGENCY CENTRES

Chemical emergency response may be a function of poisons centres or of separate chemical emergency centres specifically designed to provide assistance in the event of a chemical accident and holding only that health information needed by emergency responders. In the UK, the National Chemical Emergency Centre at Harwell has compiled the CHEMDATA database to help identify hazards and appropriate remedial actions in the event of an uncontrolled chemical release. This includes information from manufacturers and published literature for over 65 000 chemicals, on personal protection, hazards (whether absorbed through skin, toxic, carcinogenic, etc.) and first aid measures. It is available for use on microcomputer by fire brigades, emergency services and local authorities. A second database, HAZDATA, contains information on classification of hazards, risks, toxicity data, safety precautions, occupational exposure limits, monitoring requirements and health surveillance requirements, with literature references.

United Nations

INTERNATIONAL PROGRAMME ON CHEMICAL SAFETY

The International Programme on Chemical Safety (IPCS) was established by the World Health Organization (WHO), the United National Environment Programme (UNEP) and the International Labour Organization (ILO) to provide an internationally evaluated scientific basis on which countries could develop their own chemical safety measures and to strengthen national capabilities for prevention and treatment of harmful effects of chemicals and for managing health aspects of chemical emergencies. IPCS brings together international groups of experts to produce critical evaluations of chemicals and pesticide residues which are published in different types of document adapted to the needs of the user, ranging from scientist and technical expert, administrator and decision-maker to the person on the shop floor.

WORLD HEALTH ORGANIZATION

The World Health Organization (WHO) is concerned with environmental health and the prevention of environmental pollution. Many of its publications are concerned with the effects of chemicals on human health. GEENET (Global Environmental Epidemiology NETwork) is a WHO project which aims to strengthen education, training and research on the health effects of environmental hazards, by promoting collaboration between institutions in developed and developing countries.

INTERNATIONAL REGISTER OF POTENTIALLY TOXIC CHEMICALS

The International Register of Potentially Toxic Chemicals (IRPTC) is part of UNEP in Geneva. IRPTC supplies information on chemical hazards in the environment to those concerned with human health and environmental protection. It maintains a database of information about health and environmental effects of chemicals, treatment of poisoning and regulations and standards.

INTERNATIONAL AGENCY FOR RESEARCH ON CANCER

The International Agency for Research on Cancer (IARC) promotes and co-ordinates international research on the causes of cancer and its prevention.

Governmental organizations

The health and safety directory (Croner Publications, 1993) is a guide to organizations with health and safety functions, mainly UK-based, but with some coverage of organizations in the European Union and countries with a national centre for occupational safety and health.

National governments have a responsibility to protect the public and workers from exposure to potentially harmful substances. Responsibilities related to the effects of hazardous chemicals on health are usually divided between several different agencies or departments. For example, in the UK the Department of Health, Division of Health Aspects of Environment and Food, is concerned with assessment of hazards to health posed by environmental chemical hazards. Protection of workers and the public from those risks to health and safety from chemical exposure arising out of a work situation is the responsibility of the Health and Safety Executive (HSE) and the Health and Safety Commission. Chemical hazards in the home environment are the concern of the Department of Trade and Industry's Consumer Safety Unit.

In the USA there are two main federal centres within the Public Health Service of the US Department of Health and Human Services concerned with effects of hazardous chemicals on human health. The Agency for Toxic Substances and Disease Registry (ATSDR), is concerned with protecting workers and the public from exposure and/or the adverse health effects of hazardous substances in storage sites or after accidental release. Non-occupational environmental health problems, the control of environmental illnesses and investigations of the possible relationships between environmental hazards and health effects are the concern of the Center for Environmental Health and Injury Control, a division of Centres for Disease Control. These agencies collect, analyse and disseminate information relating to human exposure to toxic or hazardous substances. They are concerned with the provision of medical care of exposed individuals, the investigation of the relationship between exposure to toxic substances and illness and the evaluation of health risk from hazardous substance incidents.

University-based institutes

University-based institutes concerned with occupational health and safety are another important source. The Robens Institute of Industrial and Environmental Health and Safety, University of Surrey, Guildford, Surrey, is concerned with human health aspects of workplace, environment and commercial product safety, including toxicology, and one of its functions is provision of advice. The Institute of Occupational Health, University of Birmingham, runs an Occupational Health and Toxicology Information service which will provide information about toxic effects of chemicals.

Industry

Industry has a responsibility to provide reliable information on the chemicals stored, handled, reprocessed, manufactured and distributed or otherwise used in the workplace. This information includes toxicological properties. National and international industrial associations for manufacturers of chemical products can be useful sources of information.

Audiovisual materials

GEENET produce an *Inventory of audiovisual materials in the environmental and occupational health field* (WHO, 1990) covering mainly those produced in the UK and USA.

References

Kimbrough, R.D. *et al.* (1989) Clinical effects of environmental chemicals: a software approach to etiological diagnosis. New York: Hemisphere Publications.

CHAPTER FOUR

The effects of pollutants on wildlife

KATHERINE WESENBERG

In this chapter, selected sources of information which address the effects of pollutants on wildlife are reviewed. Although naturally occurring plant and animal toxins also affect wildlife, the focus of this review is xenobiotic toxicants. Xenobiotic substances are chemicals introduced into the environment in the form of pesticides, heavy metals, polychlorinated biphenyls (PCBs), and other by-products of human activities. The science of examining the effects of these substances on animal and plant life is multi-disciplinary in nature and contributors to the literature in this field include toxicologists, wildlife and aquatic ecologists, chemists and those in the veterinary and medical professions.

General reference works and monographs

An underlying knowledge of toxicology, the study of adverse effects of chemicals on living organisms, is essential to understanding the more specialized fields of ecotoxicology, aquatic toxicology, and wildlife toxicology. A classic textbook on general toxicology is *Casarett and Doull's toxicology: the basic science of poisons* (5th edn, McGraw-Hill, 1995) edited by Curtis D. Klaassen, designed for courses on toxicology, but also widely used in courses on environmental health and related areas. It provides information on the principles, concepts and thought patterns that are the foundation of toxicology. Another useful reference work is titled *Introduction to biochemical toxicology* (Appleton & Lange, 1994) edited by Ernest Hodgson and Patricia E. Levi. The emphasis of this introductory textbook is on events that occur at the molecular level when toxic compounds interact with living organisms.

Topics covered include the biochemistry, uptake, distribution, metabolism, mode of action and elimination of toxicants.

Ecotoxicology, as defined by David Hoffman *et al.* in *Handbook of ecotoxicology* (Lewis, 1995) is the science of predicting effects of potentially toxic agents on natural ecosystems and nontarget species. The *Handbook* is used as a reference for students and researchers in the areas of ecotoxicology, terrestrial wildlife toxicology, and aquatic toxicology. It includes 34 chapters with contributions from more than 50 internationally recognized experts. A useful general textbook by Wayne G. Landis and Ming Ho-Yu is *Introduction to environmental toxicology: impacts of chemicals upon ecological systems* (2nd edn, Lewis, 1995) where chapters build upon underlying concepts to provide an understanding of effects of chemical pollution as it pertains to ecological systems.

An overview of wildlife toxicology can be found in *Wildlife toxicology* (Van Nostrand Reinhold, 1991) by Tony Peterle. The ecosystem approach to studying environmental contaminants is emphasized, and a history of the science of wildlife toxicology is provided. It includes information documenting the various lethal, chronic, or subclinical effects of toxic substances on wildlife, as well as regulatory information. This book is based on literature collected only until the early 1980s, so other more recent literature should be used to supplement it. In *Noninfectious diseases of wildlife* (2nd edn, Iowa State Press, 1996) edited by Anne Fairbrother, Gerald Hoff and Louis Locke, leading wildlife toxicologists discuss the effects of oil, cyanide, mercury, selenium, pesticides, dioxins, and lead on terrestrial wildlife.

In regard to aquatic toxicology, Rand and Petrocelli's *Fundamentals of aquatic toxicology* (Hemisphere, 1985) is geared specifically for use as a textbook for courses in aquatic and environmental toxicology; an updated version, also by Gary Rand, *Aquatic toxicology: effects, environmental fate, and risk assessment* (Taylor & Francis, 1995) is designed similarly. Scientists and managers from academia, government and industry contributed chapters on toxicity testing and effects of toxicants in aquatic environments. *Aquatic toxicology: molecular biochemical and cellular perspectives* (Lewis, 1994) reports on the response of aquatic systems to insults from environmental contaminants. *Marine pollution* (2nd edn, Oxford University Press, 1989) by R.B. Clark resulted from an introductory course of lectures on marine pollution. This book examines various pollutants in detail including oil, metals, pesticides and PCBs. Other references include *Aquatic chemistry* (American Chemical Society, 1995) and *Standard methods for the examination of water and wastewater* (19th edn, American Public Health Association, 1995) which is particularly useful for the standardized toxicity test procedures that are listed for various aquatic species.

Toxicity testing is essential to determine the effects of pollutants on animals and several references on this topic exist. Early approaches to toxicity testing focused on dosage studies or residue level analyses to determine toxicity. Examples of such studies include *Lethal dietary toxicities of environmental contaminants and pesticides to coturnix* (US Fish and Wildlife Service, 1986) by Elwood Hill and Michael Camardese and *Manual of acute toxicology: interpretation and data base for 410 chemicals and 66 species of freshwater animals* (US Fish and Wildlife Service, 1986) by Foster Mayer. *Animal biomarkers as pollution indicators* (Chapman and Hall, 1992) by David Peakall deals with the growing field of the use of animal biomarkers which provide an indication of the physiological or biochemical impact of chemicals in the environment. *Biomarkers: biochemical, physiological, and histological markers of anthropogenic stress* (Lewis, 1992) by Robert Huggett is a comprehensive work on the use of biomarkers as a method to assess environmental stress.

Ecological toxicity testing: scale, complexity, and relevance (CRC, 1994) edited by John Cairns and B.R. Niederlehner focuses on the development and validation of predictive methods for estimating the ecological consequences of toxic chemicals. *Environmental contaminants in wildlife: interpreting tissue concentrations* (Lewis, 1996) edited by W. Nelson Beyer, Gary Heinz and Amy Redmon provides information on determination of toxicity levels from various pollutants.

Specialized materials

In addition to the more general materials, a specialized body of literature deals with the toxic effects of various pollutants including pesticides, heavy metals, oil and industrial contaminants on living organisms.

The scientific literature on the impacts of pesticides on wildlife parallels the development of these various compounds. Wayland J. Hayes, Jr. in his book *Toxicology of pesticides* (Williams & Wilkins, 1975) includes a section on the impact of pesticides on domestic animals and wildlife. There is a strong emphasis on chlorinated hydrocarbons such as DDT and DDE. An expanded and updated three-volume publication edited by Wayland J. Hayes, Jr. and Edward R. Laws, Jr. titled *Handbook of pesticide toxicology* (Academic Press, 1991) covers a multitude of pesticides including herbicides, rodenticides, fungicides and fumigants, in addition to organophosphates and carbamates. There is an entire chapter describing situations where non-target wildlife species were impacted by exposure to pollutants.

Toxicity of pesticides in animals (CRC Press, 1991) edited by T.S.S. Dikshith describes effects of organochlorines, organophosphates, carbamates and other compounds on mammals. Fumio Matsumura, author of *Toxicology of insecticides* (2nd edn, Plenum, 1985), devotes an entire chapter to the subject of effects of pesticides on wildlife and also discusses organophosphates, carbamates and chlorinated hydrocarbons. *Cholinesterase-inhibiting insecticides: their Impact on wildlife and the environment* (Elsevier, 1991) edited by Pierre Mineau is a comprehensive review of the literature on the effects of cholinesterase-inhibiting pesticides on wildlife and other non-target species.

Farm chemicals handbook (Meister, 1995) contains LD_{50} data for rats and rabbits and has a section on environmental and safety that categorizes toxicity of chemicals in birds and fish. Other sections include a pesticide and fertilizer dictionary, a regulatory file and addresses of chemical manufacturers. A similar reference from Europe is *The Pesticide manual: a world compendium* (10th edn, British Crop Protection Council, 1995) which provides a comprehensive listing of pesticides understood to be in current use or under active development there.

Pesticide effects on terrestrial wildlife (Taylor & Francis, 1990) edited by L. Somerville and C.H. Walker reviews the effect of the introduction of pesticides into biological ecosystems and considers suitable test methods for evaluating such effects. *Handbook of toxicity of pesticides to wildlife* (2nd edn, Fish and Wildlife Service, 1984) by Rick H. Hudson, Richard K. Tucker and M.A. Haegele is a compendium of pesticide toxicity data presenting acute and chronic effects on selected wildlife species.

Information unique to specific pollutants is available in the National Biological Service's biological report series titled *Contaminant hazard reviews* by Ronald Eisler. Reports on thirty different contaminants have been published, beginning in 1985. These include agricultural pesticides, heavy metals and industrial contaminants. Each report typically includes a description of uses of the product, its environmental chemistry and lethal and sublethal effects on mammals, birds, amphibians, reptiles and aquatic organisms.

Governmental agencies with land stewardship responsibilities have been historically involved in studying the effects of specific pollutants on the environment. The United States Environmental Protection Agency produces publications such as the *Wildlife exposure factors handbook* (EPA, 1993) by Margaret McVey *et al*. The Canadian government is charged with evaluating information on the effects of contaminants on natural resources important to Canada and have produced publications such as *Pyrethroids: their effects on aquatic and terrestrial ecosystems* (National Research Council of Canada, 1986) *An atlas of contaminants of eggs of fish-eating colonial birds of the Great Lakes (1989–1992)* (Canadian Wildlife Service, 1994) and *Contaminants in Canadian seabirds* (Environment Canada, 1990).

Wildlife is threatened by acute contaminant spills. *Before & after an oil spill: the Arthur Kill* (Rutgers University Press, 1994) edited by Joanna Burger provides detailed studies of the effects on plants and animals from the 1990 oil spill in the Arthur Kill Waterway between New York and New Jersey. Because biologists had been monitoring this waterway before the spill, baseline data were available on invertebrates, birds and fish. This was compared to data gathered over a two-year period following the spill. The 1989 Exxon Valdez oil spill has also generated literature on the effects of oil on wildlife. Two recent publications on this topic include *Marine mammals and Exxon Valdez* (Academic Press, 1994) edited by Thomas R. Loughlin and the *Sea otter symposium* (US Fish and Wildlife Service, 1990) edited by Keith Bayha and Jennifer Kormendy. These document the effects of the oil spill on sea otters, harbour seals, whales and other cetaceans.

Conference proceedings

Conferences allow scientists to exchange information on the effects of environmental contaminants and some of these conferences generate publications or proceedings that can be useful resources. One example is *Wildlife toxicology and population modeling: integrated systems of agroecosystems* (CRC Press, 1994), a textbook resulting from 1990 conference titled 'The Population Ecology and Wildlife Toxicology of Agricultural Pesticide Use: A Modeling Initiative for Avian Species'. This conference was jointly held by the Conservation Foundation and the Society for Environmental Toxicology and Chemistry (SETAC). Its purpose was to integrate population ecology with wildlife toxicology through new approaches to modelling. The resulting publication reflects these goals and is particularly useful as a reference for performing risk assessments of avian exposure to xenobiotics.

Environmental toxicology and risk assessment: third volume is the most recent of the toxicology publications of the American Society for Testing and Materials (ASTM) and is the 17th consecutive annual ASTM symposium to address environmental toxicology and related issues. Examples of other titles in this series include *Aquatic toxicology and risk assessment* and *Aquatic toxicology and hazard assessment*. These conferences were initiated in response to a need for knowledge about the impact of chemicals and contaminants on aquatic ecosystems. Two other ASTM conferences were organized for those interested in the effects of toxicants on wildlife populations. These were the *Avian and mammalian wildlife toxicology: first conference* (ASTM, 1979) and *Avian and mammalian wildlife toxicology: second conference* (ASTM, 1980).

Organized by the British Crop Protection Council, *Field methods for the study of environmental effects of pesticides* (BCPC, 1988) is a collection of papers dealing with methods for studying long-term effects of toxicants on populations of non-target species. It includes sections on effects of pesticides on birds, mammals, invertebrates and aquatic ecosystems.

The problem of lead poisoning in birds has been recognized in at least 21 countries. The majority of poisonings result from the ingestion of lead shot or lead fishing weights. *Lead poisoning in waterfowl: proceedings of an IWRB workshop* (International Waterfowl and Wetland Research Bureau, Brussels, 1991) edited by Deborah J. Pain documents the extent of lead poisoning in waterfowl throughout the world and provides possible solutions to the problem.

Scientific journals

Scientific journals that report on impacts of pollutants on animals and their environment overlap several disciplines including ecology, aquatic and wildlife studies and toxicity testing.

Broad disciplinary journals that cover the effects of environmental contamination include *Environmental Toxicology and Chemistry*, the official publication of the Society of Environmental Toxicology and Chemistry which is dedicated to furthering scientific knowledge and disseminating information on environmental toxicology and chemistry. Springer-Verlag publishes three journals which all deal with environmental contamination: *Archives of Environmental Contamination and Toxicology*, the *Bulletin of Environmental Contamination and Toxicology*, and *Reviews of Environmental Contamination and Toxicology*. These differ in the length and depth of articles, but all deal with similar subject matter. Chapman & Hall's *Ecotoxicology* has an international focus and is geared toward research on the effects of toxic chemicals on populations, communities and terrestrial, freshwater and marine ecosystems.

For references on detection and monitoring of pollutants, two outstanding journals are the American Chemical Society's *Environmental Science and Technology* and Pergamon's *Chemosphere*. Both emphasize analytical chemistry.

Two Elsevier journals are of great value in coverage of pollution effects. *Environmental Pollution* is useful for topics on toxicants contamination of wildlife, while the *Marine Pollution Bulletin* is a valuable source for articles that deal with the effects of toxicants on marine life and the marine environment. Pergamon's *Aquatic Toxicology* deals with the mechanisms of toxicity in aquatic environments in addition to specific responses to toxic agents.

General toxicology journals also include articles of interest on the subject of aquatic and wildlife toxicology. Hemisphere's *Journal of*

Toxicology and Environmental Health reports on the toxicological effects of various environmental pollutants. Two publications of the Society of Toxicology (USA) are *Toxicology and Applied Pharmacology*, which covers research dealing with the action of chemicals, drugs, or natural products on the structure or function of animal tissues and cells, and *Fundamental and Applied Toxicology*, which specializes in articles that assess the risk of harmful effects from exposure to chemicals and other substances on organisms. Elsevier publishes *Toxicology*, which also focuses on the effects of chemicals on living systems.

Journals that concentrate on aquatic and terrestrial wildlife often have articles that deal with the effects of pollutants. *Journal of Wildlife Diseases*, published by the Wildlife Disease Association, includes research and observations dealing with the health and survival of free-living or captive populations of wild animals. This is a good source for reports of the effects of environmental contamination on wildlife. *Journal of Wildlife Management*, the official publication of The Wildlife Society deals principally with population ecology of wildlife and occasionally contains papers on contaminants. *Diseases of Aquatic Organisms*, published by Inter-Research, reports on aquatic organisms as indicators of man's detrimental impact on nature.

Online databases

Many computerized online databases are available through host providers such as Dialog, STN, DataStar and BRS. AQUATIC SCIENCES AND FISHERIES ABSTRACTS provides coverage of the literature on the science, technology and management of marine and freshwater environments. A subsection is based on a print publication entitled *Aquatic pollution and environmental quality* which is produced by the US National Oceanic and Atmospheric Administration (NOAA).

BIOSIS PREVIEWS provides comprehensive worldwide coverage of research in the biological and biomedical sciences and CAB INTERNATIONAL, formerly the Commonwealth Agricultural Bureau, provides bibliographic information and abstracts of scientific research on animal health, veterinary medicine, the environment and many facets of agricultural research.

RTECS (Registry of Toxic Effects of Chemical Substances) is produced in the USA by the National Institute for Occupational Safety and Health and provides chemical toxicity data measured on humans and various animal species. TOXLINE deals with literature on the adverse effects of chemicals, drugs, and physical agents on living systems. It is derived from MEDLINE which is compiled in the US National Library of Medicine.

CD-ROM and other databases

National Information Services Corporation (NISC) has incorporated information from the US National Biological Service's print publications of *Wildlife Review/Fisheries Review* into CD-ROM format. *Wildlife Review/Fisheries Review* is a compilation of citations from scientific literature that deal with all aspects of information on wildlife. Coverage is extensive; the print version was first started in 1935 for the benefit of the United States Biological Survey and CD-ROM coverage dates from 1971 to the present. Another product, WILDLIFE WORLD-WIDE, is a compilation of *Wildlife Review*, the Fish and Wildlife Reference Service's database and DUCKDATA produced by the US National Biological Survey. Another NISC CD-ROM offering is the ENVIRON-MENTAL PERIODICALS BIBLIOGRAPHY which provides citation information on 450 000 citations, collected since 1972, that deal with environmental issues and research. This is produced by the Environmental Studies Institute of the International Academy at Santa Barbara, California. This corresponds to the print version titled *Environmental periodicals bibliography*. It is also available as an online database.

Pro-Cite software is the vehicle for distributing several environmentally oriented databases such as the National Biological Service's DUCKDATA and ABSEARCH's databases that list journal articles published by various societies such as the Wildlife Society and the Ecological Society. These are also available on CD-ROM.

Current awareness services

Current references dealing with the impact of toxicants on wildlife and the environment can be obtained through the Institute for Scientific Information's Current Contents. This is available in paper, diskette and CD-ROM versions. Table of contents information for over 938 journals is provided in the multi-disciplinary edition titled *Current contents for agriculture, biology, and environmental sciences*, and toxicology information appears in the *Current contents for clinical medicine* and in *Current contents for life sciences*.

An Internet-based current awareness service is Knight Ridder's UnCover. UnCover is available over the Internet by telnetting to database.carl.org. It is also offered through BH Blackwell's CONNECT Service and through Readmore's ROSS. UnCover can be dialled directly (in the USA) at +1 303 756 3600. The database contains five million articles from 1989 to the present that are available through an online order system. The database can be scanned for free and users only pay for the articles they request. UnCover's Reveal Alert Service is a fee-based system which allows subscribers to receive table of contents or results from user-created searches directly to an e-mail address.

Internet resources

The Extension Toxicology Network (EXTOXNET) is a cooperative effort between the University of California, Davis, Oregon State University, Michigan State University and Cornell University to provide Internet access to toxicology information. Some of the goals of EXTOXNET are to stimulate dialogue on toxicology issues, develop and make available information relevant to extension toxicology and facilitate the exchange of toxicology-related information in electronic form. EXTOXNET is available via ALMANAC, GOPHER, or the World Wide Web. The address for accessing EXTOXNET through the World Wide Web is http:/sulaco. oes. orst.edu 70/1/ext/extoxnet.

A database containing over 25 000 bibliographic citations dealing with fish and wildlife is available through the World Wide Web at http://www.fws.gov/htdocs/fwrefser.html. Documents that correspond to these citations are housed with the US FWS Reference Service, the producer of this database, and are available for a fee.

An internet listserver called *WildlifeHealth* is available through the National Wildlife Health Center in Madison, Wisconsin. A list server connects the electronic mail addresses of the subscribers allowing for exchange of information. *WildlifeHealth* specifically deals with case histories, questions and concerns regarding wildlife health issues. To subscribe to this list, send an e-mail message to Karen_Cunningham @nbs.gov with the message "SUBSCRIBE Wildlife Health <first names> <lastname> substituting first and last name in the spaces provided. Subscribers from many different countries already utilize this forum to pose questions and comment on issues in wildlife health.

Useful organizations

Several research centres of the US National Biological Service Centers do research on contaminants and their effect on wildlife. These include the Patuxent Environmental Science Center, the Midwest Science Center and the National Wildlife Health Center. Patuxent Environmental Science Center, located near Laurel, Maryland, was established in 1936 as one of the first federal wildlife research centers. Scientists study the effects of agricultural, industrial and other chemical contaminants on wildlife. In Columbia, Missouri, at the Midwest Science Center, a major research area is the study of impacts of pesticides, industrial and agricultural chemicals and other contaminants on aquatic ecosystems. The National Wildlife Health Center in Madison, Wisconsin, has as its focus the prevention, detection and management of wildlife disease in free-living wildlife through diagnostic and research activities.

The Institute for Wildlife and Environmental Toxicology (TIWET) at Clemson University in Pendleton, South Carolina, aims to seek out the best scientific data possible as a foundation for resolving ecological conflicts between aquatic and terrestrial wildlife resources and toxic substances released into the environment.

The US Department of Agriculture's Denver Wildlife Research Center works to develop new wildlife damage management techniques, methods and devices to resolve problems caused by the interaction of wild animals and society. Chemicals potentially useful in animal control applications are examined as to their fate in the environment, residues in animal and plant tissues and general hazards to non-target species.

The Canadian Cooperative Wildlife Health Center is a national organization that provides information on matters pertaining to the health of free-living wild animals in Canada to federal, territorial and private organizations and individuals. Advice and information on wildlife disease is available through a toll-free telephone line at +1 800 567 2033. Wildlife health services are provided to all parts of Canada by four regional centres located at Canada's four veterinary colleges. The headquarters of the cooperative is located at the University of Saskatchewan, Saskatoon, Saskatchewan; telephone: +1 306 966 5162.

The Toxicology Documentation Center of the Environmental Toxicology Department at the University of California, Davis, consists of over 5000 items dealing with toxicology and related topics. The library also maintains a pamphlet collection on agricultural chemicals, environmental pollution, heavy metals, food toxicants, toxicology, pesticides and trace elements.

CHAPTER FIVE

Environmental effects on oceans, rivers and inland waters

LINDA NOBLE, IAN PETTMAN AND ALLEN VARLEY

Note

Please note that this chapter was last substantially revised in 1994.

Introduction

For more than one hundred years many countries have endeavoured to develop an institutional basis for managing their aquatic resources. However, it is only over the past quarter century that concerns over environmental pollution and conservation of oceans, estuaries, rivers and inland waters, and the over-exploitation of renewable living resources such as fish, have been recognized as matters of urgent public concern.

Upwards of 50 000 scientific and technical documents are published each year on the aquatic (i.e. the marine and freshwater) sciences. This figure includes the grey, semi-published and report literature, and the subject scope encompasses the biology, ecology, fisheries, aquaculture, oceanography, hydrography, pollution, conservation, law, policy and economics of seas, estuaries, rivers, lakes and inland waters. There is no up-to-date guide to aquatic environmental information sources and resources, though Moulder (1990) covered the marine pollution literature, and Nieuwenhuysen (1989) reviewed documentary and information systems. The bibliography published by FAO (Varley and Freeman, 1990) was the first attempt to organize in a comprehensive manner the published information about the subject. An extremely good basis for a constantly updatable guide appeared in February 1994. This is John Bostock's *Fishing for information: a listing of network and on-*

line resources in aquaculture and aquatic science. It has already been so updated once at the time of writing and the author welcomes further notification of any new or omitted services. The latest version of this listing is available on the Internet via anonymous FTP from *'ftp.stir.ac.uk'*. It is in the directory *'/aqua'* and has the file name *'online.txt'*. For those who are new to online and network services and need further guidance on how to use Internet tools, a printed version is available from John Bostock at the Institute of Aquaculture, University of Stirling, Stirling, Scotland FK9 4LA.

Perhaps 15 per cent of the annual production of aquatic sciences literature is directly concerned with pollution, environmental protection and conservation, and it is this portion of the literature which will be considered here, together with some of the major sources covering wider aspects.

Aquatic pollution is caused through man's introduction of substances directly or indirectly, deliberately or accidentally, into the aquatic environment, resulting in hazards to health, harm to animals, plants, living and non-living resources, affecting activities such as fishing, impairing water quality and reducing amenities. Although the borderline is unclear to non-specialists, pollution scientists may distinguish between pollution and contamination, the latter being the presence of concentrations of substances in water, organisms or sediments that are above the natural background level.

Conservation and environmental protection are concerned not only with the prevention or alleviation of pollution, but also with the promotion of long-term sustainability. Aquatic conservation is therefore based on the three main objectives of the World Conservation Strategy defined by the International Union for the Conservation of Nature and Natural Resources (IUCN), the United Nations Environment Programme (UNEP), and the World Wide Fund for Nature (WWF) in 1980:

- to maintain essential ecological processes and life support systems;
- to preserve genetic diversity;
- to ensure the sustainable use by us and our children of species and ecosystems.

Major causes of aquatic pollution include the discharge of sewage, industrial and agricultural wastes, both organic and inorganic; mining, dredging and china clay wastes; fertilizers and pesticides washed off the land by rain; spills of oil, chemicals and other toxic substances from ships, waterside installations and road tankers; heat from power station cooling outlets; radioactivity; atmospheric fall-out, acid rain and irrigation.

The major concerns of aquatic conservation and environmental protection embrace a wide range of issues including surveys and monitoring; habitat and community classification; status of rare and endangered species; management of habitats; water quality standards; impact assessment; rehabilitation; scientific and/or political strategies; and the legal framework.

Much of the primary and secondary scientific literature and many of the associated information systems and services encompass the aquatic environment as a whole, though some deal exclusively with marine aspects, while others are devoted only to freshwater matters. In the sections that follow efforts are made to distinguish between general aquatic, specifically marine and specifically freshwater sources. Information resources covering wetlands have been included in the general aquatic category since the term incorporates both marine (estuaries, salt marshes, mangrove swamps, etc.) and freshwater (bogs, mires, fens, etc.). Salt lakes are included in the freshwater category since they are inland waters.

Agencies and organizations

International, regional and national bodies (both governmental and non-governmental) sponsor scientific investigations and research and formulate policy and legislation. These bodies disseminate information through their own series of reports, conference proceedings and other publications. Their researchers serve on advisory bodies, exchange information at meetings and through personal networks and contribute papers to the scientific literature.

International

International and United Nations agencies with strong interests in the aquatic environment include the Food and Agriculture Organization of the United Nations (FAO) and the United Nations Environment Programme (UNEP), while the International Atomic Energy Agency (IAEA), the World Health Organization (WHO) and the International Union for the Conservation of Nature and Natural Resources (IUCN) are among those with wider responsibilities. Several large international and educational programmes have included both marine and freshwater elements. One of the earliest was the International Biological Programme (IBP) which was established in 1964 by the International Council of Scientific Unions (ICSU). After a decade of work the Programme terminated in 1974 and in the following years a series of volumes were produced which synthesized the results (e.g. Le Cren and Lowe-McConnell, 1980).

Unesco's Man and the Biosphere (MAB) Programme was initiated in 1971 and has a long range goal to create an international network of biosphere reserves that will collectively represent the world's major ecological systems. A considerable body of work on both the marine and freshwater habitats has been undertaken within the scope of this Programme and the results published in the journal and report literature.

The IUCN Wetlands Programme focuses on the conservation and management of wetland ecosystems. It does this in collaboration with its members and with other international institutions with a specific wetland mandate, especially the Ramsar Convention Bureau and the International Waterfowl and Wetlands Research Bureau (IWRB). The IUCN publishes reports, directories, conference proceedings and leaflets (e.g. Dugan, 1993; Jones, 1993).

A new non-governmental organization was formed in 1992 – the Aquatic Ecosystem Health and Management Society (AEHMS). It aims to focus on aquatic ecosystem health from a holistic and sustainable perspective (marine, freshwater and estuarine) and to promote an understanding of the functioning, recovery and rehabilitation of stressed ecosystems from the impact of contaminants/nutrients in atmosphere, water and sediments.

Marine

The Intergovernmental Oceanographic Commission of Unesco (IOC), the International Maritime Organization (IMO), the International Hydrographic Organization (IHO) and the United Nations Office for Ocean Affairs and the Law of the Sea (UNOALOS) are specifically concerned with the seas.

Freshwater

The freshwater environment is also well served at the international level. Unesco's activities include the International Hydrological Programme (IHP) – initially set up as the International Hydrological Decade (IHD) in 1964 and converted to a long-term programme in 1974 with the general objective of improving the scientific and technological basis and the human resource base for the rational development and management of water resources, including the protection of the environment. Many reports and conference proceedings have arisen from IHP and in 1993 the first book in the International Hydrological Series was published as a joint venture between IHP and Cambridge University Press (Bonell, Hufschmidt and Gladwell, 1993).

Pollution of water resources had already been recognized as a major hazard to man and the environment when the Global Environmental Monitoring System (GEMS) was established within UNEP in 1975. As one of the key components of GEMS, the Global Water Monitoring

Project (GEMS/WATER) was launched in 1977. The network consists of more then 300 stations worldwide based on rivers, reservoirs and groundwaters. Monitoring long-term trends in water quality at a few representative locations is one of the prime objectives of the project. A first assessment has been published (Meybeck, Chapman and Helmer, 1989).

There is also a wide range of non-governmental international organizations. The International Association of Theoretical and Applied Limnology (SIL) is concerned with all categories of inland waters, not just lakes as its title might suggest. The International Consortium for Salt Lake Research (ICSLR), although concentrating on inland saline lakes, does also publish material on salination effects on stream ecosystems. The International Lake Environment Committee (ILEC) was established specifically to promote the environmentally sound management of lakes. ILEC's activities are currently concentrated in four areas: preparation of guideline books on lake management (Jorgensen, 1993); the compilation of world lake environment data (Lake Biwa Research Institute and ILEC, 1988–1991); the promotion of training courses; and the support of conferences.

The International Association on Water Quality (IAWQ), known as the International Association on Water Pollution Research and Control until 1992, has broadened its interests to include environmental restoration, diffuse pollution and water quality management, in addition to its more traditional fields of wastewater treatment technology. It has many specialist groups and produces a wide range of publications.

The International Association of Hydrological Sciences (IAHS) includes water quality within the scope of its objectives. It organizes many symposia and publishes the proceedings (e.g. Van de Ven *et al.*, 1991).

The Aquatic Plant Management Society is an international organization whose objectives are to assist in promoting the management of nuisance aquatic plants. It was originally called the Hyacinth Control Society when founded in 1961.

Other international agencies with an interest in freshwater environmental protection include the International Commission on Large Dams (ICOLD); the International Institute for Hydraulic and Environmental Engineering (IHE); and the International Commission on Irrigation and Drainage (ICRD).

Regional

GENERAL AQUATIC

At the regional level the Commission of the European Communities, the South Pacific Commission and the Arab League Educational, Cultural and Scientific Organization are examples of bodies concerned with all aspects of the environment. The International Centre for Living Aquatic Resources Management (ICLARM) in Manila, the Philippines, serves users mainly, but not exclusively, within the region, and operates successful research, advisory, training and information programmes.

MARINE

Organizations active in the aquatic and marine environment include the International Council for the Exploration of the Sea (ICES) (for the North Atlantic and adjacent waters), the Commission Internationale pour l'Exploration Scientifique de la Mer Mediterranée (CIESM), the Baltic Marine Environment Commission, and regional fisheries commissions such as the International North Pacific Fisheries Commission and the Northwest Atlantic Fisheries Organization. FAO, IOC and UNEP also operate at regional level through subsidiary bodies.

UNEP initiated the Regional Seas Programme in 1974. The aim is to follow a regional approach to the control of marine pollution and the management of marine and coastal resources, and to develop regional action plans. UNEP's Regional Seas Programme now includes ten regions: Mediterranean, Kuwait Action Plan Region, West and Central Africa, Wider Caribbean, East Asian Seas, South-East Pacific, South-West Pacific, Red Sea and Gulf of Aden, East Africa, and South-West Atlantic. It is regarded as an action-oriented programme concerned not only with the consequences but also with the causes of environmental degradation, and aims to combat environmental problems through the active management of marine and coastal areas. Regional action plans cover the parallel development of regional legal agreements, together with actions related to the quality and management of the marine and coastal environment. The activities of the various regions include an information component which results in the production of directories and bibliographies, as well as the dissemination of technical reports, training documents and the background papers to legal agreements.

The IMO/UNEP Regional Marine Pollution Emergency Response Centre for the Mediterranean (REMPEC) and the Euro-Mediterranean Centre on Marine Contamination Hazards, both based in Malta, can be mentioned as examples of regional bodies active in information dissemination, as can CONCAWE, the oil companies' European organization for environmental and health protection, with headquarters in Brussels, and the International Centre for Living Aquatic Resources Management (ICLARM), Manila.

The Estuarine Research Foundation (ERF) is a North American organization with five constituent Canadian and US estuarine research societies.

FRESHWATER

Since there are at least 215 international river basins (i.e. shared by more than two nations) and these basins comprise about 50 per cent of the available land and 40 per cent of the world's population, freshwater regional groups should be numerous. Unfortunately, this is not yet the case and the picture is very patchy. UNEP, in addition to its Regional Seas Programmes, has helped foster co-operation to protect some of the planet's shared rivers, lakes and aquifers. In 1985 UNEP jointly with WHO, Unesco and WMO conceived the Environmentally Sound Management of Inland Waters Programme (ENINWA). This Programme aims to support sustainable development in river basins. UNEP's first project in this area (1987) was the Zambezi River Action Plan involving eight riparian countries. Similar schemes are being planned for the Lake Chad Basin, the Aral Sea, the Nile, and river basins in Latin America.

There have been some regional groups in Europe since the 1950s and, within the framework of the political changes of the 1980s and 1990s, new ones are slowly being formed. In 1956, under the umbrella of the International Association of Limnology (SIL), the Internationale Arbeitsgemeinschaft Donauforschung (International Working Group on Danube Research) was formed and several research projects have been initiated. An overview of one of these is given in Humpesch (1992). Several organizations exist to stimulate regional co-operation for the Rhine Basin (e.g. the International Commission for the Hydrology of the Rhine Basin, CHR, and the International Commission for the Protection of the Rhine against Pollution, ICPR) (Wagenaar-Hart, 1994). In 1957 FAO set up the European Inland Fisheries Advisory Commission (EIFAC) and in 1962 a Working Party on Water Quality Criteria for European Freshwater Fish was formed. Its function is to produce critical reviews on substances known to have caused damage to fisheries in European rivers in order to derive appropriate water quality criteria or standards (e.g. Howells, 1994). The European Water Pollution Control Federation (EWPCA) was founded in 1981 and publishes a newsletter, journal and occasional reports.

The European Union has funded a research project called EURO-WATER under its Environment Research Programme. The Directorate-General of Science, Research and Development, DG XII, of the Commission of the European Communities is responsible for managing this project. Although mainly concerned with the institutional framework of water management, the project is expected to cover environmental policies and a European conference for the dissemination of the research results took place in 1995.

Co-operation between organizations in Canada and the USA provided the basis for the International Association for Great Lakes

Research (IAGLR) which was founded in 1966. Although still primarily concerned with North America's Great Lakes, it is now dedicated to the promotion of research on large lakes worldwide.

Regional initiatives in Africa include The International Decade for the East African Lakes (IDEAL) and the Working Group on African Great Lakes.

National

Most nations have a range of government departments, research institutions, university departments, societies and private sector/industrial organizations which monitor, advise, prepare legislation, undertake and sponsor research, etc. National directories specific to the aquatic, pollution or conservation organizations are available for some countries (e.g. for the UK, Water Services Association, 1993). Some of the very large organizations at national levels are well known internationally: the United States Environmental Protection Agency (EPA); National Oceanic and Atmospheric Administration (NOAA); and National Marine Fisheries Service; Environment Canada Department of Fisheries and Oceans; and the Institut Français de Recherche pour l'Exploitation de la Mer (IFREMER).

The journal literature

Some 5000 journals and serials are monitored for the AQUATIC SCIENCES AND FISHERIES ABSTRACTS (ASFA) international database, though very few of the titles are concerned exclusively with aquatic pollution. Citation analyses of the literature of marine biology and oceanography have been carried out by Garfield (1980, 1987) and Fuseler-McDowell (1988). More recently Pudovkin (1993) has examined citation relationships between marine biology journals and those in freshwater, environmental and pollution fields. Haas (1993), Resh (1985) and Gorham (1968) have considered the limnological literature. Some 6000 titles are listed in the *International directory of serial publications in aquatic sciences and fisheries* (Food and Agriculture Organization, 1993). A product of the international Aquatic Sciences and Fisheries Information System (ASFIS), the directory gives details which include abbreviated title, issuing body, publisher and place of publication, year first published, former title if a continuation, frequency, language of text and of summaries, and ISSN.

In the subject area considered here, the most productive journals are:

Aquatic Conservation: Marine and Freshwater Ecosystems
Aquatic Toxicology
Environmental Biology of Fishes

Environmental Toxicology and Water Quality
European Water Pollution Control
Journal of Aquatic Ecosystem Health
Journal of the Institution of Water and Environmental
  Management
Marine Environmental Research
Marine Pollution Bulletin
Regulated Rivers Research and Management
Water Environment and Technology
Water Environment Research
Water Research
Water Science and Technology

Major titles from the general marine literature include:

Biologiya Morya
Canadian Journal of Fisheries and Aquatic Sciences
Deep-Sea Research
Estuaries
Estuarine, Coastal and Shelf Science
ICES Journal of Marine Science (Journal du Conseil)
Journal of Experimental Marine Biology and Ecology
Journal of Plankton Research
Marine Biology
Marine Chemistry
Marine Ecology Progress Series
Marine Policy
Ocean and Coastal Management

Freshwater titles include:

Aquatic Botany
Aquatic Sciences
Archiv fur Hydrobiologie
Freshwater Biology
Hydrobiologia
Hydrological Processes
International Journal of Salt Lake Research
Internationale Revue der Gesamten Hydrobiologie
Journal of Freshwater Ecology
Journal of Great Lakes Research
Journal of the North American Benthological Association
Limnologica: Ecology and Management of Inland Waters
Limnology and Oceanography
Phycologia
Polskie Archiwum Hydrobiologii
Revue d'Hydrobiologie Tropical

> *Verhandlungen Internationale Vereinigung fur Theoretische und Angewandte Limnologie*

General ecology titles that contain a considerable amount of aquatic information include:

> *Ecological Monographs*
> *Ecology*
> *FEMS Microbiology Ecology*
> *Journal of Ecology*
> *Journal of Animal Ecology*
> *Microbial Ecology*
> *Oecologia*
> *Oikos*

From the general pollution literature the following are important sources of aquatic pollution papers:

> *Applied and Environmental Microbiology*
> *Archives of Environmental Contamination and Toxicology*
> *Bulletin of Environmental Contamination and Toxicology*
> *Chemosphere*
> *Ecotoxicology and Environmental Safety*
> *Environmental Pollution*
> *Environmental Research*
> *Environmental Science and Technology*
> *Environmental Toxicology and Chemistry*
> *Science of the Total Environment*
> *Toxicity Assessment: an International Journal*
> *Toxicology and Applied Pharmacology*
> *Water, Air and Soil Pollution*

A wide range of journals of varying quality, some fortunately short-lived, are published on conservation and the environment. Those of scientific value which contain papers on marine and freshwater pollution and conservation include:

> *Ambio*
> *Biological Conservation*
> *Environmental Conservation*
> *Environmental Monitoring and Assessment*
> *Field Studies*
> *Vie et Milieu*

From the general scientific literature, as well as *Nature*, *Science* and *New Scientist*, mention should be made of:

> *Analytica Chimica Acta*
> *Biogeochemistry*

Comparative Biochemistry and Physiology
Global Biogeochemical Cycles

Virtually all countries have government and university research establishments concerned with fisheries, oceanography, hydrography, marine and freshwater biology, together with conservation agencies and societies. There are many national journals covering these and related subjects which cannot be ignored when searching for aquatic environmental information concerning a specific geographic area. A few examples of the extensive range are given below:

Acta Hydrobiologica, Krakow
Amazoniana
Australian Journal of Marine and Freshwater Research
Hydrobiological Journal (Translation of *Gidrobiolocheskie Zhurnal*)
Journal of Freshwater Biology (India)
Journal of the Limnological Society of South Africa
Netherlands Journal of Aquatic Ecology
New Zealand Journal of Marine and Freshwater Research
Nordic Journal of Freshwater Research
Rivista di Idrobiologia

Books

Although only a relatively few books give overall coverage, many texts deal with particular aspects of marine and freshwater pollution and conservation. An especially large proportion of those on conservation aim at the popular market and are of limited scientific value. As in other subject areas, some titles which imply comprehensive treatment, upon examination consist merely of contributed chapters on narrow aspects of the subject, while others are found to be republications, in book form, of material which has already appeared in the journal literature.

Excellent introductory texts on marine pollution are *Marine pollution* (Clark, 1992) and *The State of the marine environment* (GESAMP, 1991). GESAMP is the recognized name for the IMO/FAO/Unesco/ WHO/WMO/IAEA/UN/UNEP Joint Group of Experts on the Scientific Aspects of Marine Pollution, and the publication originally appeared in 1990 as *Reports and Studies of GESAMP*, No.39, and *UNEP Regional Seas Reports and Studies*, No. 115.

It is impracticable to give a comprehensive listing here, but the following recently published books indicate the range of texts available: *Organic substances and sediments in water* (Baker, 1991); *The analysis of natural waters* (Crompton, 1993); *Water quality monitoring*

(Falconer, 1992); *Stream, lake, estuary and ocean pollution* (Nemerow, 1991); *Produced water: technological/environmental issues and solutions* (Ray and Engelhardt, 1992); *Pollution in tropical aquatic systems* (Connell and Hawker, 1991).

Specifically on the marine environment: *Marine pollution and international law* (Brubaker, 1993) *Pathobiology of marine and estuarine organisms* (Couch and Fournie, 1993); *Ecology of estuaries: anthropogenic effects* (Kennish, 1992); *Toxic metal chemistry in marine environments* (Sadiq, 1992); *Persistent pollutants in marine ecosystems* (Walker and Livingstone, 1992).

Texts on the pollution and conservation of freshwaters may consider the type of water body e.g. lakes (Howells and Dalziel, 1992), rivers (Boon, Calow and Petts, 1992), urban waterways (White *et al.*, 1993); the effects on organisms e.g. fish (Lloyd, 1992); invertebrates (Hart and Fuller, 1974); the industry e.g. mining (Kelly, 1988), oil (Green and Trett, 1989), electricity (Langford, 1983); or biological indicators (Hellawell, 1986; Rosenberg and Resh, 1993).

In addition, many of the books, monographs and student texts covering other or wider aspects of the aquatic environment, including marine and freshwater biology, ecology and chemistry, oceanography, hydrography, hydrology, fisheries and aquaculture, contain chapters or sections on pollution and environmental conservation and protection, as do those on analytical methods, remote sensing, and the like. Lists of the most recent and useful texts in these areas can be obtained through many university and aquatic research institute libraries.

Conference and symposia proceedings

The results of current research in aquatic pollution and conservation are disseminated in national, regional and international conferences, congresses, symposia and workshops. The meetings are sponsored and arranged by government departments, regional and international bodies, institutions and societies; the proliferation leads one to believe that, by accident or design, the primary purpose of some societies is to arrange regular conferences. The papers may or may not be subject to peer review and proceedings are published in books, reports, or as periodical special issues or supplements which may contain all the papers presented, or a selection made by an editorial committee. Abstracts or preprints of papers may be circulated to participants and these are occasionally cited in the literature, particularly when there is a long delay before the proceedings are published.

Some conferences are held annually and the published proceedings may have some of the characteristics of a serial publication; others are unique or irregular, utilizing a variety of formats.

Examples of recently published proceedings of conferences and symposia which are held regularly include the *Seventeenth Arctic and Marine Oilspill Program Technical Seminar* (Environment Canada, Environmental Protection Service, 1994) and the *Ninth Technical Seminar on Chemical Spills* (Environment Canada, Conservation and Protection, 1992); the American Society for Testing and Materials' *Fourteenth Symposium on Aquatic Toxicology and Risk Assessment* (Mayes and Barron, 1991); the fourteenth US/Japan experts' meeting on *Management of bottom sediments containing toxic substances* (Patin, 1992); the *Actes du 9e colloque international d'océanographie médicale* (Aubert and Aubert, 1991). The journal *Water Science and Technology* publishes proceedings of conferences and workshops of the International Association on Water Quality (Lijklema, Tyson and Le Souef, 1993; Olem, 1993). *Marine Environmental Research* publishes the proceedings of the international symposia on responses of marine organisms to pollutants (Stegeman, Moore and Hahn, 1993), while *Science of the Total Environment* regularly publishes the papers of relevant international symposia (Cape *et al.*, 1993; Lally *et al.*, 1993).

The European marine biology symposia always include papers related to pollution and conservation. The proceedings appear in a variety of formats: in books or as special issues of journals, according to arrangements made by the host institution (Colombo *et al.*, 1992).

The International Association for Sediment Water Science holds regular symposia on the interactions between sediments and water. The first two, 1976 and 1981, related to freshwater/sediment interaction only but from the third symposium in 1984 (Sly, 1986) both freshwater and marine interactions were covered. The proceedings of the fifth symposium in this series (Hart and Sly, 1992) is a good illustration of a publishing trend that has now become very common. The papers first appeared in the journal *Hydrobiologia* Vol. 235/236, 1992. They were then reproduced as a book in the Developments in Hydrobiology series produced by the same publisher (Kluwer). This dual publishing of conference proceedings can cause confusion for both users and librarians.

Reports and non-conventional literature

The technical, report, 'grey' or 'semi-published' literature is an important body of scientific and technical information. Normally produced in-house by the originating agency, institution, government or university department, company, etc., and issued as technical reports or bulletins, this material is not usually subject to the delays and formalities associated with publishing in books or journals. Because it is not subject to national bibliographic control, not comprehensively covered by the abstracting systems and rarely obtainable through the book trade, non-conventional literature is not easy to trace or acquire. The widespread use in both developing and developed countries of desk-top publishing software and laser printers adds to the flood of material appearing in this form. The following titles, with citations to recently published reports, are examples of some of the more important sources:

International

FAO Fisheries Technical Papers (Clark, 1992); *GESAMP Reports and Studies* (GESAMP, 1993); *IOC Manuals and Guides* (Intergovernmental Oceanographic Commission, 1993a); *UNEP on Reference Methods for Marine Pollution Studies* (United Nations Environment Programme, Intergovernmental Oceanographic Commission and International Atomic Energy Agency, 1992); *UNEP Regional Seas Reports and Studies* (Naidu *et al.*, 1991)

Regional

Baltic Sea Environment Proceedings, published by HELCOM, the Baltic Marine Environrnent Protection Commission – Helsinki Commission (HELCOM, 1993); *ICES Cooperative Research Reports* (Berman and Boyko, 1992) *ICES Techniques in Marine Environmental Sciences* (Uthe *et al.*, 1991); UNEP Mediterranean Action Plan *MAP Technical Reports* (United Nations Environment Programme, 1993) *ICLARM Technical Reports*, issued by the International Centre for Living Aquatic Resources Management, Manila (Chia, 1992).

At the annual meetings of the International Council for the Exploration of the Sea (ICES), upwards of 500 Committee Meeting Papers (known as C.M. Papers) are presented. Copies are available at the meeting for the participants, but are otherwise obtainable only in microfiche form from ICES headquarters in Denmark. The forty or so papers given each year under the auspices of the Marine Environmental Quality Committee, together with those of relevance from the other committees, are a valuable source of information and are frequently quoted in the scientific literature, although copies are held in only relatively few libraries.

National

Canadian Technical Reports of Fisheries and Aquatic Sciences (Harding, 1992); *Scientific Series Inland Waters Directorate Water Quality Branch, Ottawa* (Kent and Pauli, 1991); *Publications de l'Institut Français de Recherche pour l'Exploitation de la Mer* (Joanny *et al.*, 1993); *Technical Reports of the US National Oceanic and*

Atmospheric Administration (Ribic, Dixon and Vining 1992); UK Ministry of Agriculture, Fisheries and Food Directorate of Fisheries Research *Aquatic Environment Protection: Analytical Methods* series (Andrews and Sutton, 1993); reports of the UK National Rivers Authority (1992) and of the Danish Riso National Laboratory (Aarkrog *et al.*, 1992).

Abstracts

The most relevant and widely used information source is the Aquatic Sciences and Fisheries Information System (ASFIS), the international co-operative system aiming to offer a set of products and services covering the science, technology and management of marine and freshwater environments. It is designed as an integrated system concerned with the collection and dissemination of information and includes the bibliographic database and abstract journal AQUATIC SCIENCES AND FISHERIES ABSTRACTS (AFA) as its main product, together with directories, registers and current awareness publications. A decentralized global network for aquatic scientific and environmental information is the aim.

ASFIS is operated by the Food and Agriculture Organization (FAO), the Intergovernmental Oceanographic Commission of Unesco (IOC), and the United Nations Office for Ocean Affairs and the Law of the Sea (UNOALOS), with the participation of the United Nations Environment Programme (UNEP), and centres in Australia, Canada, China, France, Germany, India, Japan, Lithuania, Mexico, Norway, Portugal, Russia, Ukraine, UK and USA. From the beginning ASFIS has been recognized as the marine and freshwater component of Unesco's UNISIST concept, though it has to be said that in recent years management inadequacies and a lack of resources have delayed progress. A commercial publisher, Cambridge Scientific Abstracts, publishes ASFA and produces the database on behalf of the partnership.

ASFA is a computer-searchable bibliographic database with an equivalent printed abstract journal. It contains over half a million references and abstracts, and aims to add upwards of 35 000 new records annually. ASFA has been published monthly since 1971, when it was formed through the amalgamation of FAO's *Current bibliography for aquatic sciences and fisheries* (1959–1971) and Information Retrieval's *Aquatic biology abstracts* (1969–1971); its database consists of over 450 000 records added since 1978. The compact disc version of the database is updated quarterly, and the online database, which is updated monthly, is available on DIMDI, DIALOG, ESA, STN and other hosts. The printed version is issued in three parts: ASFA – 1 *Biological sciences and living resources*; ASFA –2 *Ocean technology, policy and non-living resources*; ASFA − 3 *Aquatic pollution and environmental quality.* In addition, two specialized journals are published as subsets, being selections from the main ASFA compilation: and *ASFA Aquaculture Abstracts* and *ASFA Marine Biotechnoloy Abstracts.* ASFA − 3 covers all aspects related to pollution and environmental quality of marine and freshwater environments: pollution monitoring, characteristics and fate, effects on organisms and environmental impact, prevention and control, man-made and natural environmental changes, conservation, wildlife management, recreation and public health.

Particular strengths of ASFA are its coverage of the non-Western and the grey literature, and its taxonomic and geographic indexing.

Other databases covering the aquatic environment include AQUALINE, WATER RESOURCES ABSTRACTS, WATERLIT, and WATERNET.

AQUALINE is produced by WRC in the UK and covers the international scientific and technical literature on water resources and supplies, water quality, monitoring, water treatment, water use, sewage, industrial effluents and the effects of pollution. Approximately 8000 abstracts are produced annually from 800 journals (plus some reports, conference proceedings and books). The database contains some 138 000 records (December 1993) dating back to 1960. It is available on CD-ROM updated quarterly and online via the ORBIT host. It is also available in a printed version called *Aqualine Abstracts* (formerly *WRC Information* from 1974 to 1985). Up to December 1993 the printed version, published fortnightly, only contained about half of the abstracts available on the database. Indexes were not provided in the fortnightly issues and no annual index had been printed since 1988. From January 1994 *Aqualine Abstracts* has appeared monthly containing most of the abstracted data together with a subject and author index. A yearly cumulative index is also published.

WATER RESOURCES ABSTRACTS is produced by the Water Resources Scientific Information Center of the US Geological Survey. It is prepared from materials collected by over 50 water research centres and institutes in the USA. The database covers ground and surface water hydrology, water resources planning, management and economics, pollution and water quality management. It contains over 250 000 abstracts dating back to 1967 and is available as a CD-ROM updated quarterly or online through the DIALOG host.

WATERLIT is compiled by the South African Water Information Centre. The database is strongest in hydrology and potable water information but it also covers water pollution control and wastewater treatment. It contains over 185 000 abstracts dating back to 1976 and about 12 000 are being added annually. The CD-ROM is updated quarterly. No online version is available.

WATERNET is produced by the American Water Works Association. It is intended mainly as a source of information for drinking water and wastewater but it does include water pollution, water quality and watershed management. The database contains approximately 35 000 records dating back to 1971 with about 3000 records being added each year. It is available as an online file on the DIALOG host.

CHEMICAL ABSTRACTS is recommended for information on specific chemicals, and BIOLOGICAL ABSTRACTS for wider biological aspects. ZOOLOGICAL RECORD and SCIENCE CITATION INDEX both contain references to aquatic environmental protection and conservation.

Useful databases for identifying and locating documents such as reports from government and other bodies, doctoral theses, technical literature, local authority publications and translations are SIGLE and NTIS. The UK input for the SYSTEM FOR INFORMATION ON GREY LITERATURE IN EUROPE (SIGLE) is prepared by British Library, and also issued monthly in hard copy in the British Reports, Translations and Theses series, the most relevant sections being Environmental Pollution Protection and Control, and Earth Sciences. The US National Technical Information Service (NTIS) aims to collect, disseminate information and provide copies of technical documents originating not only in North America, but from sources worldwide.

Reviews

Review papers survey and evaluate current knowledge in a given subject area and at the same time provide bibliographic references to the most pertinent publications. They are of great value in that they are usually compiled by acknowledged experts who are able to select, condense and interpret from the mass of available information. Some reviews of broad subject areas consider only material published in the preceding twelve months, while others on more specific topics aim for coverage in depth regardless of publication date.

Although biased towards the North American literature, the annual Literature Review published in the journal *Water Environment Research* achieved its sixtieth anniversary in 1993 (Weber, 1993), discussing 41 topics and listing over 5000 citations.

Contaminant Hazard Reviews e.g. Eisler (1994) is a series of useful reviews on the hazards of specific chemical to fish, wildlife and invertebrates. These reports are a subset of the Biological Report series produced by the US Department of the Interior, Fish and Wildlife Service.

Review articles are scattered through the periodical literature, others are published in titles devoted to reviews such as:

Reviews in Fish Biology and Fisheries
Reviews in Aquatic Sciences
Annual Review of Fish Diseases

Although the following titles may give the impression that their purpose is to give broad overviews and perspectives of current developments, their papers are normally in-depth studies of narrow and quite distinct topics, rather than wide treatments of the subject area:

> *Advances in Marine Biology*
> *Advances in Limnology*
> *Current Trends in Limnology*
> *New Dimensions in Water Environment and Ecology*
> *Oceanography and Marine Biology Annual Review*
> *Progress in Oceanography*
> *Progress in Phycological Research*
> *Progress in Underwater Science*
> *Recent Advances in Fresh Water biology*

An expansion of effort in the production of high quality reviews relating to the aquatic environment would be of great benefit. It is, therefore, encouraging to hear that WRC is planning to produce a regular series of reviews from April 1994. It is intended to search the AQUALINE database on particular topics and have a leading expert in the field review the relevant articles. The series is to be called AQUALINE REVIEWS and four issues a year are planned.

Catalogues

Library catalogues are increasing accessible online or on compact disc. The Canadian Council of Fisheries and Oceans Librarians WAVES database (Olson and Miller, 1993) has been available on CD-ROM since 1990, and more recently the Oceanographic and Marine Resources – Volume I disc has been released by the National Information Services Corporation (NISC), Baltimore. The disc, which is updated half-yearly, contains the DEEP-SEA RESEARCH OCEANOGRAPHIC LITERATURE REVIEW database (1976 to present), the library database of the UK Institute of Oceanographic Sciences Deacon Laboratory and the Proudman Oceanagraphic Laboratory, and the marine pollution and British waters databases of the Plymouth Marine Laboratory (1985 to present). Oceanography and Marine Resources – Volume II, also updated semi-annually, contains the holdings of the US National Sea Grant Depository, University of Rhode Island (30 000 records, 1968 to present) and 135 000 records from the National Oceanic and Atmospheric Administration (NOAA) Library and Information Network (1807 to present).

Current awareness

Despite its English language bias, for keeping up to date *Current Contents*, which is available as hard copy, diskette, CD-ROM, online and magnetic tape, gives reasonable and timely coverage, although not focused on the aquatic environment. *Marine Science Contents Tables* (monthly) and *Freshwater and Aquaculture Contents Tables* (quarterly), which reproduce the contents pages of core journals, are produced by FAO and distributed free to several thousand addresses worldwide. Supplements listing forthcoming meetings and symposia are issued periodically, though their coverage in recent years has not been adequate. The US National Technical Information Service (NTIS) *Environmental Pollution and Control* fortnightly bulletin in their *NTIS Alert* series is useful for the report and grey literature; the majority of the reports listed and abstracted may be purchased in hard copy or on microfiche, though non-USA customers find them expensive, particularly when obtained through agents. *Marine Pollution Research Titles*, the monthly information bulletin issued by Plymouth Marine Laboratory's Marine Pollution Information Centre, aims for comprehensive coverage (apart from legal, economic and social aspects) and lists some 2500 documents annually. References are listed in eight sections: general; petroleum hydrocarbons; metals; radioactivity; other chemicals; biological wastes; heat; solids.

The Freshwater Biological Association produces a Current Awareness Service listing between 800 and 1000 documents a month of which approximately 200 fall into the category of pollution and conservation. The Office International de l'Eau, Limoges, publishes *Information Eaux* eleven times a year. Each issue lists between 400 and 500 documents of which approximately 25 per cent relate to environmental protection and conservation.

Criteria documents and data

Criteria documents provide expert evaluations of the risks of specific chemicals to human health and environmental quality, based on a review and summary of existing data, and may form the basis for legislation. Gaps are identified in available information and recommendations are made for protective measures. Examples include publications of the National Research Council of Canada Associate Committee on Scientific Criteria for Environmental Quality (1988); the US Environmental Protection Agency (1993); the UK Water Research Centre (Mance, Norton and O'Donnell, 1988), and the Environmental Health Criteria series of the International Programme on Chemical Safety (IPCS), a joint venture of the United Nations Environment Programme, the International Labour Organization and the World Health Organization (World Health Organization, 1992).

ECDIN (Environmental Chemicals Data and Information Network) developed and maintained by the Commission of the European Communities, and AQUIRE (Aquatic Information Retrieval) sponsored by the US Environmental Protection Agency Office of Toxic Substances, are two factual databases which contain information on fate and toxicity in the aquatic environment.

AQUIRE contains actual data on acute and chronic toxicity sublethal effects and bioaccumulation in freshwater and saltwater organisms for approximately 5200 chemical substances, collected from the available literature between 1970 and 1992. Searches can be made not only for information on a particular chemical, but also for specific effects or for a named test species. Experimental conditions and bibliographic details of original sources are included. A unique feature of this database is that data quality is rated on a scale of one to four. The system is accessible through the hosts Chemical Information Systems and Numerica.

In addition to data on effects and bioaccumulation, ECIN contains files on Biodegradation and Metabolism and Bioelimination, together with the IRPTC (see below) Legal File. Coverage reflects the literature published between 1980 and 1992 for all chemical substances, and additional retrospective information is available for some. As with AQUIRE, searches can be made for concepts as well as for chemicals, and the Chemical Abstracts (CAS) Registry Number can be used to ensure accurate identification of relevant records. ECDIN is available online through DIMDI and Numerica and can also be purchased on compact disc. However, the software for the early releases of the CD-ROM version has rather restricted facilities and a limited search is more easily retrieved using the power and flexibility of ECDIN online.

Oceanographic data which may be relevant to marine pollution studies, are held in a worldwide network of National Oceanographic Data Centres, coordinated by the IOC. Major data sets are listed in the *Marine Environmental Data and Information Referral Catalogue (MEDI Catalogue)*. The MEDI system was designed by the IOC to hold technical descriptions of marine data holdings of participating organizations in standardized form. The third edition of the published catalogue (Intergovernmental Oceanographic Commission, 1993b) lists data holdings of oceanographic data centres in 26 countries and one international organization (ICES). The data centres also act as focal points for enquiries relating to data holdings of their national marine and fisheries research institutes.

Most nations have extensive freshwater data holdings. In some countries these may be cumulated, analysed and published (Institute of Hydrology and British Geological Survey, 1992). A developing trend since the 1970s has been the combination of data from a number of catchments and this has led to the formation of networks of basins whereby data may be transferred and compared. The European Water Archive has been assembled as an integral part of the Flow Regimes from International Experimental and Network Data (FRIEND) research programme and includes data from 17 European countries.

Information, advisory and referral services, directories, non-bibliographic information and networks

Information, advisory and referral services

Government departments, agencies, research institutes and international organizations normally have a mandate to collect, analyse, interpret, share and disseminate information. Aquatic pollution and environmental information should be available from national fisheries, marine and freshwater environmental, hydrographic and oceanographic research institutes and from the UN agencies with interests in the subject areas. The libraries of the institutes and organizations will usually provide bibliographic information, although increasing administrative pressures to generate income and to recover full economic costs mean that those asking for advice, analysed information or data, will often be asked to pay. Approaching an international agency can be something of a lottery and those with personal contacts are well advised to use them. However, the libraries usually respond, especially to enquirers from developing countries, and the helpfulness of some, particularly the FAO Fisheries Branch Library, Rome, and the UNEP MAP Library, Athens, is legendary.

The International Register of Potentially Toxic Chemicals (IRPTC) of the United Nations Environment Programme, based in Geneva, maintains a database and operates a Query-Response service free of charge. IRPTC uses its central files of evaluated information on toxic substances to answer questions, for example, on behaviour and effects in the aquatic environment, health hazards, waste disposal and legislation. Over 120 national correspondents, representing 116 countries provide a network through which IRPTC is able to obtain and disseminate information.

The Marine Pollution Information Centre of the Plymouth Marine Laboratory, UK, was established in 1970 following the upsurge of interest and concern resulting from the Torrey Canyon oil spill. The Centre now holds over 54 000 documents on marine and estuarine pollution and offers enquiry, bibliographic and data extraction services. Every effort is made to achieve comprehensive coverage by monitoring the world literature and acquiring or recording details of relevant publications. One of the main products of the centre, *Marine Pollution Research Titles*, has already been mentioned above. The Library and Information Service of The Freshwater Biological Association, UK, can offer similar services for information on protection and conservation of the freshwater environment.

ASFIS/ASFA centres in Australia, Canada, China, France, Germany, India, Japan, Lithuania, Mexico, Norway, Portugal, Russia, Ukraine, UK and the USA aim not only to produce input for ASFA, but also to provide output services. The ASFA database itself is used not only for bibliographic information, but also to identify institutions and their addresses and to locate experts on specified subjects. An increasing number of countries has established networks of aquatic sciences libraries to collaborate and facilitate information exchange. The International Association of Aquatic and Marine Science Libraries and Information Centers (IAMSLIC) promotes co-operation, publishes the proceedings of its annual meetings and issues a quarterly newsletter. Although the majority of its members are in North America, IAMSLIC has made commendable efforts in recent years to become truly international (Fuseler and Wiist, 1993). Its affiliate, the European Association of Aquatic Sciences Libraries and Information Centres (EURASLIC), actively seeks to improve links within Europe and its directory gives details of 514 European aquatic sciences libraries (Moulder, 1994).

In developing regions, a number of aquatic and marine information networks are operational, usually with external funding from aid agencies. They provide enquiry and current awareness services, maintain databases of regional literature and regional directories of research institutions, scientists and their research specialities.

An ASFA regional input centre is based at the Centro de Informacion Cientifica y Humanistica of the National University of Mexico and a sub-regional network, covering Barbados, Jamaica and Trinidad and Tobago, is centred in the Institute of Marine Affairs, Port of Spain, Trinidad. The Pacific Islands Marine Resources Information System (PIMRIS) was established in 1987, with headquarters in Suva, Fiji, with the support of the Canadian International Centre for Ocean Development (ICOD).

The Southeast Asian Fisheries Information System (SEAFIS) is based on operations of the Southeast Asian Fisheries Development Centre (SEAFDEC), with headquarters in Bangkok, and supports national fisheries information systems in Indonesia, Malaysia, Philippines, and Thailand. Funding and administrative problems have been experienced in recent years, although the region continues to be well served by the information activities of the International Centre for

Living Aquatic Resources Management (ICLARM), based in Manila, Philippines.

The Indian ASFA input centre and library at the National Institute of Oceanography, Goa, India, fulfil some of the functions of a regional marine information centre. The regional centre for the RECOSCIX-WIO (Regional Co-operation in Scientific Information Exchange in the Western Indian Ocean Region) project is based at the Kenya Marine and Fisheries Research Institute, Mombasa. Funded mainly by the Belgian government, the aim is to link marine scientists and information specialists in Ethiopia, Kenya, Madagascar, Mauritius, Seychelles, Somalia, Tanzania, and possibly Comores and Mozambique. A similar network, also Belgian funded, was initiated in 1993 for the Central Eastern Atlantic region. With the focal point at the Centre de Recherches Océanographiques, Abidjan, the network is burdened with the uninspiring acronym RECOSCIX-CEA.

The United Nations Environment Programme (UNEP) Mediterranean Action Plan Co-ordinating Unit is based in Athens, Greece. The Unit's Environmental Information Centre promotes the exchange of scientific and technical information among Mediterranean countries, provides information services and has produced a directory (Davaki, 1992). Literature reviews are produced and published as meeting documents by the Commission International pour l'Exploration Scientifique de la Mer Méditerranée (CIESM) (Relini, 1992). Among the working groups which operate within the CIESM framework are the Comité de Radioactivité Marine and the Comité de Lutte contre les Pollutions Marines. In late 1992 a training workshop was held in Malta for marine library and information specialists from Mediterranean and Black Sea countries. Participants strongly supported the idea of developing closer links through a regional information network.

Directories

The third edition of the *International directory of marine scientists* (UN/FAO/IOC, 1983) lists over 2500 institutions and 18 000 scientists and their research interests. Despite its undoubted value it has not been possible to update their Directory. Although there are clear possibilities of merging regional and national directories to achieve international coverage, this is not straightforward, because a concerted effort is needed, with the support and leadership of one of the UN agencies, together with standardized questionnaires and database structures.

Regional directories are available, for example, for the Southeast Asian Seas region (Chua *et al.*, 1989), for the Arab States (United Nations Environment Programme, 1990), for the Mediterranean (Davaki, 1992), and for Europe (Commission of the European Communities, 1992).

Society yearbooks and membership directories are also useful sources (e.g. International Association on Water Quality, 1992; Institution of Water and Environmental Management, 1993).

An appreciable number of countries produce national directories of aquatic marine or freshwater institutions, researchers and their subject specialities. Canada, Korea and the UK are among countries with directories of this nature (Canada Department of Fisheries and Oceans, 1989; Wells, Belore and Belore, 1985; Korea Ocean Research and Development Institute, 1989; Varley *et al.*, 1992). There are many conservation and environment directories. Some of those which are produced commercially or by pressure groups relying on responses to mailed questionnaires are inaccurate, misleading and of poor quality.

Full text and interactive information

The worldwide availability of cheap but powerful microcomputers has stimulated the distribution in electronic form of not only biblio- graphic information, but non-bibliographic and integrated information products. The IMO-VEGA compact disc database was developed jointly by the International Maritime Organization and Det Norske Veritas Classification. The disc contains full text of conventions and codes relating to safety and pollution prevention requirements, including resolutions and circulars of IMO's Marine Environmental Pollution Committee. The OIL SPILL CASE HISTORY database, developed by the US National Oceanic and Atmospheric Administration (NOAA), documents some 100 significant oil spills around the world, 1967–1991, and is available on a microcomputer diskette. UKDMAP (United Kingdom Digital Marine Atlas) is also loaded from microcomputer diskettes. Produced by the British Oceanographic Data Centre, the Atlas is being developed as a reference work on all aspects of the coastline and seas around the British Isles.

Despite the information infrastructure and perhaps because of the sheer mass of published information, scientists continue to interact directly and they are enthusiastic users of electronic networks. Omnet/ Sciencenet and Internet are favoured by aquatic scientists and their library and information colleagues for electronic mail, special interest groups, bulletin boards, access to catalogues and inventories and information and data transfer. Those relevant to the aquatic environment are listed in John Bostock's *Fishing for information*, detailed in the Introduction to this chapter.

UK

The pattern of research and development in aquatic pollution and conservation in the UK is broadly similar to that of many Western countries and the range of information sources and services is strong and diverse. Government departments, organizations and advisory bodies support, direct and conduct research and set the legal and regulatory frameworks. Research institutes, university departments, regional and local government bodies, industry and commerce carry out research and environmental monitoring, while conservation is furthered by natural history societies, trusts, pressure groups and the media. The following is an indication of the range of activities, with selected examples, but with no attempt at comprehensive coverage.

The Royal Commission on Environmental Pollution advises the government on matters of environmental concern. Pollution of estuaries and coastal waters was considered in the Commission's third and tenth reports (1972, 1984), effects of oil pollution on the marine environment in the eighth (1981) and freshwater quality in the sixteenth (1992). The Department of the Environment has a key role and includes a Water Directorate, a Marine Pollution Monitoring Management Group, Her Majesty's Inspectorate of Pollution, the North Sea Scientific Coordinating Office, and groups concerned with the development of Statutory Water Quality Objectives for estuarine and coastal waters, and other aspects of marine and freshwater pollution and conservation. Responsibility for marine pollution control is dispersed across several departments and consideration is being given to making them the responsibility of a new Environment Agency. Consideration of freshwater pollution is often undertaken in collaboration with the Welsh Office, for example, the quinquennial surveys of *River quality in England and Wales* (Department of the Environment and The Welsh Office, 1986). The Scottish Office Environment Department produce similar water quality surveys for Scotland (1992). The main fisheries laboratories of the Ministry of Agriculture, Fisheries and Food are at Lowestoft and Burnham, while the Scottish Office Agriculture and Fisheries Department maintains a marine laboratory at Aberdeen and a freshwater fisheries laboratory at Pitlochry; the Department of Agriculture for Northern Ireland has an Aquatic Sciences Research Division in Belfast.

The Natural Environment Research Council supports aquatic research, including pollution, in research institutes and universities. Among those carrying out marine and estuarine research are the Plymouth Marine Laboratory and Marine Biological Association, whose library contains the Marine Pollution Information Centre, and the Dunstaffnage Marine Laboratory and Scottish Marine Biological Association, Oban. Oceanographic research is carried out at the Institute of Oceanographic Sciences Deacon Laboratory at Wormley, which also supports a Marine Information Advisory Service, and at the Proudman Oceanographic Laboratory, Bidston, Merseyside, the latter housing the British Oceanographic Data Centre. Major centres of freshwater research are the Windermere Laboratory of the NERC Institute of Freshwater Ecology and the Freshwater Biological Association, and the Institute of Hydrology, Wallingford.

Agencies with interests in aquatic pollution include AEA Environment, Harwell; the former Warren Spring Laboratory, (the environmental resources of these two organizations, including the marine pollution monitoring, have been transferred to a new organization called the National Environmental Technology Centre created in June 1993); Hydraulics Research, Wallingford; and WRC (formerly the Water Research Centre), Marlow and Swindon. A wide range of publications is available from government supported research and advisory bodies, apart from their annual reports which give good indications of research in progress.

Marine and freshwater ecology, fisheries, aquaculture, oceanography, hydrology and environmental sciences are taught and are the subjects of research at universities. Some of them maintain research stations or house special units: Liverpool University's Port Erin Marine Laboratory, Isle of Man, the University Marine Biological Station, Millport, Isle of Cumbrae and the University of London's Monitoring and Assessment Research Centre (MARC), being examples.

The organization of the UK water industry is complex. In England and Wales water supply and sewage disposal are provided by the water companies. Regulation is carried out by the independent National Rivers Authority (NRA, from April 1996 part of the Environment Agency) which has responsibility for river basin regulation, including setting river water quality standards, consenting to discharges, monitoring compliance and for licensing abstraction. The NRA's sphere of regulation covers rivers, lakes, reservoirs, aquifers and the sea around the coast for a distance of three miles. In Scotland the Regional Councils have the functions of public water supply, sewerage and sewage disposal with the Central Scotland Water Development Board acting as a bulk supplier to six of the regional councils. Regulation comes under nine River Purification Boards. In Northern Ireland both the supply and regulatory aspects are performed by The Water Service of the Department of the Environment Northern Ireland.

Research, analysis, environmental monitoring, impact assessment and advisory services are undertaken by industry and offered by numerous firms of consultants. Zeneca Ltd, Brixham Environmental Laboratory provides services to ICI and external clients; National Power maintains a Marine and Freshwater Biology Unit at Fawley, Southampton, and the oil companies carry out environmental research.

In 1991 the Nature Conservancy Council was divided into English

Nature, the Countryside Council for Wales, and Scottish Natural Heritage and the Joint Nature Conservation Committee (JNCC). The JNCC has statutory responsibilities including the establishment of common standards, undertaking and commissioning research, advising on nature conservation and on the development and implementation of nature conservation policy. The JNCC is carrying out a Marine Nature Conservation Review and a Coastal Review of habitats and human pressures on the coastal environment. Other relevant bodies include the Field Studies Council, the Marine Conservation Society, local natural history societies and conservation trusts. A whole range of bodies and pressure groups as diverse as the Consumers Association, Friends of the Earth, Greenpeace and the Tidy Britain Group have interests in aquatic pollution and conservation.

International organizations based in London include the International Maritime Organization and the International Tanker Owners' Pollution Federation. UK scientists and policy-makers are deeply involved in European, UN and other international programmes related to aquatic pollution and conservation.

The *Directory of marine and freshwater institutions, scientists and research engineers in the United Kingdom and Republic of Ireland* (Varley *et al.*, 1992) prepared and published by members of the Britain and Ireland Association of Aquatic Sciences Libraries and Information Centres (BIASLIC) lists some 450 institutions, departments and companies primarily or partly engaged in marine and estuarine scientific research, together with over 2400 researchers and their subject interests. *Estuaries and coastal waters of the British Isles: an annual bibliography of recent scientific papers*, published since 1977, lists over 1000 papers each year. *Hydrobiological papers on British freshwaters* the annual freshwater equivalent, published since 1976, lists approximately 350 papers each year (Freshwater Biological Association, 1994). Details of UK aquatic sciences libraries, their services and facilities, are listed in the *EURASLIC directory of European aquatic sciences libraries and information centres* (Moulder, 1994).

References

Aarkrog, A. *et al.* (1992) *Environmental radioactivity in the North Atlantic region including the Faroe Islands and Greenland, 1988 and 1989.* Roskilde: Riso National Laboratory.

Andrews, D.J. and Sutton, G.A. (1993) An automated NaI 'well' counting system for the determination of radiocaesium. *Aquatic Environment Protection: Analytical Methods,* 9.

Aubert, M. and Aubert, J. (1991) Actes du 9e colloque international d'océanographie médicale 22–24 Octobre 1990, Nice (France). *Revue Internationale d'Océanographie Médicale,* 101–104.

Baker, R.A. (1991) (ed.) *Organic substances and sediments in water.* (3 vols.) Michigan: Lewis Publishers.

Berman, S.S. and Boyko, V.J. (1992) ICES seventh round intercalibration for trace metals in biological tissue. *ICES Cooperative Research Reports,* 189.

Bonell, M., Hufschmidt, M.M. and Gladwell, J.S. (1993) *Hydrology and water management in the humid tropics: hydrological research issues and strategies for water management.* Cambridge: Cambridge University Press.

Boon, P.J., Calow, P. and Petts, G.E. (1992) (eds) *River conservation and management.* Chichester: John Wiley.

Brubaker, D. (1993) *Marine pollution and international law: principles and practice.* London: Belhaven Press.

Canada Department of Fisheries and Oceans (1989) Directory of marine and freshwater scientists in Canada – 1989. *Canadian Special Publication of Fisheries and Aquatic Sciences,* 104.

Cape, J.N. *et al.* (1993) (eds) Chemical analysis of natural waters: collection of papers presented at an international conference: Analytical solutions to current problems, held at the Institute for Terrestrial Ecology, Merlewood Research Station, Grange-over-Sands, Cumbria, UK, September 1991. *Science of the Total Environment,* 135, ix.

Chia, L.S. (1992) Singapore's urban coastal area: strategies for management. *ICLARM Technical Reports,* 31, xii.

Chua, T.E. *et al.* (1989) *Directory of institutions and scientists in the ASEAN region involved in research and/or management related to coastal areas.* Manila: International Center for Living Aquatic Resources Management.

Clark, J.R. (1992) Integrated management of coastal zones. *FAO Fisheries Technical Paper,* 327, viii.

Clark, R.B. (1992) *Marine pollution* 3rd edn. Oxford: Clarendon Press.

Colombo, G. *et al.* (1992) (eds) *Marine eutrophication and population dynamics: Proceedings of the 25th European Marine Biology Symposium* (Ferrara, Italy, 10–15 September 1990). Fredensborg: Olsen and Olsen.

Commission of the European Communities (1992) *European directory of fisheries and aquaculture research.* Dordrecht: Kluwer Academic Publishers.

Connell, D.W. and Hawker, D.W. (1991). (eds) *Pollution in tropical aquatic systems.* Boca Raton: CRC Press.

Couch, J.A. and Fournie, J.W. (1993) *Pathobiology of marine and estuarine organisms.* Boca Raton: CRC Press.

Crompton, T.R. (1993) *The analysis of natural waters* (2 vols.). Oxford: Oxford University Press.

Devaki, A. (1992) Directory of Mediterranean marine environmental centres. *Map Technical Reports Series,* 65.

Department of the Environment and The Welsh Office (1986) *River quality in England and Wales 1985.* London: HMSO.

Dugan, P.J. (1993) (ed.) *Wetlands in danger.* London: Mitchell Beazley (in conjunction with IUCN).

Eisler, R. (1994) Famphur hazards to fish, wildlife, and invertebrates: a synoptic review. *Contaminant Hazard Reviews,* 27, iii.

Environment Canada, Environmental Protection Serv ice (1994) *Proceedings of the Seventeenth Arctic and Marine Oilspill Program Technical Seminar* (Vancouver, British Columbia, 8–10 June 1994). Ottawa: Environment Canada, Environmental Protection Service.

Environment Canada, Conservation and Protection (1992) *Proceedings of the Ninth Technical Seminar on Chemical Spills* (Edmonton, Alberta, 8–9 June 1992). Ottawa: Environment Canada, Conservation and Protection.

Environmental Protection Agency (1993) *Ambient aquatic life water quality criteria for aniline (CAS Registry Number 62–53–3).* Narragansett, Rhode Island: Environmental

Research Laboratory.
Falconer, R.A. (1992) (ed.) *Water quality monitoring*. Aldershot: Ashgate Publishing.
Food and Agriculture Organization (1993) *International directory of serial publications in aquatic sciences and fisheries*. Rome: Cambridge Scientific Abstracts, for FAO. (ASFIS Reference Series No. 12).
Freshwater Biological Association (1994) *A list of hydrobiological papers on British freshwaters published in 1993*. Ambleside: FBA.
Fuseler, E. and Wiist, S. (1993) (eds) *Aquatic information resources: tools of our trade: Proceedings of the 18th Annual IAMSLIC Conference* (Bremerhaven, Germany, 5–9 October 1992). Fort Collins, Colorado: IAMSLIC.
Fuseler-McDowell, E. (1988) Documenting the literature of marine biology. In *Marine science information throughout the world: sharing the resources*, eds C.P. Winn, R.W. Burkhart and J.C. Burkhart, pp. 45–60. St. Petersburg, Florida, IAMSLIC.
Garfield, E. (1981) The literature of marine biology. *Biologiya Morya*, 3, 3–20 (in Russian). [English translation in *Soviet Journal of Marine Biology*, 7, 137–152, 1981].
Garfield, E. (1987) Journal citation studies. 47. What oceanography journals make the biggest waves? *Current Contents*, 30 (48), 3–11.
GESAMP (1991) *The state of the marine environment*. Oxford: Blackwell Scientific Publications.
GESAMP (1993) Impact of oil and related chemicals and wastes on the marine environment. *GESAMP Reports and Studies*, 50, ix.
Gorham, E. (1968) Journal coverage in the field of limnology. *Limnology and Oceanography*, 13, 355–369.
Green, J. and Trett, M.W. (1989) (eds) *The fate and effects of oil in freshwater*. London: Elsevier.
Haas, S.C. (1993) Core journals in limnology: a reassessment. *ASLO Bulletin*, 2 (1), 7–8.
Harding, G.C. (1992) A review of the major marine environmental concerns off the Canadian east coast in the 1980s. *Canadian Technical Reports of Fisheries and Aquatic Sciences*, 1885, vi.
Hart, B.T. and Sly, P.G. (1992) (eds) *Sediment/water interactions: Proceedings of the Fifth International Symposium*. Dordrecht: Kluwer Academic Publishers.
Hart, C.W. and Fuller, S.L.H. (1974) (eds) *Pollution ecology of freshwater invertebrates*. New York: Academic Press.
HELCOM (1993) Study of the transportation of packaged dangerous goods by sea in the Baltic Sea area, and related environmental hazards. *Baltic Sea Environment Proceedings*, 51, v.
Hellawell, J.M. (1986) *Biological indicators of freshwater pollution and environmental management*. London Elsevier.
Howells, G. (1994) (ed.) *Water quality for freshwater fish: further advisory criteria*. Amsterdam: Gordon and Breach Science Publishers.
Howells, G. and Dalziel, T.R.K. (1992) (eds) *Restoring acid waters: Loch Fleet 1984–1990*. London: Elsevier.
Humpesch, U.H. (1992) Ecosystem study Altenwörth: impacts of a hydroelectric power-station on the River Danube in Austria. *Freshwater Forum*, 2 (1), 33–58.
Institute of Hydrology and British Geological Survey (1992) *Hydrological data United Kingdom 1991 yearbook: an account of rainfall, river flows, groundwater levels and river water quality January to December 1991*. Wallingford: Institute of Hydrology.
Institution of Water and Environmental Management (1993) *1993 Yearbook*. London: IWEM.
Intergovernmental Oceanographic Commission (1993a) Chlorinated biphenyls in open ocean waters: sampling, extraction, clean-up and instrumental determination. *IOC Manuals and Guides*, 27.
Intergovernmental Oceanographic Commission (1993b) Marine environmental data

information referral catalogue (MEDI catalogue) 3rd edn. *IOC Manuals and Guides*, 16, vi.

International Association on Water Quality (1992) *Yearbook 1992–93 and directory of members*. London: IAWQ.

Joanny, M. *et al.* (1993) *Qualité du milieu marin littoral*. Brest: Institut Français de Recherche pour l'Exploitation de la Mer.

Jones, T. (1993) *A directory of wetlands of international importance* (4 vols.). Gland: IUCN.

Jorgensen, S.E. (1993) (ed.) *Guidelines of lake management. Vol. 5. Management of lake acidification*. Otsu, Shiga: ILEC.

Kelly, M. (1988) *Mining and the freshwater environment*. London: Elsevier.

Kennish, M.J. (1992) *Ecology of estuaries: anthropogenic effects*. Boca Raton: CRC Press.

Kent, R.A. and Pauli, B.D. (1991) Canadian water quality guidelines for captan. *Scientific Series Inland Water Directorate, Ottawa*, 188.

Korea Ocean Research and Development Institute (1989) *Directory of marine scientists in Korea*. Seoul: KORDI.

Lake Biwa Research Institute and ILEC (1988–1991) (eds) *Data book of world lake environments – a survey of the state of world lakes. Interim reports I–IV* (4 vols.). Otsu, Shiga: ILEC.

Lally, A.E. *et al.* (1993) (eds) Environmental radiochemical analysis: a collection of papers from the 6th international symposium on environmental radiochemical analysis, September 1990, Manchester, UK. *Science of the Total Environment*, 130/131, xi.

Langford, T.E. (1983) *Electricity generation and the ecology of natural waters*. Liverpool: Liverpool University Press.

Le Cren, E.D. and Lowe-McConnell, R.H. (1980) *The functioning of freshwater ecosystems*. Cambridge: Cambridge University Press. (International Biological Programme No. 22).

Lijklema, L., Tyson, J.M. and Le Souef, A. (1993) (eds) INTERURBA: interactions between sewers, treatment plants and receiving waters in urban areas: proceedings of the IAWPRC workshop held in Wageningen, The Netherlands, 6–10 April 1992. *Water Science and Technology*, 27 (12).

Lloyd, R. (1992) *Pollution and freshwater fish*. Oxford: Fishing News Books.

Mance, G., Norton, R. and O'Donnell, A.R. (1988) Proposed environmental quality standards for List II substances in water: vanadium. *Technical Report, Water Research Centre* (TR 253).

Mayes, M.A. and Barron, M.G. (1991) (eds) *Aquatic toxicology and risk assessment: volume 14*. Philadelphia: American Society for Testing and Materials.

Meybeck, M., Chapman, D. and Helmer, R. (1989). *Global environment monitoring system, Global freshwater quality: a first assessment*. Oxford: Blackwell.

Moulder, D.S. (1990) A review of the marine pollution literature. In *Oceanic processes in marine pollution. Volume 6. Physical and chemical processes: transport and transformation*, eds. D.J. Baumgartner and I.W. Duedall, pp. 13–21. Malabar, Florida: Krieger.

Moulder, D. (1994) (ed.) *Directory of European aquatic sciences libraries and information Centres* 2nd edn. Madrid: Instituto Español de Oceanografia, for European Association of Aquatic Sciences Libraries and Information Centres (EURASLIC).

Naidu, S. *et al.* (1991) Water quality studies on selected South Pacific lagoons. *UNEP Regional Seas Reports and Studies*, 136, iv.

National Research Council of Canada Associate Committee on Scientific Criteria for Environmental Quality (1988) *Pyrethroids: their effects on aquatic and terrestrial ecosystems*. Ottawa: National Research Council of Canada Associate Committee on Scientific Criteria for Environmental Quality (NRCC No. 24376).

National Rivers Authority (1992) The influence of agriculture on the quality of natural waters in England and Wales. *Water Quality Series, National Rivers Authority*, 6.

Nemerow, N.L. (1991) *Stream, lake, estuary and ocean pollution* 2nd edn. New York: Van Nostrand Reinhold.

Nieuwenhuysen, P. (1989) (ed.) *Scientific and technical water-related documentary and information systems in the Unesco International Hydrological Programme*. Paris: Unesco. (*Technical Documents in Hydrology* SC-89/WS-49).

Noble, L. (1994) *Estuaries and coastal waters of the British Isles: an annual bibliography of recent scientific papers* No. 18. Plymouth: Plymouth Marine Laboratory and Marine Biological Association.

Olem, H. (1993) (ed.) Diffuse pollution: proceedings of the IAWQ 1st international conference on diffuse (nonpoint) pollution: sources, prevention, impact, abatement, held in Chicago, Illinois, USA, 19–24 September 1993. *Water Science and Technology*, 28 (3–5), xiii.

Olson, P.L. and Miller, G. (1993) Ways and WAVES: bibliographic control of Canadian fisheries literature. In Fuseler and Wiist (1993), pp. 71–76.

Patin, T.R. (1992) (ed.) *Management of bottom sediments containing toxic substances: Proceedings of the 14th US/Japan Experts Meeting* (Yokohama, Japan, 27 February – 1 March 1990). Vicksberg, Massachusetts: Army Engineers Waterways Experiment Station.

Pudovkin, A.L. (1993) Citation relationships among marine biology journals and those in related fields. *Marine Ecology Progress Series*, 100, 207–209.

Ray, J.P. and Engelhardt, F.R. (1992) (eds) *Produced water: technological/environmental issues and solutions*. New York: Plenum Press.

Relini, G. (1991) Rapport bibliographique sur le zoobenthos de la Méditerranée (1988–1990). *Rapports et Procès-Verbaux des Réunions, Commission Internationale pour L'exploration Scientifique de la Mer Méditerranée*, 32 (2), 17–62.

Resh, V.H. (1985) Periodical citation in aquatic entomology and freshwater benthic biology. *Freshwater Biology*, 15, 757–766.

Ribic, C.A., Dixon, T.R. and Vining, I. (1992) Marine debris survey manual. *NOAA Technical Report NMFS*, 108, vi.

Rosenberg, D.M. and Resh, V.H. (1993) (eds) *Freshwater biomonitoring and benthic macroinvertebrates*. New York: Chapman and Hall.

Royal Commission on Environmental Pollution (1972) *Pollution in some British estuaries and coastal waters*. London: HMSO (Cmnd 5054).

Royal Commission on Environmental Pollution (1981) *Oil pollution in the sea*. London: HMSO (Cmnd 8358).

Royal Commission on Environmental Pollution (1984) *Tackling pollution – experience and prospects*. London: HMSO (Cmnd 9149).

Royal Commission on Environmental Pollution (1992) *Freshwater quality*. London: HMSO (Cmnd 1966).

Sadiq, M. (1992) *Toxic metal chemistry in marine environments*. New York: Marcel Dekker.

Scottish Office Environment Department (1992) *Water quality survey of Scotland 1990*. Edinburgh: the Scottish Office.

Sly, P.G. (1986) (ed.) *Sediments and water interactions*. New York: Springer.

Stegeman, J.J., Moore, M.M. and Hahn, M.E. (1993) (eds) Responses of marine organisms to pollutants: proceedings of the sixth international symposium, held at Woods Hole Oceanographic Institution, Massachusetts, 24–26 April 1991. *Marine Environmental Research*, 34 (1–4), xiv [part one]; 25 (1–2), xi [part two].

United Nations Educational Scientific and Cultural Organization, Food and Agriculture Organization and Intergovernmental Oceanographic Commission (1983) *International Directory of Marine Scientists*, 3rd edn. Paris: UNESCO.

United Nations Environment Programme (1990) *Directory of marine scientists and marine environmental centres in the Arab States*. Nairobi: UNEP.

United Nations Environment Programme (1993) Selected techniques for monitoring biological effects of pollutants in marine organisms. *MAP Technical Reports*, 71, vii.

United Nations Environment Programme, Intergovernmental Oceanographic Commission and International Atomic Energy Agency (1992) Determination of petroleum hydrocarbons in sediments. *UNEP Reference Methods for Marine Pollution Studies*, 20, iii.

Uthe, J.F. *et al.* (1991) Temporal trend monitoring: introduction to the study of contaminant levels in marine biota. *ICES Techniques in Marine Environmental Sciences*, 14.

Van de Ven, F.H.M. *et al.* (1991) (eds) *Hydrology for the water management of large river basins*. Wallingford: IAHS (IAHS publication no. 201).

Varley, A. and Freeman, R.R. (1990) A bibliography on information services, systems and centres for marine and freshwater resources and environment. *FAO Fisheries Circular*, 830, iv.

Varley, A. *et al.* (1992) (eds) *Directory of marine and freshwater institutions, scientists and research engineers in the United Kingdom and Republic of Ireland*. Windermere: Freshwater Biological Association, for Britain and Ireland Association of Aquatic Sciences Libraries and Information Centres.

Wagenaar-Hart, A.M. (1994) International Commission for the Hydrology of the Rhine Basin (CHR). *Water Science and Technology*, 29 (3), 375–378.

Walker, C.H. and Livingstone, D.R. (1992) (eds) *Persistent pollutants in marine ecosystems*. Oxford: Pergamon Press.

Water Services Association (1993) *Who's who in the water industry 1993*. London: Water Services Association.

Weber, A.S. (1993) The Literature Reviews's sixtieth anniversary. *Water Environment Research*, 65 (4), 289–605.

Wells, P.G., Belore, R.C. and Belore, E.L. (1985) *Canadian directory of aquatic toxicologists and related specialists*. Ottawa: Environment Canada, Environmental Protection Service.

White, K.N. *et al.* (1993) *Urban waterside regeneration: problems and prospects*. New York: Ellis Horwood.

World Health Organization (1992) Trichlorfon. *Environmental Health Criteria*, 132.

CHAPTER SIX

Environmental effects on the atmosphere

MARY F. CAMPANA AND SHIRLEY M. SMITH

Introduction

The subject of atmospheric sciences encompasses an enormous range of disciplines and areas of study, and includes highly theoretical work as well as research on pressing practical issues. The information generated from these endeavours is produced in every conceivable format: paper, data tapes, CD-ROM, online numeric and bibliographic databases, and, increasingly, the Internet and World Wide Web. It is gathered, analysed, processed and distributed by a very large number of companies, universities, governments and international agencies. The amount of information is growing rapidly, and research emphases and funding shift as new concerns are identified. This chapter describes some of the key resources in atmospheric sciences available to information seekers and providers. In addition to general meteorological sources, global climate change and air quality are highlighted.

A quick review of terms clarifies some of the basic aspects of the science:

- atmosphere refers to the physical envelope of air surrounding the planet
- meteorology is the study of all aspects of the atmosphere
- climatology is the study of climate, and is considered a major branch of meteorology

While the term global warming is often seen, the term used here is the less charged global change. Air quality encompasses more than air pollution and is used as the preferred term.

Basic standard sources

The dispersed nature of the atmospheric sciences and the many
potential approaches to the information require broad, even eclectic,
location and retrieval strategies. Therefore, the use of standard
reference materials as a part of information gathering is important;
they provide good overviews and outlines of organizations and
products.

World of learning (Europa, annual) is organised by country and lists
the learned societies and academies where the major meteorological
institutions can be found with their addresses founding dates,
telephone numbers and major publications.

Europa yearbook (Europa, annual) contains the structure of the
government, including dates and secretariats, for each country.

CD-ROMs in print (E.N. Desmarais, ed., Meckler) lists discs
alphabetically and indexes by subject, supplier and online service,
enabling the user to discover the major meteorological products in that
format. The *Gale directory of databases online* (Gale) provides
similar information for online databases.

The Yearbook of international organisations (Saur, annual) is a
source for international organizations and programmes. Volume 3 is
the subject index, and the majority of the regional and international
organisations concerned with atmospheric sciences can be located
under the terms Climatology, Geophysics and Meteorology. Entries
within the text volumes provide addresses, telephone and fax numbers,
outline the organizational structure and describe component
programmes and publications. Organizations such as Council of
Europe, EC, UNEP and Unesco which have atmospheric concerns are
found here.

World treaty index (P.H. Rohn, ed., ABC-Clio) is a source of
international and regional agreements. Volume 5 contains the key
word index and searching the terms atmosphere and meteorology calls
up a lengthy list. Another tool for searching international agreements
is the online/print index PAIS.

Specific organisations and publications

A major source of information on worldwide meteorology is the World
Meteorological Organization (WMO, Case Postale 2, CH-1211
Geneva, Switzerland, URL: http://www.wmo.ch/). WMO has been in
existence since 1950 and most nations are members. Its purpose is to
ensure the production, standardisation, publication and distribution of
meteorological research, both basic and applied. WMO publishes a
number of series: technical notes, technical regulations, atlases,

observational and data processing information and operation manuals such as the *International meteorological codes*. Additionally WMO sponsors and co-sponsors several international meetings each year on various aspects of meteorology and publishes the proceedings of these conferences. WMO extensively co-operates with major national and international agencies. One consideration in using WMO publications is the eccentric and difficult-to-follow numbering systems of their various series.

The American Meteorological Society (AMS, 45 Beacon St., Boston MA 02108, URL: http://www.atm.geo.nsfgov/AMS/) publishes journals, books, monographs, conference proceedings and *Meteorological and Geoastrophysical Abstracts*. While including many unique sources, it is updated irregularly and without a thesaurus of indexing terms precise and comprehensive retrieval is somewhat difficult. It is advisable to include other databases with the *Abstracts* when searching for information.

The coverage of AMS is international and it is the US distributor of WMO publications. The *Bulletin of the AMS*, May issue, publishes a complete list of AMS and WMO publications and is therefore a useful collection tool. The *Bulletin* also lists a Calendar of Meetings which includes both US and international meteorological conferences.

The AMS publishes several primary atmospheric sciences journals which are international in scope. *Journal of Applied Meteorology* covers applied research in all aspects of meteorology, while *Journal of the Atmospheric Sciences* emphasizes quantitative and deductive basic research. Climate data analysis, modelling and prediction are the subjects of *Journal of Climate*.

The UK Meteorological Office (UKMO, London Road, Bracknell, Berkshire RG12 2SZ, URL: http://www.meto.govt.uk/home.html) publishes a variety of materials, including the online data-base MOLARS of the holdings of the UK National Meteorological Library. Records date from 1971 and are updated monthly. It is available through the European Space Agency Information Retrieval Service in Rome. Research produced by the UKMO appears in its *Annual Report* as well as in *Meteorological Magazine*, and the Royal Meteorological Society's publication *Meteorological Applications*. UKMO also produces a primary atmospheric sciences journal *International Journal of Climatology*, which encompasses global and regional climatic studies.

The online database HMSO Official British Publications is the source for identifying UK government materials, as well as European and international publications for which it is the distributing agent.

Another US organisation, the American Geophysical Union (AGU, 2000 Florida Ave. SW, Washington DC 20009, URL: http:// earth.agu.org/kosmos/homepage.html) publishes a primary journal in atmospheric sciences, the multi-part *Journal of Geophysical Research*, which is international in scope. In particular *JGR: Atmospheres* publishes papers on the physics and chemistry of the atmosphere, as well as atmospheric, biospheric, lithospheric or hydrospheric research.

A major producer of atmospheric sciences data is the National Climate Data Center (NCDC, URL: http://ncdc.noaa.gov) run by NOAA in Asheville, North Carolina. It produces *Climatological Data*, a monthly summary of US climate records. In cooperation with WMO, NCDC produces *Monthly Climatic Data for the World* which is organised by continent, country and data collection station.

Several US agencies participate in atmospheric sciences research: National Oceanic and Atmospheric Administration (NOAA,URL:http: / /www.noaa.gov), National Science Foundation (NSF, URL: http://www.nsf.gov), National Aeronautics and Space Administration (NASA, URL: http://www.nasa.gov), US Department of Agriculture (USDA, URL: http://www.usda.gov). They publish a variety of documents and much of the research is global in scope. Online databases such as the Government Publication Office (GPO, URL: http://www.gpo.gov) GPO Monthly Catalog. GPO Publications and National Technical Information service (NTIS, URL: ttp://fedworld.gov/ntis/nthome.html) are primary sources for locating information produced by these organizations. The National Center for Atmospheric Research (NCAR, Boulder, CO, URL: http://www.ucar.edu) is arguably the premier atmospheric sciences research centre in the USA; its research is worldwide. Information published by NCAR is indexed in *NTIS* and *Meteorological and Geoastrophysical Abstracts* as well as the internal NCAR database. NTIS is the National Technical Information Service.

Air & Waste Management Association (AWMA, One Gateway Center, 3rd flr., Pittsburgh PA 15227, URL: http://www.awma.org/) is a non-profit organisation and a neutral forum for presenting all viewpoints of an environmental management issue (technical, scientific, economic, social, political and public health). AWMA attracts decisionmakers from government agencies, industry and the academic and research communities. Fifty countries are represented in the membership. A major air quality journal, *Air & Waste*, is produced monthly. The Association also publishes a useful *Directory* which includes meetings and publications, indexes the membership in a variety of ways, provides a buyer's guide section and a government agency directory section of the USA and Canada.

Electronic information

Electronic access (WWW, Internet, CD-ROM, online databases) is rapidly becoming the primary venue for both the identification and presentation of atmospheric science information. The emergence and rapid growth of the World Wide Web and the availability of easy-to-use browsing tools have had a major impact on the presentation and access of atmospheric science information. In less than three years, there has been exponential growth in Web-based atmospheric science information. Much of what was available only in print can now be retrieved in a few clicks of a mouse. The potential of the WWW/Internet for entirely new kinds of data presentation is enormous, and is fundamentally changing the way atmospheric science information is compiled, stored, displayed and used.

It is important to note that the Internet currently is not comprehensively or systematically indexed, and that available search engines are less powerful than engines available through most online database vendors. Finding information can be time consuming and frustrating. However, the huge amount of atmospheric sciences and air quality information present on WWW pages, on gophers, and through ftp mandates the use of this resource.

The Web sites provided in this chapter are just a few of thousands of pages in existence on this subject. Searching the term weather on the Lycos search engine in April, 1996, retrieved 77,945 documents. The term climate retrieved 23,398 documents.

There have been some attempts to locate and link to atmospheric science homepages to create a comprehensive index. The European Centre for Medium-range Weather Forecasting (ECMWF) has a page called Meteorology on the Internet, ECMWF member state WWW sites (URI.: http://www.ecwmfint/docs/meteo_sites.html). NASA has created a page called WWW servers with global change, environmental data and information (URL http://gcmd.gsfc.nasa.gov/gcmdonline.html).

The United Nations Environmental Programme/World Meteorological Organization Information Unit on Climate Change (IUCC) and the secretariat for the UN Framework Convention on Climate Change (UNFCCC) manage a Web page that contains official documents and archives of various conferences and conventions on climate change. (URL: http://www.unep.ch.iucc.html)

NOAA has a number of pages describing their atmospheric programmes. The Global Climate Perspectives System (GCPS) page includes the global maximum-minimum temperature dataset, and the NOAA baseline climatological datasets. (URL: http://ncdc.noaa.gov/gcps/gcps.html). The Climate Prediction Center is chartered to maintain a continuous watch on short-term climate fluctuations. Its page contains information on predictions, assessments, a link to the US regional climate centers' pages and a products list. (URL: http://nic.fb4.noaa.gov).

In addition to Web pages, there are newsgroups, listservs, gopher sites and documents available through ftp. Communications technology is constantly evolving, and it remains to be seen what form Internet access will take in a year, or even if there will be an Internet as we know it in a year or two. Anyone interested in atmospheric science information, however, will have to contend with this diverse and developing medium.

CD-ROMs in meteorology generally contain numeric/data information. Products include the series of discs produced by NCDC, especially the International Station Meteorological Climate Survey, which provides basic information from 640 stations worldwide and 5434 world wide airfield summary stations. Also produced by NCDC is World WeatherDisc: Climate Data for the Planet Earth, a comprehensive description of world weather, based on 17 data sets, from 1740 to the present.

World Climate Disc from the Climatic Research Unit, University of East Anglia, UK, has data from 7000 stations worldwide, from the 1800s to the present, and software which enables users to map the data of any area in the world.

Online databases, usually produced by commercial vendors or government agencies, contain a wide array of atmospheric information, much of it bibliographic and/or full text, but also data/ numeric information.

The authors conducted two searches in Knight-Ridder Dialog using databases which contain primarily juried journal articles, scientific reports and conference proceedings. (see Tables 6.1 and 6.2).

Approaching atmospheric sciences information from another direction, a major source of both bibliographic and full text material is PTS Newsletter database (KR Dialog file 636). This database is useful for locating newsletter and report information, from both organizations or publishers specifically interested in the atmosphere, as well as business publications which include such material. PTS Newsletter is updated daily and is continually incorporating new materials, so it provides a very current and unique source of information.

Full text coverage of several air quality and global change newsletters is included, for example, *Air/Water Pollution Report* and *Global Environmental Change Report.*

Air/Water Pollution Report is published weekly by Business Publishers, Silver Spring MD. It covers legislative, regulatory and business news for companies involved in or affected by pollution controls in the USA. It highlights issues such as risk assessment and EPA developments. Company scientific advances, mergers and acquisitions and publications are given lengthy coverage. The report also announces AWMA and other organizations' conferences.

Table 6.1 Results of Dialog literature search, April 1996

Search strategy: global(w)change*	
Database	**#Cites**
SCISEARCH (1974)	1894
ENERGY SCIENCE 7 TECHNOLOGY (1974)	1505
GEOREF (1785)	1121
GEOBASE (1980)	628
MET ABSTRACTS (1970)	525
NTIS (1964)	510

*Note: each database was searched separately, in its entirety; removal of duplicates was not used.

Table 6.2 Results of Dialog literature search, April 1996

Search strategy: (air(w)quality)/ti*	
Database	**#Cites**
ENERGY SCIENCE 7 TECHNOLOGY (1974)	3878
CA SEARCH (1967)	2101
NTIS (1964)	1936
POLLUTION ABSTRACTS (1970)	1399
SCISEARCH (1974)	1231
ENVIRONLINE (1970)	1075
AEROSPACE DATABASE	824

Note: each database was searched separately, in its entirety; removal of duplicates was not used

Primarily a professional newsletter it is valuable for companies involved in air quality concerns in the USA.

Global Environmental Change Report is published biweekly by Cutter Information Arlington MA. Aimed at professionals and academics specialising in global change issues, it is also useful for and understandable by interested laypersons. Unlike *Air/Water Pollution Report*, this report is worldwide in its coverage. In each issue there are a couple of lengthy articles, followed by shorter news stories. In addition to US coverage, there is a great deal on European countries and EC projects, GATT and Asia, both at governmental and scientific research levels.

Government publications, which often must be mined for specific nuggets of information, are important sources, especially for internal and/or project reports. NTIS is a valuable source for locating government scientific information; the Federal Register database should also be considered for US material. A unique source available through STN (STN c/o Chemical Abstracts, 2560 Olentangy River Rd., Box 3012, Columbus OH 43210) is IGL (System for Information on Grey Literature in Europe). It covers most EC countries and includes earth sciences and aeronautics information from 1981 to the present and is updated monthly.

Books

Despite the breadth of information on this subject, there are some standard as well as benchmark works which are central to any collection of atmospheric science materials.

Compendium of meteorology (AMS, 1951) was designed to 'take stock of the present position in meteorology . . . summarize and appraise the knowledge available . . . [and] indicate avenues of further research'. Every aspect of the science from composition of the atmosphere to radiometeorology is covered thoroughly. It is international in scope and authorship.

Handbook of meteorology (Berry, 1945) was written to 'furnish a convenient text reference for data, fundamental theory and weather analysis and forecasting, [with emphasis on the] scientific and engineering aspects of meteorology rather than on current techniques'. It contains data, calculations, instruments, an explanation of the scientific basis for modern meteorology and discussions of clouds, climatology and all other aspects of the discipline.

Handbook of applied meteorology (Houghton, 1985) is a 'reference for meteorological knowledge and technology, designed for professionals and technicians outside the meteorological field. It is also a standard reference for meteorological fundamentals, measurements and applications, including air quality. It lists major meteorological information collections and libraries in the USA.

The physics of clouds (2nd edn., Mason, 1971) is concerned with those processes which are responsible for the formation of clouds and the release of precipitation, and microphysical processes.

The physics of rainclouds (Fletcher, 1962) covers the basic principles of cloud modification.

Physics of the air (Humphreys, 1929) deals with the physical phenomena of the earth's atmosphere.

Weather and climate modification (Hess, 1974) presents technical discussions of the major fields of weather modification.

The collected works of Irving Langmuir (Langmuir, 1962) is an invaluable resource because of Dr Langmuir's long association with General Electric Research Laboratory as a research scientist and his intense curiosity about natural phenomena in an industrial environment. He received the 1932 Nobel Prize for Chemistry.

Air quality on the global scale (Schaefer, 1976) is the final report on worldwide air quality patterns of aerosols.

Berkeley symposium of mathematical statistics and probability (volume 5, University of California, 1967) deals with the physical background of weather modification.

Air Pollution (Stern, 1976) is addressed to engineers, chemists, physicists, physicians, meteorologists, lawyers, economists, sociologists, agronomists and toxicologists. It covers the cause, effect, transport, measurement and control of air pollution.

Conclusion

Atmospheric sciences, like all scientific subjects, is in the midst of an information revolution, unanticipated a few years ago. Information is more and more often solely available in electronic form. Possibilities for display of information have mushroomed. What information will continue to be provided, how it will be accessed, how that access will be controlled, where funding for electronic products will come from, and what will happen to traditional formats are all questions for which there are, at present, no answers. Information seekers in this field must be willing to incorporate new delivery methods into their repertoire if they are to carry out comprehensive searches.

References and Bibliography

American Meteorological Society Committee on the Compendium of Meteorology (1951) *Compendium of meteorology.* Boston: AMS.

Berry, F.A. (1945) *Handbook of Meteorology.* New York: McGraw-Hill.

Byers, H.R. (1965) *Elements of cloud physics.* Chicago: University of Chicago Press.

Fletcher, N.H. (1962) *The physics of rainclouds.* Cambridge: Cambridge University Press.

Hess V.N. (1974) *Weather and climate modification.* New York: Wiley–Interscience.

Houghton, D.D. (ed.) (1985) *Handbook of applied meteorology.* New York: Wiley–Interscience.

Humphreys, W.J. (1929) *Physics of the air* 2nd edn. New York: McGrawHill.

Huschke, R.E.) (1959) *Glossary of meteorology.* Boston: AMS.

Langmuir, I. (1962) *The collected works of Irving Langmuir* (12 vols.). New York: Pergamon Press.

Mason, B.J. (1971) *The physics of clouds* 2nd edn. Oxford: Clarendon Press.

Schaefer, V.J. (1976) *Air quality on the global scale* Washington DC: National Science Foundation.

Stern, A.C. (1976) *Air pollution* 3rd edn. (5 vols.). New York: Academic Press.

Berkeley symposium of mathematical statistics and probability (1967) (5 vols.) Berkeley: University of California Press.

CHAPTER SEVEN

Wastes management

DIANA MASLIN

Introduction

Wastes management may seem, at first, to be a very specific and even
specialized field, but it is one of the most wide-ranging and important
aspects of environmental management. Every process, every activity
generates waste which has to be dealt with in an acceptable manner.
Today, developed countries are as interested in waste minimization
and cleaner technologies as in 'final' disposal. The EU hierarchy for
waste management, as stated in the Waste Framework Directive (1),
places prevention or reduction of waste first, followed by recovery of
waste by recycling, reuse or reclamation. The EC 5th Environmental
Action Programme (2) continues the hierarchy with safe disposal of
any waste which cannot be recycled or reused in ranking order –
combustion as fuel, incineration and landfill. Most developed
countries now have national waste management hierarchies.

The range of information sources available on waste management is
as diverse as the subject. The Waste Management Information Bureau
(WMIB) houses a large collection of sources on all aspects of waste
management (3). The remainder of the present chapter discusses the
relative merits of a selection of the more useful and important sources
from this collection.

Directories

There has been a marked increase in the number of environment-
related directories published in recent years. There are a number of
specialized directories as well as the more general environmental ones

which, nevertheless, often have waste-related sections. There is one general European environmental directory which is particularly useful –the *ENTEC directory of environmental technology, European edition* (4). It lists a large number of companies, with names, addresses and telephone/fax numbers for each company. The layout consists of tables of company names against activities for each country. Waste management is very well sub-categorized. General European directories are less useful for comprehensive coverage of individual countries than are country-specific directories. However, given the difficulty in obtaining these outside one's own country and, of course, given the language barrier, the main benefit of the *ENTEC Directory* is its extensive geographical coverage.

Of the many UK environmental directories available, two annuals of great practical value are *Information for Industry's Environment business directory* (5) and Macmillan's *Environment industry yearbook* (6). There are two publications which are useful for information on recycling companies and organizations – *Materials recycling handbook* (7) is published annually by EMAP Maclaren, who also publish the journal *Materials Recycling Week* (8), both aimed at the reclamation industries. The Handbook is more than a directory since it covers codes of practice, standard classifications and specifications and other useful information about the reclamation of chemicals and oils, glass, paper, metal, textiles, plastics and rubber. There is also a trade names listing. Companies are listed separately for each material and are organized regionally.

An excellent publication to use alongside *Materials recycling handbook*, but covering the subject from a different point of view, is the *National directory of recycling information* by Waste Watch (9). This lists local authority recycling facilities and local groups involved in recycling projects. Again, it is arranged regionally and also has a list of useful addresses organized by type of material.

The USA is covered in the *American recycling market – directory/ reference manual*. It lists companies involved in recycling a wide range of materials, including vehicle dismantlers, the demolition industry and composting. It covers brokers, exporters and consumers of recycled materials and a useful section of data including chemical composition of alloys, specifications and pricing data. A reference section gives details of associations, resource recovery agencies and a glossary of terms which is particularly helpful to the non-American researcher. The *Annual buyer's guide* is published as a supplement to the main manual, to be used as a quick reference 'yellow pages' directory.

A useful US-published directory is the *World environmental directory – North American edition* (11) which covers companies, organizations and individuals involved in the main environmental activities in the USA and Canada. The information is divided into large sections, which can be difficult to use as the category indexes are divided into only ten categories, listing companies alphabetically. The fields of specialization which are listed under each company are not indexed separately. However, the Directory's comprehensiveness is its main value. It covers federal and state government agencies, product manufacturers, professional services, a large number of organizations, including educational establishments and environmental databases.

There are a number of valuable specialized directories. The *Directory of environmental consultants* (12) by Environmental Data Services is a well-organized list of around 400 UK consultancies. Each entry contains details of turnover, number of projects and extent of experience in subject categories, including waste management, and 18 industry sectors. There is also an interesting guide on how to commission an environmental consultancy.

Aspinwall has compiled the database *Sitefile* (13) of authorized waste treatment and disposal facilities in England, Wales and Scotland. The printed form, *The sitefile digest* (14), published by Macmillan, is extremely useful for finding waste management facilities in defined regions. Each entry gives details of category of site, (landfill, transfer station, incinerator, etc.) site classification and types of waste approved for handling at the site. Codes are given for waste types and there is a comprehensive list of wastes against their respective code. A major drawback of the publication is the lack of any index to the sites. The site list is arranged geographically by county and town. If one needs to locate sites by category, operator or waste type, Aspinwall will carry out a search of the database for a fee. The directory is updated by subscription and is claimed to be the only published list of waste management facilities in Great Britain.

Updating services and yearbooks

There is a trend towards publishing certain reference materials in looseleaf format and providing updates by subscription. In general, this format tends to be suitable for information which changes frequently, such as legislation. One of the most useful publications in this category is *Croner's waste management* (15) which acts as a first-stop reference manual. It is aimed at a wide audience, including the waste producer. It is divided into five sections, the first of which covers UK and relevant EC legislation. This section is useful to those with little prior knowledge and includes summaries of the legislation under subject headings which follow the order of the Acts and Regulations. Section two is entitled Practical Waste Management and is a clear overview of the options for waste management. It is divided into categories which follow the waste management hierarchy and starts with a guide to compliance with duty of care. In section three there is a series of helpful waste charts covering the hazards, handling, storing, labelling, treatment and disposal of categories of waste which are based on the Special Waste regulations, 1980. Section four is a directory of contractors, consultants, recyclers, local and central government bodies and associations. Section five is an appendix of useful information such as lists of publications and abbreviations.

Garner's environmental law (16) is a well-known encyclopaedia of UK and EU environmental legislation which is a must for anyone who deals regularly with such issues. It is a complete compilation of the texts of the Acts, Statutory Instruments, codes of practice, departmental circulars and other such publications relating to the environment. It also refers to case law and covers relevant EU law The International Solid Waste and Public Cleansing Association (ISWA) is a prolific publisher of useful information. The *International directory of solid waste management – the ISWA yearbook* (17) is packed with good quality, up-to-date information on a wide variety of topics. There are a number of general articles followed by sections from ISWA working groups. Each section contains a report from the working group and several articles from members covering the subject in a selection of countries. The directory section can be useful for finding a few companies from countries and often covered by the more major directories.

Dictionaries

An excellent dictionary of waste management terms is published by ISWA, *1000 Terms in solid waste management* (18) Not only is it comprehensive, but its authorship gives it credence. Each term is described in English and then listed in German, Spanish, French and Italian, with indexes in each of these languages. There is also a useful classification of wastes, described in each language, and a list of definitions of waste by some of the major legalistic/authoritative bodies.

Another dictionary published by an authoritative body on the subject of wastewater is the *Glossary*, which is part of the series Handbooks on UK Wastewater Practice by the Institution of Water and Environmental Management (IWEM), (19). Each term is comprehensively described and cross-referenced.

Monographs and reports

Market research reports are often useful as an up-to-date introduction to a subject, as well as being obvious sources for data on a particular market; they can also be extremely expensive. However, a few reasonably priced general waste management market reports are published. One particularly helpful document is the *MSI data report: waste management: UK* (20). It contains a large number of useful tables on waste arisings, collection, recycling, treatment and disposal. All the major issues are covered, including an outlook for the future of the industry. There is a comprehensive section covering the major waste management companies operating in the UK.

A number of guides have been published recently, directed at business and industry, covering the whole spectrum of waste and environmental issues. These can be useful in breaking down subjects into their component parts and usually have helpful tables and checklists. One such publication is a *Waste minimization guide*, published by the Institution of Chemical Engineers (21). Although written for UK industry, much of the information has been taken from US publications and the authors state that the techniques and examples are universally applicable. The subject is covered step by step and the guide is clearly written.

Some of the more useful reports are written by committees and work working groups of major organizations and industries, or are compiled by consultancies on behalf of government departments. These publications are therefore usually good quality, authoritative sources of information. A study on the *Management of plastic wastes in the ECE region* has been carried out by the United Nations Economic Committee for Europe (UNECE) Working Party on the Chemical Industry (1992) (22). Most of the enquiries on plastic wastes received by any library could be satisfied to some extent by this publication. The study covers a large number of European countries and also information from the USA. The report is full of tables, charts and figures and there is a useful summary of current recycling projects and key national recycling centres in Western Europe in an appendix.

Landfill gas: from environment to energy (23) is considered by professionals to be an indispensable publication. It is in the form of a report from the Commission of the European Communities, but is physically an 865-page book. It covers the subject from the composition and genesis of landfill gas through to the economics of its exploitation. The environmental impact of landfill gas is covered exhaustively and the book is full of case studies and examples.

There are two particularly useful publications on recycling in Europe. *Recycling in member countries* (24) is a state-of-the-art report written by the ISWA Working Group on Recycling. The report contains contributions from Denmark, Italy, Norway, UK, Spain and Sweden. Each chapter covers national policy and legislation and outlines the state of recycling for a variety of materials in that country. Each chapter ends with a table of data from a number of recycling plants in that country. Elsevier has published a comprehensive report *Municipal solid waste recycling in Western Europe to 1996* (25) which contains a great deal of information and data on legislation, waste arisings and management and recycling by country and by material. There are also useful chapters on suppliers and organizations. The EU countries are covered, together with Finland and Sweden.

The UK Department of the Environment (DoE) publishes a series of reports and other material from their Controlled Wastes Management (CWM) research programme. The programme is managed by Wastes Technical Division which lets a number of research contracts each year. The final reports from these contracts are published as CWM Reports, and can be purchased for a small fee. Each report also has a corresponding Project Summary which is available free of charge. When a contract is let, the contractor publishes a Project Profile, which is a short pamphlet-type publication discussing the aims and objectives of the research. There are also Technical Summaries and Technical Reviews published in the same series as the Profiles and all are free of charge.

Serials

There seems to be a new environmental journal published every month. A large number of general environmental, waste management and specialized journals, have application to the waste management field, but as the general environmental journals will have been covered elsewhere in the book, this chapter will concentrate on the specifically waste-oriented journals.

WMIB publishes *Waste & Environment Today* (26), a monthly news and bibliographic journal in two parts. The news journal covers relevant events from around the world, special sections on EU news and news from the UK Department of the Environment, book reviews, a diary of forthcoming events and occasional longer articles and case studies. The bibliographic section contains a selection of the items which have been entered on to the WASTEINFO database that month (see Databases section below).

An excellent technical journal on the subject is *Waste Management & Research* (27) which is ISWA's bi-monthly journal. This also contains a calendar of events and book reviews. The national trade associations and professional bodies also tend to publish their own journals and magazines (see section below on information services and organizations).

World Wastes (28) is an American monthly waste management journal which has a useful news section on trends in the industry, as well as a number of longer articles which are often practical in their outlook. An annual buyers' guide is published within the journal. An international edition of *World Wastes* is published bi-monthly in English with French and German summaries. Another bi-monthly US journal is *Hazardous Waste Consultant* (29), which is particularly good at covering regulatory and legal issues and for keeping an eye on the activities of the US Environmental Protection Agency (EPA) and new technologies.

Müll and Abfall (30) is a German waste management journal. The technical articles have summaries in German with English and French keywords. *Waste Magazin* (31) is an Austrian journal covering all aspects of waste management in Austria with a full English translation of each article.

An international journal covering the environment in general which should also be mentioned here is *International Environment Reporter* (32). This is a key international journal with an excellent manual index which is published quarterly. The journal is published fortnightly and is truly international in coverage. A wide range of enquiries can be answered through reference to this publication, it is a first source for information on any country outside Western Europe or the USA. The subscription includes periodic publication of reference file sections on individual countries, the complete text of international treaties, bilateral agreements, European conventions and EC legislation. In 1993, reference file material on individual countries was published for Sweden, Netherlands, Taiwan, UK, Austria, Belgium, Finland, France, Germany and Greece.

Recycling as an issue in its own right, is covered by an increasing number of journals, one of the most readable is *Warmer Bulletin*, published by the World Resource Foundation (formerly the Warmer Campaign) (33). It is international in coverage and published four times a year. Although the emphasis is on recycling, wider issues on the management of wastes are also covered. There is a series of useful factsheets published within the journal from time to time on subjects such as incineration, glass recycling, life cycle analysis and nappies (diapers). There are a number of good recycling journals for the USA, two of the more well known being *Biocycle* (34) and *Resource Recycling* (35). Both are very readable and have useful national news sections, although there are often articles about other countries, particularly in Europe. *Biocycle* also publishes a special international issue. Elsevier produce a good international, technical journal on recycling, *Resources, Conservation and Recycling* (36).

Conference proceedings

Diaries of events which are included in many relevant journals are good sources of information about conferences. Conference proceedings provide useful information on recent technologies. Five conferences have been chosen for discussion here – all of which are highly respected and long-standing with full conference proceedings published. CISA Environmental Sanitary Engineering Centre, Sardinia, Italy, holds a biannual conference on landfill, commonly known as 'the Sardinia conference' (37). This is an international event which covers every aspect of landfill and is considered the major conference on the subject.

Polmet is another well-known more general conference covering issues of urban pollution control. It is held every three years in Hong Kong by the Hong Institution of Engineers (38). Waste management figures very highly, including topics such as practical recycling, sludge disposal and chemical waste management.

Waste management international (39), published by EF-Verlag für Energie-und Umwelttechnik, provides a thorough exploration of recycling of industrial and domestic wastes. Despite its title, it concentrates on recycling and previous editions were entitled *Recycling international*. The book is a collection of conference papers from the triennial International Recycling Congress, although the conference details do not appear anywhere in the publication.

There are two US national conferences relevant to this chapter. Purdue University, Indiana, holds an annual Industrial Waste Conference (40) and there is an annual Mid-Atlantic Industrial Waste Conference (41) held at one of the Mid-Atlantic universities. Both are comprehensive, covering topics from waste minimization through to site remediation together with regulatory issues.

Official publications and statistics

Legislation is covered elsewhere in this book, but there are several official UK publications which must be mentioned here. The principle of 'duty of care' was officially imposed in the Environmental Protection Act 1990 on 'any person who produces, imports, carries, keeps, treats or disposes of controlled waste'. This is a particularly important part of the Act and official guidance has been published in the form of a code of practice by the Department of the Environment (DoE) *Waste management: the duty of care: a code of practice* (42). There is currently a new edition in draft form. Guidance documents on a variety of subjects are published from time to time by the DoE, the most important to those involved in waste management being the Waste Management Papers series. These documents are updated and the series is added to as necessary. At present there are 28, dealing with a range of issues. *Waste management paper no. 1* (43) is a review of the options available for waste treatment and disposal; *No. 28* is a memorandum for local authorities on recycling (44). Other titles in the series cover subjects such as the licensing of waste management facilities, landfill and landfill gas.

Obtaining meaningful statistics can be difficult and in many cases they are not available in an easily accessible form. For the UK, the source of official published statistics on the environment is the *Digest of environmental statistics*, published annually by HMSO for the DoE (45). Waste and recycling are covered in a single chapter, which in-cludes figures on waste arisings, disposal licences, imports of hazard-ous waste, weights of various recovered scrap materials and other recycling data. The Scottish Office and Welsh Office also publish their own *Digests* (46, 47). The DoE also publishes *The UK environment* (48) with a further edition in 1997. Waste and recycling are again covered together and the statistics are, understandably, from the same sources. However, the presentation of the data is much more accessible and readable than in the *Digest* and more background information is given, including details of contracts.

The Chartered Institute of Public Finance and Accountancy (CIPFA) produces two useful statistical publications – *Waste disposal statistics* and *Waste collection statistics*. These are compiled from returned data from local authorities.

Eurostat regularly publishes *Environment statistics* (49) in German, French and English, through the EU Official Publications Office, covering the EU countries, USA and Japan. Figures are given, where available, for domestic and industrial waste arisings. In some cases figures are given for a fairly detailed breakdown of waste categories. Disposal routes and the recycling of a range of materials are also covered. Eurostat collaborates with the OECD and obtains data through joint questionnaires and compilation of the data. The biennial *OECD environmental data* (50) contains, to a large extent, the same information, in English and French. However, it also includes supplementary details of the percentage of the population served by municipal waste services and numbers of waste treatment and disposal installations. There is also a more detailed breakdown of industrial waste arisings and more countries are covered – Canada, Austria, Finland, Norway, Sweden, Switzerland and Poland.

Databases

WMIB produces the bibliographic database *WasteInfo* (51) which covers all aspects of non-nuclear waste management and is available online, on CD-ROM and by contacting WMIB directly. There are general environmental databases available online and on CD-ROM, which are covered elsewhere in this publication. There are also industry-specific databases which will have some information on the subject where it relates to that industry, for example, *Rapra* (52) covers plastics and rubber and *Pira* (53) covers paper and packaging.

The specialized environmental database directory *ECO Directory of Environmental Databases in the United Kingdom* (54) is particularly useful in that it covers databases which are available only by contacting the producer, as well as those available online and on CD-ROM.

Information services and organizations

The Waste Management Information Bureau (WMIB) (55) is the national referral centre for information and advice on all aspects of non-nuclear waste management. It also provides an international service to any organization or individual who needs to know about the subject. WMIB will answer short enquiries free of charge, but can also provide an online search and consultancy service. The reference collection is open to the general public on request. WMIB is also the Special Sectoral Source for information on waste management for the United Nations Environment Programme (UNEP) INFOTERRA network. UN government bodies and other organizations can obtain information on the environment, often free of charge especially in the case of developing countries, if their enquiry is directed through their national focal point, or the INFOTERRA Programme Activity Centre in Nairobi (see Chapter 1).

The International Solid Waste and Public Cleansing Association (ISWA) (56) has already been mentioned as the publisher of a journal, yearbook, working group reports and conferences. It is a non-profit, membership organization dedicated to promoting acceptable waste management practices. Membership comes from the whole spectrum of individuals, companies and national bodies involved in waste management. It also interacts with other international organizations.

Many countries have waste management industry associations and relevant professional bodies. In the UK these are the Environmental Services Association (ESA) (57), formerly the National Association of Waste Disposal Contractors (NAWDC), and the Institute of Wastes Management (IWM) etc. (58). Both publish journals, newsletters, guidance documents/codes of practice, etc. and hold conferences and courses. NAWDC is a member of the European Federation of Waste Management (FEAD) (59) whose membership comprises European national waste management associations. In the USA the industry is represented, among others, by the Solid Waste Association of North America (SWANA), (60) the National Solid Waste Management

Association (NSWMA) (61), and the Air and Waste Management Association (A&WMA) (62).

Other industry-sponsored associations and councils are also useful sources of information on that particular industry's impact on the environment. Some industries have special bodies dedicated to the environment issues surrounding their activities. There are many such national organizations which also belong to European or international organizations. For example, in the UK many of the industries involved in packaging material support the Industry Council for Packaging and the Environment (INCPEN) (63), which is also a founder member of the European Organization for Packaging and the Environment (EUROPEN) (64).

Environmental pressure groups can be helpful sources of information. Both Friends of the Earth (65) and Greenpeace (66) are international organizations which publish useful leaflets, posters, newsletters and other material.

References

1. Council Directive of 18 March 1991 (91/56/EEC) amending Directive 75/442/EEC on waste. *Official Journal of the European Communities L,* 34 (78), 32–37, 26 March 1991.
2. Commission of the European Communities (1992) *Towards sustainability* (vol. 2) COM (92) 23. Office for Official Publications of the European Communities L-2985 Luxembourg.
3. Waste Management Information Bureau, AEA Technology, F6 Culham, Oxon. OX14 3DB, UK. Tel: +44 1235 463162. Fax: +44 1235 463004.
4. The Entec Press (1993) *ENTEC directory of environmental technology. European edition.* London: Kogan Page.
5. Information for Industry (1995) *Environment business directory 1995/6.* London: Information for Industry.
6. Macmillan Publishers (1996) *Environment industry yearbook 1995.* London and Basingstoke: Macmillan Publishers.
7. EMAP Response Publishing (1995) *Materials recycling handbook 1995.* Peterborough: EMAP Response Publishing.
8. *Materials Recycling Weekly.* EMAP Maclaren Ltd., PO Box 109, Maclaren House, Scarbrook Road, Croydon, Surrey CR9 1QH, UK. Tel: +44 181 688 7788.
9. Waste Watch (1995). *National directory of recycling information* 4th edn. London: Waste Watch.
10. Recoup (1993) *American recycling market – directory/reference manual* 9th edn. Ogdensburg, NY: Recoup.
11. Business Publishers Inc. (1994) *World environmental directory: North America,* 7th edn. Silver Spring: Business Publishers.
12. Environmental Data Services Ltd (1995) *Directory of environmental consultants* 4th edn. London: Environmental Data Services.
13. *Sitefile.* Aspinwall and Co., Ltd., Walford Manor, Baschurch, Shrewsbury SY4 2HH.
14. Aspinwall and Company (1995) *The Sitefile digest.* London and Basingstoke: Macmillan.
15. Croner Publications Ltd., quarterly updated, *Croner's waste management.* Kingston-upon-Thames: Croner Publications.

16. Garner, J.F., Harris, D.J., Henderson, H. McN. and Doolittle, I.G. (1976–1993) (eds) *Garner's environmental law*. London: Butterworths.
17. International Solid Waste and Public Cleansing Association (1994) *International directory of solid waste management 1994/5 – the ISWA yearbook*. London: James and James Science Publishers.
18. Skitt, J. (1992) (ed.) *1000 terms in solid waste management*. Copenhagen: ISWA.
19. Institution of Water and Environment Management (1993) *Glossary* 2nd edn. Handbook of UK Wastewater Practice. London: IWEM.
20. Marketing Strategies for Industry (UK) Ltd. (1995)   *MSI data report: waste management: UK*. Chester: MSI.
21. Crittenden, B.D. (1992) *Waste minimisation guide*. Rugby: Institution of Chemical Engineers.
22. United Nations Economic Commission for Europe Chemical Industry Committee (1992) *Management of plastic wastes in the ECE region*. New York: United Nations.
23. Gendebien, A. *et al.* (1992) *Landfill gas from energy to environment*. Brussels: Office for Official Publications of the European Communities.
24. ISWA Working Group on Recycling (1992)   *Recycling in member countries*. Copenhagen: ISWA.
25. Elsevier Advanced Technology (1992) *Solid waste recycling: municipal solid waste recycling in Western Europe to 1996*. Oxford: Elsevier.
26. *Waste & Environment Today*. Waste Management Information Bureau. Tel: +44 1235 463097.
27. *Waste Management & Research*. Academic Press, 24–28 Oval Road, London NW1 7DX, UK.
28. *World Wastes*. PO Box 41369, Nashville, TN 37204-1094, USA. International ed, Circulation Dept, 6151 Powers Ferry Road NW, Atlanta, GA 30339, USA. Tel: +1 404 955 2500.
29. *Hazardous Waste Consultants*. McCoy & Associates Inc., 13710 West Jewell Evenue, Suite 202, Lakewood, Colorado 80228, USA. Tel: +1 303 987 0333.
30. *Müll und Abfall*. Erich Schmidt Verlag GmbH & Co., Genthiner Strasse 30G, W-1000, Berlin 30, Germany. Tel: +49 30 25 00 85 0.
31. *Waste Magazin*. Gruppe Umwelttechnik und technische Betriebe, A-1010 Wien, Doblhoffgasse 9, Austria.
32. *International Environment Reporter*. The Bureau of National Affairs Inc., 1231 25th Street NW, Washington, DC 20037, USA. Tel: +1 202 452 4200.
33. *Warmer Bulletin*. World Resource Foundation, Bridge House, High Street, Tonbridge, Kent TN9 1DP, UK. Tel: +44 1732 368333.
34. *Biocycle*. J.G. Press Inc., 419 State Ave, Emmaus, PA 18049, USA. Tel: +1 215 967 4135.
35. *Resource Recycling*. 1206 NW 21st Ave, PO Box 10540, Portland, OR 97210, USA. Tel: +1 503 227 1319.
36. *Resources, Conservation and Recycling*. Elsevier Science Publishers BV, PO Box 1527, 1000 BM Amsterdam, The Netherlands. Tel: +31 20 5803258.
37. CISA Environmental Sanitary Engineering Centre (1995) *Fifth International Landfill Symposium*. (S. Margherita di Pula (Cagliari), Sardinia, Italy, 2–6 October 1995). Cagliari, Sardinia: CISA.
38. Hong Kong Institution of Engineers *Polmet 94 – pollution in the metropolitan and urban environment* (Hong Kong, 14–17 November 1994). Hong Kong: Hong Kong Institution of Engineers.
39. Thomé-Kozmiensky, K.J. (ed.)   *Waste management international*. Neuruppin, Germany: EF-Verlag für Energie-und Umwelttechnik.
40. Purdue Research Foundation (1995)   *Proceedings of the 49th Industrial Waste Conference* (Purdue University, 1995). Chelsea, Michigan: Lewis Publishers.
41. Huang, C.P. (1994) (ed.) *Hazardous and industrial wastes: Proceedings of the 26th mid-Atlantic Industrial Waste Conference* (Newark, 7–10 August 1994). Lancaster, Pennsylvania: Technomic.

42. Department of the Environment (1991) *Waste management: the duty of care: a code of practice*. London: HMSO. (Consultation draft of revised code of practice).
43. Department of the Environment (1992) *Waste management paper no 1: a review of options*. London: HMSO.
44. Department of the Environment (1991) *Waste management paper no 28: recycling*. London: HMSO.
45. Department of the Environment (1995) *Digest of environmental statistics, no 17*. London: HMSO.
46. Scottish Office (1995) *The Scottish environment – statistics no 5*. Edinburgh Scottish Office.
47. Welsh Office (1996) *Environmental digest for Wales, no 9*. Cardiff: Welsh Office.
48. Brown, A. (1992) (ed.) *The UK environment*. London: HMSO. (2nd edn. due 1997).
49. Chartered Institute of Public Finance and Accountancy (CIPFA) (1995) *Waste Disposal Statistics 1993–94 Actuals*. London: CIPFA.
50. Chartered Institute of Public Finance and Accountancy (CIPFA) (1995) *Waste collection statistics 1993–94 Actuals*. London: CIPFA.
51. Eurostat (1992) *Environment statistics 1991*. Luxembourg: Office for Official Publications of the European Communities.
52. OECD (1995) *OECD environmental data 1993*. Paris: OECD.
53. *WasteInfo* (available from Questel.Orbit and SilverPlatter).
54. *Rapra* (available from Dialog/Data Star, Questel.Orbit, ESA-IRS, STN and RAPRA).
55. *Pira* (available from Dialog/Data Star, STN, Questel.Orbit and Dialog OnDisc).
56. Barlow, M., Fleming, P., Button, J. (1994) (eds) *ECO directory of environmental databases in the United Kingdom*. Bristol: ECO Trust.
57. Waste Management Information Bureau, AEA Technology, F6 Culham, Oxon. OX14 3DB, UK. Tel: +44 1235 463 162. Fax: +44 1235 463004.
58. International Solid Waste and Cleaning Association (ISWA), Bremerholm 1, DK 1069 Copenhagen K, Denmark. Tel: +45 33 91 44 91.
59. Environmental Services Association (formerly National Association of Waste Disposal Contractors (NAWDC), Mountbarrow House, 6–20 Elizabeth Street, London SW1W 9RB, UK. Tel: +44 171 824 8882.
60. Institute of Wastes Management (IWM), 9 Saxon Court, St Peter's Gardens, Northampton NN1 1SX, UK. Tel: +44 1604 20426.
61. European Federation of Waste Management (FEAD – Federation Européene des Activities du Dechet), Avenue des Nerviens 117/69, B-1040 Brussels, Belgium. Tel: +32 2 732 16 01.
62. Solid Waste Association of North America (SWANA), PO Box 7219, Silver Spring, MD 20910, USA. Tel: +1 301 585 2898.
63. National Solid Waste Management Association (NSWMA), 1730 Rhode Island Ave, NW, Suite 1000, Washington, DC 20036, USA. Tel: +1 202 659 4613.
64. Air & Waste Management Association (A&WMA), PO Box 2861, Pittsburgh, Pennsylvania 15230, USA. Tel: +1 412 232 3444.
65. Industry Council for Packaging and the Environment (INCPEN), Tenterton House, 3 Tenterton Street, London W1R 9AH, UK. Tel: +44 171 409 0949.
66. European Organisation for Packaging and the Environment (EUROPEN) see Industry Council for Packaging and the Environment (INCPEN).
67. Friends of the Earth (FoE) Ltd, 26–28 Underwood Street, London N1 7JQ, UK. Tel: +44 171 490 1555.
68. Greenpeace Ltd, Canonbury Villas, London N1 2PN, UK. Tel: +44 171 354 5100.

CHAPTER EIGHT

Noise as a pollutant

IAN H. FLINDELL

Introduction

Noise is usually defined as unwanted sound. There is one important difference from other pollutants in that noise does not usually leave a permanent trace in the environment. This is because the amount of physical energy involved is usually very small. The effects of noise are only meaningful when measured in terms of biological response and this is often quite variable from one person to another. Matters of physical acoustics do not often lead to disagreement but the same is not always true when considering the effects of noise on people. One can often find plausible and even convincing articles to support both sides of a particular controversy, and the reader must always be on guard against this. At the end of the day, the selection of a particular noise level threshold for any regulatory purpose often involves as much consideration of what is practicable and reasonable in the social and political climate of the time as consideration of the results of basic research.

The starting point for the recent history of the problem of noise in the UK was the publication of the Wilson Report in 1963: *Noise – final report of the Committee on the problem of noise* (Chairman Sir A. Wilson, Cmnd 2056, London: HMSO). This report set out the basis of a system of noise criteria and regulation which is still in use, albeit with some modification. The Wilson Report recognized that 'noise problems must involve people and their feelings', and are not simply a matter of physical measurement and engineering control. The Report also set out to define objective criteria wherever possible, since otherwise there could be no fair basis of comparison between different problems in different parts of the country. In *Noise and man* (1968, 2nd edn 1973,

John Murray) provided an excellent summary of many of the issues originally covered by the Wilson Committee.

Not all primary sources of information are readily available to the general public as a large proportion of research in this area has been carried out for commercial and government sponsors who have not always been as keen on dissemination as perhaps they should have been. This means that there will often be useful research reports buried in small libraries and archives and many key materials are now out of print. The keen student may need to exercise some ingenuity to obtain copies of all relevant material. Some technical and scientific journals occasionally publish collections and anthologies of classic works on particular topics and such volumes can usually be recommended.

It is unusual to find an expert who is fully conversant with all the scientific and engineering disciplines which are relevant to a complete understanding of noise issues. Most experts nowadays specialize in one or more particular areas such as physical acoustics, electroacoustics, engineering acoustics, architectural acoustics, transportation noise or auditory acoustics.

Physical acoustics

Sound travels from a source to a receiver as a wave motion in the atmosphere. All sound waves are generated by some kind of mechanical disturbance or vibration at the source. The science of the generation and subsequent behaviour of sound waves in the atmosphere is known as physical acoustics. Physical acoustics is a relatively mature science. Most of the fundamental mathematical relationships were set out by J.W. Strutt, (Baron Rayleigh), in the first important work in acoustics *The theory of sound* (2nd edn, 1894, Macmillan). There have been many good basic and more advanced textbooks published since. Examples are *Fundamentals of acoustics* (2nd edn, 1962, John Wiley) by L.E. Kinsler and A.R. Frey, and *Basic acoustics*, by D.E. Hall (1987, Harper & Row), which is generally easier to follow for the non-expert.

However, many problems in physical acoustics are quite complex due to the three-dimensional nature of space and the interactions of sound waves of different wavelengths with the physical dimensions of solid objects, and the fact that the temperature and composition of the atmosphere varies from place to place. This means that advanced research is continuing into many areas of physical acoustics.

The two leading scientific journals which deal with physical acoustics and other matters are the *Journal of the Acoustical Society of America* and the *Journal of Sound and Vibration*.

Electroacoustics

Instrumentation

All measurements in acoustics depend on precision microphones and instruments. Bruel and Kjaer of Denmark stand out among manufacturers of acoustic instruments for producing a wide range of technical literature to explain the operating principles and correct usage of their products. Textbooks published in Denmark by Bruel and Kjaer such as *Acoustic noise measurements* (5th edn, J.R. Hassall and K. Zaveri, 1988), *Frequency analysis* (1987) and many other titles can all be recommended, notwithstanding an understandably large number of references to their own products. The company has been reorganized and it remains to be seen whether the large amount of resources allocated to the preparation and publication of these useful handbooks will continue.

Other manufacturers produce useful literature but it is generally less wide-ranging in scope. The Acoustics Branch of the Division of Radiation Science at the National Physical Laboratory provides calibration and other assistance with all areas of acoustic instrumentation. It is hoped that this service will continue after the announcement of reorganizations.

Loudspeakers and music systems

It has been estimated that there are at least ten loudspeakers in use for each member of the population of Western industrialized societies. The modern music industry depends entirely on the development of electronic means of recording and broadcasting sound and is directly responsible for a considerable amount of neighbourhood noise nuisance. Audio public address systems often provide the only effective means of communication with large crowds of people in public places such as sports stadia, railway stations, airports and shopping malls, particularly in emergency situations. There are a large number of small to medium-sized companies involved in specialist areas of electroacoustic development and a smaller number of much larger, usually Pacific Rim based, companies exploiting developments for the mass market. Most of the basic theory was covered by L.L. Beranek in *Acoustics* (McGraw Hill, 1954) and there have been a large number of textbooks dealing with different areas at varying levels of sophistication since. Most new developments in audio electroacoustics are reported in the *Journal of the Audio Engineering Society*, but commercial pressures do not always allow manufacturers to be completely open and there are areas (particularly in stereophonic techniques) where not all experts agree.

The Sound and Communications Industries Federation have recently published a *Code of Practice for the assessment, specification, maintenance and operation of sound systems for emergency purposes at sports grounds and stadia in pursuit of approval by licensing authorities* (Slough, 1992), in an effort to encourage higher standards of engineering design for public address systems.

Active noise and vibration control

A new and promising area in recent years has been the development of active noise and vibration control (see *Active control of Sound* by P.P. Nelson and S.J. Elliott, Academic Press, 1992). At its simplest, active control depends on the use of loudspeakers to generate additional sound waves which cancel out the original sound waves to a greater or lesser extent. The technique is quite simple for sounds with large wavelengths in enclosed spaces and becomes progressively more complex as the size of the space increases and the wavelength reduces. Active control techniques can also be used to control vibration in solid objects and to modify and potentially improve the sound quality of stereophonic systems.

Engineering acoustics

Engineering acoustics is the art and science of noise and vibration control. There are many ways in which noise levels can be reduced, and it is usually necessary to achieve a compromise between maximum quiet and lowest cost. The best place to start is at the source where the elimination or reduction of vibration of solid objects and pulsation or turbulence in air flow will reduce noise. The next stage is to increase the resistance to the passage of sound between the source and the receiver by interposing increased distance or some form of physical barrier. Finally, the receiver can be protected to a certain extent by restricting exposure to the noise in some way, by using ear plugs and ear defenders, and even (although this is sometimes controversial) by changing attitudes to the noise and the noise source.

L.L. Beranek set out many of the principles in his classic text on the subject *Noise reduction*, 1960 (McGraw Hill). There are now a number of comprehensive guides and handbooks which detail practical solutions to engineering noise control problems: *Handbook for industrial noise control*, NASA SP-5108 (HMSO, 1981); *100 practical examples of noise reduction methods*, report by HM Factory Inspectorate for the Health & Safety Executive, (HMSO, 1983); *Noise control*, adapted from a publication of the Swedish Workers Protection Fund (Bruel and Kjaer, 1986). Most manufacturers of engineering noise control products publish comprehensive literature describing the uses and performance of their products, but expert interpretation and experience is often required.

There are a number of journals that carry articles which, while not in the front rank for academic complexity, are directly useful for engineering purposes. *Applied Acoustics* falls into this category.

Architectural acoustics

Traditionally, architectural acoustics has been more concerned with the acoustics of grand buildings and concert halls than with everyday homes and offices. While concert hall acoustics is still important, there is an increasing emphasis on improving the indoor acoustic environment for shops, schools, factories and houses. Many architects leave acoustic design to a specialist in the same way as they would delegate structural engineering calculations. There are four main areas of interest:

- acoustic insulation against external noise break-in;
- acoustic insulation of internal partitions;
- control of internal reverberation;
- control of mechanical plant and other building services noise.

There are a number of basic textbooks on architectural acoustics. Most tend to deal adequately with the fundamentals and selection is a matter of personal preference. There are a number of cookbook-style texts, with lots of diagrams and cross-sectional drawings and a minimum of mathematics and engineering formulae, whereas others take the opposite view. Either style of book can provide useful information in simple cases, while difficult cases usually require an expert with considerable experience of the specific type of problem. A typical example of the cookbook-style genre is M.D. Egan's *Architectural acoustics* (McGraw Hill, 1988). A textbook offering a little more in the way of mathematical explanation is *Noise control in building services*, Sound Research Laboratories, ed. Alan Frey (1988, Pergamon Press) and there are many others.

Manufacturers of building materials which have applications in the acoustics field generally publish comprehensive information about their products. This type of information is used as basic design data for many purposes and is usually available directly from the manufacturer or supplier. A good example is *Glass and noise control* (Pilkington Glass, 1993).

The Building Research Establishment (BRE) has a small research group concerned with building and environmental acoustics which has published a considerable amount of information on practical solutions to building acoustics problems. BRE have been using audio and video publications in recent years and the latest series of BRE Information Papers are somewhat brief and do not give full details of the research.

Transportation noise

Motor vehicles, jet aircraft and, to a lesser extent, railways all produce their own particular noise problems. *Transportation noise reference book*, edited by P.M. Nelson (Butterworth, 1987) has become the standard reference, with specialist chapters by a wide range of different experts. The memorandum *Calculation of road traffic noise*, Department of Transport (HMSO, 1988), sets out the UK method of calculating road traffic noise to determine entitlement to statutory compensation for new road development and for other purposes. There are numerous specialist reports published by the Department of Transport, the Civil Aviation Authority, the Motor Industry Research Association, the Transport Research Laboratory and the British Rail Research Department which deal with specific aspects.

Despite the fact that advances in engineering have steadily reduced source noise levels over the last twenty years, the demand for mechanized transportation continues to increase, alongside public expectations of peace and quiet. This means that transportation noise is a continuing problem. Reports and documents on the subject include J.B. Ollerhead *et al.*, *Report of a field study of aircraft noise and sleep disturbance*, Civil Aviation Authority for the Department of Transport (HMSO, 1992); *Assessing the environmental impact of road schemes*, D.A. Wood, Department of Transport (1992); *The UK environmental foresight project – the future road transport noise agenda in the UK*, Centre for Exploitation of Science and Technology (HMSO, 1994); *The design manual for roads and bridges – volume 11 section 3 part 7 – traffic noise and vibration*, Department of Transport (HMSO, 1993).

New research is often required to support environmental assessment of new transport infrastructure. The increasing involvement of the private sector has meant that government departments are tending to take less interest in specific transportation noise problems than hitherto. There remains, however, a large body of statutory accountability where, for example, the Civil Aviation Authority continues to take responsibility for aircraft noise at the major London airports. A recent emphasis on deregulation has tended to accelerate the process of the devolution to individual developers. Taken overall, the twin processes of devolution and deregulation mean that the available information is becoming more fragmentary and harder to locate. There is an increasing tendency for noise matters to be dealt with on an individual, case-by-case basis as at major public inquiries, or by specially convened industry working parties. The disadvantage of this process is that there is no one body to which an interested observer can turn for comprehensive and impartial advice.

Auditory acoustics

Auditory acoustics includes both psychological and physiological response to noise. A great deal of research into noise annoyance and noise nuisance over many years has shown that whereas individual response is unpredictable, it is possible to establish noise levels at which either small or large percentages of the population describe themselves as highly annoyed. It is often difficult to strike a fair balance between the freedom of the individual to continue making the noise and the interests of the person who is being unreasonably exposed to a noise nuisance. A large number of social surveys of community response to noise have been carried out in many countries around the world to try to inform such decisions.

The different capabilities of the human listener to hear various types of sound are well understood. Brian Moore provides a good grounding of the psychological aspects of human hearing in *Introduction to the psychology of hearing* (2nd edn, 1982, Academic Press). Jens Blauert has written the definitive text to date *Spatial hearing* (MIT Press, 1983) on those aspects of binaural hearing which allow us to localize sources in space. The masking effects of noise on speech are discussed in *Method for calculating the articulation index* (ANSI). There have been many recent developments (Speech Transmission Index – STI and RASTI) to allow for automated measurement, although the final correlation with speech intelligibility as measured with real people remains quite low in many cases.

Noise can cause difficulty in going to sleep, interfere with actual sleep, and create difficulty in returning to sleep once awoken (for whatever cause). Many research studies of noise and sleep have been carried out in laboratories and people appear to be very much more sensitive to noise while asleep in a laboratory than when exposed to familiar noises in their own homes. It appears that many people can get used to noise at night to a certain extent, but there are no data to indicate whether or not there is some other cost to the individual or to long-term health. This means that the general area of noise and sleep has been particularly controversial in recent years.

Another difficult area is noise and health. It is well known that excessive exposure to high level noise can permanently damage the hearing organs. The Noise at Work Regulations, (HMSO, 1989), as written under the Health and Safety at Work, etc. Act, 1974, set out action levels to control excessive exposure at work. The corresponding

Noise Guides (HMSO) provide a large amount of useful background information. There is also available a great deal of specialist information from the suppliers of hearing conservation equipment and from industrial noise control manufacturers. However, problems remain in that leisure and other non-work activities can make a significant contribution to overall noise exposure. There is a potential risk to hearing by less usual sounds which were not fully represented in the original research and might not be adequately represented by the existing regulations. In addition, a small minority of the population are believed to have sensitive ears which are more easily damaged at lower exposure levels. The problem here is that there is no reliable method for detecting those with sensitive hearing in advance of exposure.

The other potential effects of noise on health remain unproven. The levels of physical energy involved in most noise exposures are too low to cause direct physical damage to any of the tissues of the body. On the other hand, it is possible that a stress reaction to noise, such as startle to unexpected loud sounds, or continued annoyance to a lower level distant road traffic noise, could have a long-term effect on psychiatric or physiological health. There are many hypotheses and a large number of research studies in the literature, but the statistical problems of controlling for the many hundreds or even thousands of potentially confounding variables are very difficult and the majority scientific opinion still remains to be convinced. Articles on noise and health appear in a wide range of journals.

Standards and regulations

The World Health Organization (WHO) published a comprehensive review of noise criteria for environmental health in 1980. A draft revision of the document was prepared by Professors Berglund and Lindvall from Stockholm in 1992 and after review by a team of international experts in 1992 a final draft was circulated for comment in 1993. It is hoped that the final revised version will be published by WHO, but the task of collating the expected large number of comments from around the world is expected to be enormous. The final document will include a comprehensive bibliography of original source materials.

No national guidelines will carry the same prestige as the new version of the WHO document. On the other hand, the final draft version of the WHO document recognizes that individual countries will wish to set their own guidelines and criteria in the light of national experience and makes no comment where these might be different. Many people feel that the new WHO guidelines tend to err on the side of caution, suggesting criteria to cover particular noise effects where those effects are not universally accepted as proven. On the other hand, the main reason for not adopting stricter criteria is usually cost and sometimes inconvenience to the noise producer and there is rarely any advantage to accept higher noise levels.

There are a large number of individual British, European, American and international standards which deal with most aspects of noise measurement, assessment and control. The reader is again cautioned that many of these are constantly under revision in the light of new research data as they become available; it is important to be certain that the latest version or edition of the standard is being consulted.

Advice on national regulations will normally be available from the representatives of the ministry concerned. With hindsight, there are some national regulations in the UK and elsewhere which might appear to be a little arbitrary. There are others which remain as justifiable today as when they were first written and readers must form their own opinions in the light of wider consultation if in doubt.

Practical advice

The first port of call is normally the reference library but (at least in the UK) there is usually an environmental health officer available at the local government offices who may be able to assist with particular noise problems. The three main government research establishments which deal with noise issues (the National Physical Laboratory, the Building Research Establishment and the Transport Research Laboratory) are able to provide a limited amount of advice over the telephone or in response to a written enquiry.

It is unlikely that the local volunteer advice centre will have sufficient expertise to be able to deal directly with any problem which involves more than simple communication between disputants, but it should be able to point people in the right direction. A number of universities have specialist departments which can offer a certain amount of free advice, but eventually an enquirer may have to engage a specialist consultant for a professional fee. The UK Institute of Acoustics maintains a register of members and members' organizations and lists a large number of specialist consultants who may be able to assist in particular cases. The reader is cautioned that not all consultants have expertise in all aspects of noise pollution because it is such a wide-ranging topic.

CHAPTER NINE

Energy and mineral resources

GRAHAM McKENNA

A major factor in economic development and progress is the ability to identify and exploit a range of natural resources, all of which constitute a part of the environment within which we exist. In this existence, minerals, water and energy resources all represent critical elements. From the earliest times man has learnt that knowledge of, and ready access to, these elements is essential to survival. Today the same holds true but resources are often viewed on a more global scale. In recent times, the downside to the increasingly successful exploitation of resources has been recognized. Badly organized extraction of resources from the environment creates a variety of hazards for future generations. Abandoned mines, spoil heaps, waste tips and polluted water leave behind a legacy long after the initial gain. Uncontrolled use of fuel resources is liable to pollute the environment with emissions contributing to acid rain and global warming. Consumption at a local level is seen to affect the global environment.

Given the diversity of natural resources and their relationship to the environment, it follows that the range of organizations involved is broad and that information resources are both varied and extensive. On the one hand a number of governmental bodies is involved. Their interests include planning, construction, health and safety, pollution, trade, environmental protection and legislation. On the other hand a cross-section of non governmental organizations is involved. These include commercial companies in the extractive and fuel industries, trade associations, professional societies, publishers and information vendors. This chapter concentrates largely on the scene in the UK but cites examples of international organizations which are active in the field. In some instances local UK organizations, recognized as experts in their field, have an international as well as a local remit.

The natural resources cover materials such as oil, gas, coal, ores, road and building stones, aggregates, china clay, gypsum and underground water. In view of the range of natural resources, processes and interests involved it is hardly surprising that information formats and sources on the subjects are extensive. The information itself ranges from the raw numerical data resulting from, say, the hydrocarbon exploration process to a multi-volume published work on ore deposits of the world. In between information is disseminated in the form of serials, technical reports, reviews, theses, directories, maps, borehole or well logs, databases, CD-ROMs, abstracting and indexing services, photographic archives, mineral specimens, field survey records, etc. Seeking information in the natural resources sector, the researcher can look to both expert organizations and the published literature to solve any problems. This chapter deals with both sources. It does not attempt to be comprehensive but rather to identify major organizational sources and to select items from the published literature which illustrate the range of information available.

Organizational sources

The two main government departments in the UK which are active in natural resource management in the broadest sense are the Department of the Environment (DOE) and the Department of Trade and Industry (DTI) which now includes the areas previously covered by the former Department of Energy. The DTI publishes the pre-eminent source of information on the UK energy scene in the two-volume annual *Energy report* (HMSO). The first volume reviews the whole energy market and includes a section dealing with issues relating to energy and the environment. Volume 2 is the continuation of *Oil and gas resources of the United Kingdom* (the 'brown book') which details activity providing facts and figures on exploration, reserves, licences and production from the UK resources of hydrocarbons. In addition to this annual, the DTI statistical services also publish the *Digest of UK energy statistics* and the monthly *Energy trends*.

As well as statistical data the DTI also releases field data from offshore exploration activity in the microfiche publication *UK Continental shelf oil well records* (HMSO). The Department's wider role in energy policy and research has resulted in two overviews, *An assessment of renewable energy for the UK* and *An appraisal of UK energy research, development, demonstration and dissemination* (HMSO, 1994). The latter volume examines the energy technologies relevant to the UK and their future prospects and reviews R & D programmes supporting each technology. The series of Energy Papers covers various aspects of energy applications. No. 61 for instance, *Energy technologies for the UK*, (HMSO), 1994) assesses the technologies available to meet the UK's energy requirements over a 40-year time horizon.

General news of renewable energy developments appears in *New Review*. This magazine covers the whole spectrum of renewable energy sources including hydro-electric and geothermal.

The Department of Environment (DOE), with specialist divisions dealing with the minerals and water sectors, has as part of its remit areas such as environmental protection, planning, the countryside and the environmental impact of the construction industry. The DOE commissions research to inform the development of policy, monitors the effectiveness of existing policy relating to the environment and provides guidance on good practice. Mineral workings constitute a significant area of activity. Surface minerals such as aggregates represent an essential element as far as the construction industry is concerned but the extraction of sand, gravel and stone can have a major impact on the environment.

The DOE publications range from guidelines in the form of Minerals Planning Guidance Notes (MPG) to commissioned research reports such as the *Environmental effects of surface mineral workings* (HMSO, 1992) and *Low level restoration of sand and gravel workings* (HMSO 1989). The Guidance Note, *Environment Act 1995: review of mineral planning permissions* (HMSO, 1995) provides timely advice to minerals planning authorities and the minerals industry on the statutory procedures to be followed under the Act. The first of the reports looks not only at the effects of working on local residents but also on the landscape and groundwater resources and recommends good practice. A valuable bibliography comprising almost 500 items is included.

The restoration of sites after working contaminated land and the effects on agriculture are also among topics covered by the DOE's series of Circulars and Science and Technology Information Notes. A joint initiative between DTI and DOE created the Joint Environmental Markets Unit which has issued a report on the UK environmental industry in the worldwide context, *The UK Environmental industry: succeeding in the changing global market* (HMSO, 1994). This report illustrates how technologies applied to environmental processes have become a major global industry with many commercial opportunities. Useful data from the DOE are to be found in the *Digest of environmental protection and water statistics* (HMSO) which also includes summary information from the 1982 Survey of Land for Mineral Working in England. Still with statistics, UK production figures for coal, mineral oil, natural gas and a variety of minerals can be found in the Business Monitor series from the Central Statistical Office.

Moving beyond the government departments a number of statutory bodies and organizations are closely involved with environmental activity at a policy, research and practical level. In some cases the organizations also have a regulatory role. Public funds in one way or another finance a good deal of activity in this sector. Bodies represented here include the British Geological Survey and the Institute of Hydrology, both institutes of the Natural Environment Research Council, English Nature, Scottish Natural Heritage, the Countryside Council for Wales and the Joint Nature Conservancy Committee. Regulatory activity is centred on bodies such as the National Rivers Authority (NRA), (from April 1996 NRA has merged into the new Environment Agency) the Coal Authority and the Offices of Gas Supply, Electricity Regulation and Water Services.

The information and data resources of this sector are considerable. While some of the output is formally published, a very significant quantity of grey literature and unpublished data complements the publications. This information may come in the form of raw data, manuscript records, digital databases and indices, photographs, maps, technical reports or CD-ROM compilations.

A long-standing organization, the British Geological Survey, founded in 1835, provides a good illustration of the breadth of information resources available. The Survey's research activity covers topics such as mineral reconnaissance, groundwater resources, natural radioactivity, land use planning, geothermal resources, coastal zone management, contaminated land and hazard assessment, to name but a few. Its publications include thematic maps at various scales, in many cases accompanied by explanatory memoirs. Specialist map series include hydrogeology, engineering geology, mineral reconnaissance and applied geology, the latter series displaying the inter-relationship of environmentally significant factors. Some specialized mapping is published in the form of atlases such as the *Geochemical atlas of the Lake District* (1992). The whole range of thematic mapping in print is listed in the annual *Catalogue of maps*.

New technical reports and publications, including maps, are to be found in the bimonthly *New Releases*. Recent technical reports reflect the international nature of BGS activity; *Jersey groundwater—year 4 monitoring and consolidation* (1994) and *A mineralogical and petrographic study of a Nigerian dune profile* (1994). Useful sources of information on mineral production, consumption and trade are the *United Kingdom minerals yearbook*, the *Directory of mines and quarries*, covering the UK and *World mineral statistics*.

Other major reports series from BGS on minerals are the Mineral Assessment Reports, Mineral Reconnaissance Programme Reports, Mineral Dossiers, and the Overseas Geology and Mineral Resources series. Water resources are covered by the Water Supply Papers and earlier series based on county areas. A concise guide to mineral sources in Britain can be found in the BGS *Exploration for metalliferous and related minerals in Britain: a guide* (1990). In collaboration with the Association of Geoscientists for International Development (AGID),

BGS has published a review of minerals in 30 developing countries, *Industrial minerals in developing countries* (1994).

As well as publishing technical information BGS also issues two house journals which contain brief articles on BGS activities, *Earthwise* and *Earthworks*. Some issues are devoted to specific topics, for example the February 1993 issue of *Earthwise* dealt with the topic of groundwater. All the BGS published output is complemented by a vast archive of field and analytical data in a variety of formats. The National Geosciences Information Service provides access to the whole resource.

Organizations dealing with conservation are often linked to minerals activity. English Nature, the Countryside Council for Wales and Scottish Natural Heritage designate and manage Sites of Special Scientific Interest (SSSIs) and Regionally Important Geological Sites (RIGS). News about the organizations is published in house journals such as *English Nature*. Aspects of surface water and groundwater resources are covered by bodies such as the Institute of Hydrology which, with the BGS, publishes *Hydrological data UK* containing information from the National Water Archive. The National Rivers Authority, see previous page, (NRA) had among its responsibilities the monitoring of water quality and controlling pollution. In some areas this links to mineral workings. In its *Water Quality Series*, reports 14 and 15 (1994) deal with abandoned mines and contaminated land respectively. A new series of groundwater vulnerability maps at 1:100,000 scale is titled *Policy and practice for the protection of groundwater*. This map series was commissioned by the NRA from BGS, the Soil Survey and the Land Research Centre. As in the case of the British Geological Survey, the information resources of these bodies is far greater than the purely published output. The regulatory body for the coal industry is now the Coal Authority which has as one of its responsibilities 'to provide information on a wide range of topics'. The Authority holds the main collection of mine plans and associated records at Bretby.

Alongside the public bodies a wide range of information sources is to be found in the professional and commercial sector. Associations and learned societies often have extensive libraries and produce a range of publications and services. In the field of mineral resources is the Institution of Mining and Metallurgy which publishes *Transactions of the IMM, Minerals Industry International, IMM Abstracts* and its parallel on-line service IMMAGE. The *IMM Abstracts* include coverage of articles on a world-wide basis in terms of regional resources. Useful sections contain abstracts on economic geology and the environment. Of particular interest is the inclusion of entries of overseas thematic maps such as the *Geological Resource Map of New Zealand* series.

Elsewhere the Institute of Petroleum, the Petroleum Exploration

Society of Great Britain, the Institute of Quarrying and the Sand and Gravel Association, are all potential information suppliers. Learned societies such as the Geological Society of London have a wide programme of publication including journals such as *Petroleum Geoscience* and the *Quarterly Journal of Engineering Geology*. A recent title in the Geological Society's Special Publication series is devoted to *European coal geology* (1995) and covers both resource and environmental aspects of coal as a fuel. The *Geologist's directory*, published annually by the Geological Society, contains a useful listing of government, academic and commercial contacts. The Mineralogical Society of Great Britain publishes *Mineralogical Abstracts*. This is issued quarterly and includes abstracts of both site-specific resource analysis and environmental studies. The major body in the water industry is the Chartered Institution of Water and Environmental Management which publishes its *Journal* six times per annum.

On occasion information sought may relate to a particularly local area. In such cases local geological societies such as the Yorkshire Geological Society, museums and local archive and library services hold, or can advise on, unique local data sources. Specialist centres on a national basis may also be helpful. Resources such as the Natural History Museum in London, the National Stone Centre in Derbyshire or the Beamish Open-Air Museum in Northumberland should not be overlooked.

In the commercial sector, the availability of information is not always widely broadcast and access, especially where matters of commercial value are concerned, may not be straightforward. Large energy-based organizations such as Esso UK do release news features via their Public Affairs departments. *Esso View* for instance in its June 1995 issue highlights the measures taken by the company to protect the environment around its marine oil terminal at Fawley.

As in many scientific disciplines, a large part of the total information resource is generated by commercial publishers, in some cases on behalf of learned societies or associations. In this area it is more helpful to consider groups of material belonging to a particular format. Sections follow which deal with journals, abstracting and indexing services, directories, and monographs and maps.

Journals

Journals span the whole range of environmental interests connected with minerals, energy and water. Starting with initial resources policy is *Resources Policy*, dealing with mineral resources and sustainable development issues. *Nature and Resources* provides a general global approach but with thematic issues such as water quality and availability.

Energy Policy addresses among other topics the environmental aspects of energy supply and utilization. At the exploration and production level, journals such as *World Oil, Petroleum Times Energy Report* and *Petroleum Review* provide both news and technical articles on aspects of the hydrocarbons industry. Geological aspects of the hydrocarbon resources are dealt with in *Petroleum Geoscience*. A good example from overseas is *Petromin,* which covers the Asian sector of the market. The minerals industry has a similar range of journals with international content. *Industrial Minerals, Minerals Industry International* from IMM and *Mining Journal* and the *Mining Magazine* are major sources; *Metals & Minerals Annual Review* provides a useful overview. Specific areas such as coal, stone and aggregates have their own specialist journals such as *International Coal Report* and *Quarry Management.* The latter includes a list of environmental consultants in its buyers' guide section. The planning aspects of the minerals industry are covered by *Mineral Planning* which has regular sections on aggregates and energy minerals. A sister journal *Waste Planning* also contains relevant information for the extractive industries. At a worldwide level, the key scientific journal dealing with mineral resources is the Society of Economic Geologists' *Economic Geology.*

Groundwater resources are often dealt with in the more general journals of the water industry. *Water Resources Research,* for example, carries a wide range of scientific articles which include items on subsurface hydrology, hydrogeochemistry and water policy. *World Water and Environmental Engineer* and the *Journal of the Chartered Institution of Water and Environmental Management* have a technical bias and the latter contains major articles on such topics as the management of groundwater resources in France and European water policy.

Abstracting and indexing services

The science underlying the mineral, energy and groundwater sectors is so diverse that relevant literature maybe abstracted or indexed in services aimed more generally at chemistry or fuel technology. A useful guide to the area is *World Databases in Energy and the Environment* from the British Library. Core services of a specialized nature are as follows

GEOREF available as an online service via DIALOG and also as a three-disc CD-ROM product is arguably the biggest database with nearly two million citations. Together with its print version*Bibliography and index of geology,* it is an invaluable bibliography scanning over 3000 journals on a worldwide basis with concentration on North America, including most of the output of the US Geological Survey. Another indexing service

GeoArchive, is also international in coverage but has better coverage of UK regional items. In terms of abstracting services the main general service is GEOBASE with its print version *GeoAbstracts*. Specialized services are available in a number of areas. For mineral-related information *IMM Abstracts* with the on-line service IMMAGE and *Mineralogical Abstracts*; for energy-related information such services as *Coal Abstracts* and *International Petroleum Abstracts*; for water-related items AQUALINE and *Selected Water Resource Abstracts*. An energy-related service with over two million citations is to be found in DOE ENERGY, accessible on DIALOG. This dataset is compiled by the US Department of Energy. A valuable historical index dealing with mineral resources worldwide is the *Minerals Index* compiled by staff on the British Geological Survey. Available only as a card index, it is held in the BGS Library at Keyworth. Under index sources it is worth while pointing out that with the development of online catalogues and the Internet, it is now possible to search for information across the network. Many major library catalogues can be accessed remotely including those of several national geological surveys and other research bodies.

Directories

Information on companies, suppliers and consultants is to be found in many general trade directories. A number of publications are however aimed at particular industries and markets. Titles range from the *Offshore oil and gas directory* (Miller Freeman) to the *Natural stone directory* (Herald House). Some such as the *Directory of mines and quarries* deal with the UK while others such as the *FT oil and gas international year book* (Longman) have a broader geographical remit. The *Water services yearbook* (International Trade Publications) is a good example of the range of content. As well as providing details of the water companies in the UK, it lists relevant government departments and trade associations together with a section on consultancy services and an extensive buyers' guide.

Aimed rather more at the environmental aspects of the sector are titles such as the *ENTEC directory of environmental technology* (Kogan Page) and the *Environment industry yearbook* (Environment Press) which includes laboratory analysis services and specialist legal advisrs in its listings. The worldwide minerals mining industry is covered by a number of sources. Prominent among these are the *Financial Times mining international year book* (Longman) and the *Industrial minerals directory* (Metal Bulletin Books) which list producers and provide some statistical detail. Aimed at the market for specific minerals the *Roskill's reports on metals and minerals* cover some 80 metals and minerals in depth reporting on production, trade, consumption and companies active in the market.

Monographs and maps

As might be expected in key resource areas, each sector is supported by an extensive literature ranging from the bibliographic to the research-level monograph. In the field of minerals, C.F. Park's *The geology of ore deposits* (W.H. Freeman, 1986) provides a general overview of metalliferous mineral deposits. J.D. Ridge's multi-volume work *Annotated bibliographies of mineral deposits* (Geological Society of America, 1972; Pergamon Press, 1976–) also provides coverage on a worldwide basis. Volumes in the *Mineral deposits of Europe* (1979–) series are published by the IMM and the Mineralogical Society. Each volume covers serveral countries and volume 1 includes Great Britain and Ireland. Still at a national/regional level, many countries are covered by single works, often produced by the local geological survey. Examples here are the *Mineral deposits of Southern Africa* (1986) from the Geological Survey of South Africa and the Irish Association for Economic Geology's *Geology and genesis of mineral deposits in Ireland.* (1986). Within the UK local studies from the British Geological Survey include *The metalliferous mining region of South-West England* (HMSO, 1956; 1994 reprint) and the two-volume *Geology of the Northern Pennine orefield* (HMSO, 1948, 1985). Offshore mineral resources, together with the complications of exploiting them, are dealt with in D.S. Cronan's *Underwater minerals.* A major review of mineral deposits is the multi-volume *Handbook of strata-bound and stratiform ore deposits* (Elsevier, 1976–). While not comprehensive, this is an authoritative work and the chapters include valuable lists of further references. At a specific level, texts such as *Phosphate deposits of the world* by P.J. Cook and J.H. Shergold (Cambridge University Press, 1986) provide specialist coverage.

Several general atlases of mineral deposits are available. Perhaps more useful at an operational level are various series of mineral maps. Within Europe the *Carte metallogenique de L'Europe* (1968) published by UNESCO and BRGM and the *Carte des gites Mineraux de la France* (BRGM) at 1:500,000 scale represent useful sources of information. *GEOKATALOG–Geosciences*, published by Geocenter in Stuttgart, is an invaluable source of information on the availability of thematic mapping world wide.

In the field of energy resources, publications range from general texts to studies of specific regions from bodies such as the American Association of Petroleum Geologists (AAPG) and the Circum-Pacific Council for Energy and Mineral Resources. At the general level, two standard texts by E.N.Tiratsoo are *Natural gas* (Scientific Press, 1979) and *Oilfields of the world* (3rd edn, Scientific Press, 1984). The latter title reviews the situation by region and contains an appendix detailing oil reserves. Using the Pacific region as an example of the type of material available, a wide review is to be found in M.T. Halbouty's *Energy resources of the Pacific region* (AAPG, 1981). Published as No. 12 in the series AAPG Studies in Geology, this title ranges in its content from coal in Australia to geothermal resources in Taiwan. A number of volumes in the Earth Science series from the Circum-Pacific Council for Energy and Mineral Resources deal with the geology and resources of areas in the Pacific Region. Specifically covering hydro-carbons is No.10 in the series, *Petroleum resources of China and related subjects* (1988). This is a substantial technical study which deals with both onshore and offshore resources.

Geothermal energy resources received a good deal of attention in the early 1980. Texts published at that time still provide good background information on this resource. H.C.H. Armstead's *Geothermal energy* (2nd edn, Spon, 1983) provides a general review and contains a chapter on the the environmental impact of this energy source. R. Bowen's *Geothermal Resources* (2nd edn, Applied Science, 1979) includes coverage of a number of national geothermal energy operations. A good example of a technical study of geothermal resources at a national level is to be found in two reports from the British Geological Survey, *An assessment of the geothermal sources of the United Kingdom* and *Atlas of the geothermal resources of the United Kingdom* (1984).

Groundwater resources information is often to be found within works on the broader topic of hydrology or water resources. A much cited work which has a significant section describing the groundwater re-sources of the UK is J.C. Rodda's *Systematic hydrology* (Newnes Butterworth, 1976). In *Groundwater resources assessment* (Elsevier, 1989) a title in the Developments in Water Science series, J. Balek outlines techniques which can be used to carry out an effective groundwater assessment of a given area. A useful current text providing a guide to the topic of groundwater is M. Price's *Introducing Groundwater* (2nd edn. Chapman and Hall, 1994). *Water resources of the world-selected statistics, 1975* published by the Water Information Center (1975) examines each country in turn and even contains a table showing the water carrying capacity of the aquaducts of ancient Rome. Eighteen years later, with its title perhaps reflecting the increasing importance of water resources in the world political and economic scene, is *Water in crisis—a guide to the world's fresh water resources* (Oxford University Press, 1993). This wide-ranging review contains sections on the contaminaton of underground water, the application of water to energy generation and regional resources. Tabular data is preponderantly North American but many parts of the world do appear, although in less detail. Underground water resource locations are often depicted in the form of hydrogeological maps published by the national geological surveys.

The increasing awareness of the whole linkage between minerals and the environment is leading to new appraisals of the whole mineral cycle. A recent example is the proceedings of a meeting in Prague entitled *Mineral deposits: From their origin to the environmental impacts* (Balkema, 1995). Still on the environmental aspects of the mining industry, a useful source is *Environmental aspects of metalliferous mining – a select bibliography –* (Technical Communications 1987). This illustrates the range of factors involved in exploitation and its consequences, covering topics ranging from environmental pollution to natural rehabilitation and colonization of mining sites and waste deposits.

The international scene

It is not possible in a single chapter to treat in depth the whole global range of information resources. This section highlights, with examples of their output, those organizations which are actively involved at a global, regional or national level. In addition, attention is drawn to some sources which are perhaps less obvious.

The United Nations and its agencies generate both statistical and descriptive publications. On the one hand there is the *Annual bulletin of coal statistics for Europe and North America* and on the other the Natural Resources/Water Series from the Department of Technical Cooperation for Development. Issues in this series are valuable summaries containing both maps and useful bibliographies. No.19 for instance, is *Groundwater in Eastern, Central* and *Southern Africa* (United Nations: 1989). The UN Economic and Social Commission for Asia and the Pacific (ESCAP) supports a good deal of activity in the mineral and water sectors. Series published include the Mineral Resources Development Series (United Nations), which provides brief descriptions of the local energy and mineral markets and the Water Resources Series (United Nations). No. 71 of this series, *Towards an environmentally sound and sustainable development of water resources in Asia and the Pacific* (United Nations), reflects some of the wider concerns which are now linked to water resource management. As well as water availability and quality, broader concerns such as deforestation, erosion and the loss of wildlife caused by water projects are raised. ESCAP has also reviewed the relationship of the minerals industry to the environment in *Mineral resources development and the environment* (1992). This covers thirteen countries in the region and provides a brief outline of minerals activity and the main environmental issues at stake in each country.

UNESCO publishes relevant items in its Earth Sciences series. No.19, *A global geochemical database for environmental and resource management* (Unesco, 1995) reports the recommendations of the International Geochemical Mapping Project and proposes a global data network to address the global environmental problems.

The International Energy Agency produces among other publications, *Coal information* (IEA), which summarizes world coal developments and also deals with emission standards.

At the European level various agencies publish relevant information. From the EU, Eurostat issues several energy related titles including *Energy: monthly statistics*. Both printed and electronic services are listed fully in the *Eurostat catalogue*. The EC Directorate for Energy reviews the regional position three times a year in *Energy in Europe: energy policies and trends in the European Community*. *Europe's Environment 1993* (European Communities, 1995) from the European Environment Agency provides an in-depth report of the state of the pan-European environment. The Council of Europe has issued *Guidelines for the protection of groundwater* (European Communities, 1995) aimed at protecting the health of the consumer.

Before moving to examples at a national level, it is worthwhile raising sources which may not be immediately obvious. Although they commission work rather than carry it out themselves, the various development banks are often involved in funding major projects in the minerals, energy and water sectors overseas. Examples of activity here include Laos and The Gambia. The Asian Development Bank in 1990 funded a review of the mineral potential of Laos. The African Development Bank has issued a review of The Gambia including a *Country environmental profile* aimed at integrating environmental concerns into the Bank's lending programmes. One topic included is water resource degradation. Not always an easy source to locate bibliographically, such publications and information sources should not be overlooked.

At a national level, most industrialized countries have organizations and information sources similar to those found in the UK and listed earlier. In the USA for instance, the Bureau of Mines' *Minerals Yearbook* has for many years been a major source of minerals information world wide. Agencies such as the US Geological Survey (USGS) and the US Environmental Protection Agency (EPA) have extensive publishing programmes. The USGS publications include major series such as the Water Supply Papers, with almost 2500 papers issued and the Water Resources Data series. Items in this series cover individual states on an annual basis. As well as providing a wealth of information on surface water resources, each volume also includes detailed data on groundwater levels at sites across the state. Other USGS series with relevant content include the Professional Papers and Open-file Reports. National geological surveys are usually good sources of thematic information such as local mineral, groundwater and hydrocarbon resources.

One general reference of relevance to the subject matter of this chapter is D.N. Wood, J.E. Hardy and A.P. Harvey (eds) *Information sources in the earch sciences* (2nd edn, 1989, Bowker-Saur).

Periodical titles (with ISSN)

Annual Bulletin of Coal Statistics Europe (0066–3808).
Bibliography & Index of Geology (0098–2784).
Coal Abstracts (0309–4979).
Digest of UK Energy Statistics (0307–0603).
Earthwise (0967–9669).
Economic Geology (0361–0128).
Energy in Europe (1017–6705).
Energy Monthly Statistics, EC (0258–3569).
Energy Policy (0301–4213).
English Nature (0966–1166).
IMM Abstracts (0019–0020).
Industrial Minerals (0019–8544).
International Petroleum Abstracts (1052–9292).
Journal of the Chartered Institution of Water and Environmental Management (0951–7359).
Mineral Planning (0267–1409).
Minerals Industry International (0308–9789).
Mining Annual Review (0076–8995).
Mining Journal (0026–5225).
Mining Magazine (0308–6631).
Nature and Resources (0028–0844).
Petroleum Geoscience (1354–0793).
Petroleum Review (0020–3076).
Petroleum Times Energy Report (0261–3883).
Petromin (0129–1122).
Quarterly Journal of Engineering Geology (0481–2085).
Resources Policy (0301–4207).
Transactions of IMM
   Mining Industry (0371–7844).
   Applied Earth Science (0371–7453).
   Mineral Processing & Extraction Metallurgy (0371–9553).
Waste Planning (0965–3147).
Water Resources Research (0043–1397).
World Oil (0043–8790).

Details of organizations referred to in this chapter are shown in the Appendix.

PART THREE

Practicalities

CHAPTER TEN

Land use

JOHN GOODIER

Introduction

Our environment is experienced on the surface of the earth and compared with its size the space occupied by living creatures is a thin film
over that surface. An understanding of the form of the land, its uses and
history are an essential part of the study of the environment. Some parts
of the landscape, specific sites, views, natural and manmade features
may themselves need protecting. In other cases a not particularly
interesting piece of land may need protection because it is home to
some particular creature or because important archaeological remains
lie beneath its surface.

In this chapter the main sources of UK information on land use are
discussed. The intention is to outline the aspects of the topic and the
many sources available. A subplot to this chapter is to suggest that, in
addition to the central environment information, historical sources and
the literature of art can be of use in the study of the environment. To
a greater or lesser extent similar sources can be found for any area of
the earth. There are, in very general terms, three sorts of information
available for the study of land use. There are the textbooks, articles,
archives and databases of traditional information. Then there are more
direct representations of the land such as maps and photographs. And
there is the land itself which can be read not only for its current use but
also for its history. In this account the three types of information will
be discussed together and historical and current information will be
considered. The chapter is divided into a number of short notes on
various land uses. Some of the sources on specific industries given in
chapter 12 on technology are also relevant here. This area of information very easily spills over into social and economic information which

can help to make sense of the physical history of the land. An introduction to the use of geographical information systems in the study of landscape is provided by Haines-Young *et al.* (1993).

I have deliberately opted for wide, if at times sketchy and anecdotal, description because I wish to outline the extensive range of material available. The way in which land use meshes with concepts such as planning and conservation is described by Mather (1986); originally an American text, this is a useful introduction to the topic. The section in Chapter 12 about urban land use should be consulted for information on Ordnance Survey (OS) maps and aerial photographs. In that chapter pre-industrial land use is not considered and so documents and maps from before the late 18th century are not considered. A useful introduction to earlier maps and documents and to secondary sources is provided by Brown (1987).

A number of the references quoted are from the Collins New Naturalist series. This is, on the whole, a good series and many of the volumes are of relevance to other chapters in this book. Marren (1995) has produced a useful summary of the series as the fiftieth anniversary volume.

In the 1930s L.D. Stamp carried out a survey of land use which was written up in popular form in 1946 (Stamp, 1967). During the 1960s Alice Coleman organised the Second Land Utilisation Survey, using volunteer records. The coverage of the country is incomplete but those maps that were made have been published (Coleman 1961), and there is a handbook describing the mapping conventions (Coleman and Maggs 1968). A sample survey of 1000 kilometre squares are being mapped for land use in the summer of 1996 by schools. For brief details see McTaggart (1996) or contact the Land Use UK Administrator at the Geographical Association. An historical overview has been provided by Rackham (1986).

The view from the sky

A general overview of land form and land use can be obtained from Landsat images. These are false colour pictures taken from satellites. The surface of the earth is scanned for several discrete bands of infra-red radiation and the subsequent picture is produced by assigning arbitrary colours to each band. The resolution is such that each pixel of the original scan is about half a hectare. Photographs taken from high altitude have a resolution of about 20cm square. However, Landsat is a lot less expensive than photography. Although Landsat pictures give some useful information about well-mapped areas like the UK, they are particularly valuable for remote expansive areas such as deserts. An introduction to the technology is given in Sheffield (1981). An account of recent developments with examples of their use in landscape history is provided by Evans (1994). A catalogue of remote images is available as File 13 on the ESA-IRS database.

Maps

The Ordnance Survey maps are used as the basis of a number of other maps. There are various series of geological maps, covering solid and surface geology, produced by the Geological Survey. These are complemented by a series of Regional Geology surveys. The Soil Survey and Land Resource Institute produce several series of soil maps at differing scales which are accomplished by texts that give a lot of general information on land use possibilities. The Ministry of Agriculture Fisheries and Food have produced maps of land capability and land use.

Geological features

The geology and scenery in Britain (Whittow, 1993) is a new version of a classic introduction to landscape. Another good account, with more emphasis on the geological history, has been produced by Fortey (1993). There are series of Regional Geology and Classic Areas of British Geology produced by the Geological Survey. Regional guides have also been produced by the British Geomorphological Research Group and the Geographical Association and published by Methuen.

Soil

Soil is a key aspect of land use from which it determines the natural and cultivated vegetation and from those, the animal life of an area. It can also have significant civil engineering effects. A comprehensive introduction is given by Wild in *Soil conditions and plant growth* (1988). The Macaulay Institute in Scotland and the Soil Survey and Land Research Centre in England and Wales have produced soil maps on various scales which are usually accompanied by a descriptive monograph.

General texts

There are very few parts of the UK which have not been subject to extensive activities by people. In fact, there are very few areas of the earth outside the polar regions that have not been extensively altered by people. Tropical rainforest is a mosaic of shifting agricultural sites in various states of regeneration. In the UK a discipline of landscape history has grown up. *Making of the English landscape* by W.G. Hoskins (1992) remains the classic text and is a good introduction to reading the landscape for information on past use. Richard Muir has provided a more extensive account in *Reading the landscape (1993)*. N. Fairbrother in *New lives, new landscapes* (1970) gives more attention to industrial and urban landscape than most authors. Books of aerial photographs tend to be aimed at the photographs-as-art market, but can be useful.

Representative examples of books with many photographs are *Yorkshire album*, by Hartley and Ingilby which is a collection of photographs from the first half of the century, and *Fell walking with Wainwright* which contains many photographs by Derry Brabbs. A possible way such books can be used is the investigation of the effects of tourists on landscape. The c1890 picture of Gordale Scar shows more vegetation on the cliffs than is present now, and Brabbs' picture of the summit of Coniston Old Man shows serious erosion.

There exist many accounts of particular areas and, in some ways older accounts, which are more dependent on text than pictures, are better than more recent guides, which tend to emphasize the picturesque and the odd. The many books published by Batsford in the 1930s and early 1940s have much to commend them. Representative examples are *West Country*, by C.H. Warren (1938) covering Somerset, Devon and Cornwall, and *British hills and mountains* by J.H.B. Bell (1940) which describes a particular landscape feature. Arthur Mee's The King's England series is aimed at a lower educational level. The series, produced for the Festival of Britain, is a somewhat superficial snapshot of post-war UK. Several volumes in Collins New Naturalist series deal with particular landscape types or particular areas (for example, the New Forest). Although they concentrate on the wild life, there is usually some account of land use and landscape history.

Series which cover the whole of the UK include The Making of Britain (Routledge and Kegan Paul) which deals with landscape in five volumes, covering historical periods, and the Making of the English Landscape (Michael Joseph: London) which deals with the UK by area. There is also a series of Disovering books for many areas published by John Donald. The Pimlico County Histories series (London House: London) provides useful historical overviews. The first titles in this series were published in 1995.

The British Association for the Advancement of Science used to publish accounts of the region where its annual meeting was held. These include chapters on geography, land use, industry, wildlife and settlement. It stopped producing them as separate publications about twenty years ago. One of the last was *The Stirling Region.* (Timms 1974). The meetings usually include a number of papers on the local area.

In the early days of photography a number of attempts were made to record local scenes as an archaeological exercise. An account of these has been produced by Taylor (1994). In addition to photographs, paintings can be a useful source of information. There is more danger of misrepresentation in paintings than in photographs, especially where the picturesque takes over from the reporting. On the whole the late 18th and early 19th century watercolours are reasonably accurate, as are the Recording Britain Series of the 1940s (see Mellor *et al*, 1990).

Woodland

The history of woodland development and management has been provided by Edlin (1970). Rackham's (1976) account is more detailed and examines the history of particular woodland types and particular tree species. The Forestry Commission has produced a wide range of books and leaflets, some of which discuss forestry systems. It also produces guides to major forests such as the New Forest and the Forest of Dean, which cover broader aspects than timber production.

Farmland

The Ministry of Agriculture, Fisheries and Food and its forerunners have been collecting UK agricultural statistics since 1866. Much of the data are available at county level and so present a reasonably detailed picture of local agricultural systems. Various accounts of regional agriculture have been produced, the earliest attempt being the Georgical survey of the Royal Society (1667), but only one full response to the questionnaire and a few responses to the shorter version were received. The survey carried out by Arthur Young between 1768 and 1770 was the first authoritative overview of the whole country. Details of Young's publications can be found in the bibliography compiled by G.D. Amery which is published as an appendix in *Old English farming books* by Fussell (1978). The Board of Agriculture carried out a postal survey in 1816; this has been reprinted. The Royal Agricultural Society carried out a survey in the late 1950s and David Rendal published The Farming Series of regional accounts in the late 1960s. The series covered the country in a number of regional volumes written by practising farmers. Examples are *Farming in Wales* by R. Howells (1965) and *Farming in East Anglia* by J. Young (1967). Coppock produced a number of books in the 1970s. Examples of Coppock's work are *An Agricultural Atlas of*

England and Wales (1962) and *The changing use of land in Britain* (1962) written with his colleague R. Best.

A good survey of farm features and regional farming is provided by Darley (1981), which contains some useful reference lists. *Hedges* (Pollard et al., 1974) gives an account of this distinctive feature of post-enclosure agriculture. A good introduction to various farming practices can be found in the frequently revised *Principles of Food and Agriculture* (Spedding, 1992). Previous editions usually referred to as 'Fream's' after the first author, provide a series of overviews of farming since 1892. There is no better way of keeping informed of what is going on in agriculture than to read the journal *Farmer's Weekly*, first published in 1934. There are several other agricultural periodicals which deal with specific aspects.

Agricultural history is a well-developed discipline, although much effort is directed towards economic history and it is not always possible to tease out the agricultural system. However, some texts do permit this; Hoskins (1957) *The Midland Peasant* gives a good account, albeit as subplot, of the system of the later middle ages. Kerridge gives the best description of the Norfolk six-shift system (what most authors call the four-course rotation) in *The agricultural revolution* (1967).

Agricultural history since the middle of the 19th century is the subject of the Rural History Centre (RHC) at the University of Reading. The RHC has a large collection of texts, a massive archive of company histories, photographs, etc, and a collection of artefacts. It also compiles a database of references in rural history which it hopes to make available in electronic medium.

Wild areas

There are few truly wild areas in the UK but several areas are designated National Parks where there are restrictions on various types of development. Guides to these areas are produced by the various parks boards and by commercial publishers. There is a tendency to overdo the photographs and underdo the text, especially in the more popular versions, but the photographs may be used as sources of information. Some areas are designated areas of scenic beauty or as Sites of Special Scientific Interest (SSSIs). The Countryside Commission has produced a Directory of Areas of Outstanding Natural Beauty (1989). The MAFF has recently designated some parts of the country as Environmentally Sensitive Areas (ESAs) and has produced leaflets on specific areas such as The Broads. A full set of leaflets and an introduction to the scheme can be obtained from MAFF (MAFF, 1994). A number of national and local nature reserves protect particular geological or natural habitats or particular species. There

are also bird sanctuaries such as those set up by the Royal Society for
the Protection of Birds. The National Trust owns a large amount of
rural land and there are restrictive covenants on the use of other areas.
These organizations produce guides to their property and hold much
historical and detailed information in their archives. English Nature
(DoE, 1996) and its Scottish and Welsh counterparts (MAFF, 1994)
publish lists of local nature reserves.

Common land is an almost unique feature of the English landscape.
A full account of its history and a reliable list of sites is provided by
W.G. Hoskins and L.D. Stamp in *The common lands of England and
Wales* (1963). Not all common land is wild land, by any stretch of the
imagination, and free access is available only on urban commons.

The Joint Nature Conservation Committee (Joint Nature Conservation Committee, 1995) is producing a series of descriptions of coastal
areas which cover land form, land use and wildlife. The Countryside
Commission has started work on a *Directory of regional landscape*
(Countryside Commission, 1994).

Parks, gardens and arboreta

Substantial portions of UK land are given over to managed landscape.
The development of landscaped parks took place in the 18th century
and many of these areas, with their lakes and wildernesses, still exist as
grounds to stately homes or institutions, or as public parks. Those in the
care of private owners, of the National Trust or English Heritage may
well have guides to their history and management. An outline history,
with many illustrations is given by S. Lasden (1991) in *The English
park: royal, private and public.*

Urban development

The history of urban development goes back to medieval times but
rapid growth occurred during the 19th and early 20th centuries. A
comprehensive introduction covering all counties, to pre-industrial
urban use, is given by Morris (1994). The more recent period is well
covered by OS maps. Photographs and local newspapers give an
account of more modern urban history. There is a danger of being
misled in trying to date buildings by their style. For example, in the
1920s some timber-framed houses were built in Kingsbury (north west
London) both in the Tudor style and manner, using unseasoned elm.
Some buildings such as the White House, Aston Munslow, Shropshire,
which hides Saxon, Norman and Tudor features behind a Georgian
facade, are more complex than they seem.

Urban developments, such as model villages and garden suburbs, are well covered by histories. The County Architectural Surveys, originally conducted by Nikolaus Pevsner (Pevsner, various dates) and now being revised, contain information on regional architectural styles and deal with extensive schemes such as schools, factories and housing development. However, the emphasis is on the best and most important buildings. Knowledge of the origins of an important building might be a key to reading the landscape. The conservation of the built heritage has its own literature. Haskell (1993) provides an overview with several examples from each county in *Caring for our built heritage*.

Recent and future urban use

Since the 1930s and more strongly since World War II, the development of planning controls has reduced some of the variability of the developing urban landscape but has provided a good source of information in local authority archives. Development plans were first produced in 1947. Current legislation requires structure plans (giving a broad framework); district local plans (which are also produced for National Parks); minerals plans; waste disposal plans; and (for metropolitan areas) a unitary development plan. The Department of Environment (DoE) has a unique collection of these documents; *Bibliography 152A*, DoE library information sheet No. 13 is an introduction to the plans (DoE, 1996). The listing of important buildings and the designation of various levels of conservation area also fixes some of the history and use.

Local information

There is a wealth of local history information available, some published in local history magazines or by the local library or educational service and some as a private printing venture. There are numerous guides to local churches and other interesting features; the scholarship is not always good but useful snippets of information are often included in the text. In theory all these documents should also be held in the British Library Humanities Collections, but in practice much will be missing. Local libraries will probably have good collections and may well have a local history section. For the London region the bibliography by Dolphin et al. (1981) is a good starting-up point. The database URBALINE hosted by ESA and produced by the London Research Centre, contains some useful urban planning information, especially if considerable detail about small areas is required. The sources mentioned on contaminated land in Chapter 12 are also relevant here.

Land use statistics have been discussed by Coppock, and town and country planning statistics have been discussed by Gebbert; these two reports form volume 8 of the *Reviews of statistical sources*. Volume 7, *Leisure and tourism*, may also be useful. Some of the other volumes have information relevant to urban land use and all volumes contain a critique of the data and a list of data sources (Maunder).

Online and CD-ROM information

Only ENVIROLINE offers general coverage of land use. For specific areas, databases on biological (e.g. BIOSIS and ECOLOGICAL ABSTRACTS), agricultural (especially CABI rural sociology and AGRICOLA) and historical and geographical databases have to be relied upon. General waste management and pollution sources will target specific problems. Many of the books and series mentioned here are aimed at the non-specialist. this seems appropriate, as the idea is to provide the historical and geographical context to environmental problems. A consequence of this is that much of the material is not included in the main online databases or CD-ROMs. *The British Library catalogue* (covering works pre-1975, including the whole of the *General catalogue*) and the *Humanities and social science* (for works post-1975) available on BLAISE will cover most (in theory all) UK publications, plus a good representation of other literature. CARTOGRAPHIC MATERIALS (MAPS) is the catalogue of the post-1974 British Library map catalogue. In addition to maps, it contains references to cover 200 remote-sensing and digital cartography databases. The collection is worldwide. It is also available via BLAISE.

Conclusions

In a short chapter one can only sketch out a topic as large as land use. What I have attempted to do here is to illustrate the range of published data and to suggest some approaches.

References

Bell, J.H.B., Bozeman, E.F. and Fairfax-Blakeborough, J. (1940) *British hills and mountains*. London: Batsford.

Best, R.H. and Coopock, J.T. (1962) *The changing use of land in Britain*. London: Faber & Faber.

Board of Agriculture (1816) *The agricultural state of the Kingdom* (Reprinted 1970) Bath: Adams and Dent.

Brown, A. (1987) *Fieldwork for archaeologists and local historians*. London: Batsford.

Coleman, A. (Director) (1961 onwards) *The second land utilisation of Britain on the scale of 1:25 000*. Ramsgate, Isle of Thanet Geographical Association. [Series of maps]

Coleman, A. and Maggs, K.R.A. (1968) *Land use survey: An explanation of the new land use survey of Britain on the scale of 1:25 000*. 5th ed Ramsgate, Isle of Thanet Geographical Association.

Coppock, J.T. (1964) *An agricultural atlas of England and Wales*. London: Faber & Faber.

Countryside Commission (1987) *Directory of areas of outstanding natural beauty*. Cheltenham: Countryside Commission.

Countryside Commission (1994) *The new map of England: a directory of regional landscape: results of a pilot study in south western England*. Cheltenham: Countryside Commission.

Darley, G. (1981) *The National Trust book of the farm*. London: Weidenfield & Nicholson.

DoE (1996) Library Information Sheet No 13: Plans and Special Collections. London: DoE.

Dolphin, P., Grant, E. and Lewis, E. (1981) *The London region: an annotated bibliography*. London: Mansell.

Edlin, H.L. (1970) *Trees, woods and man*, 3rd edn. London: Collins New Naturalist Series.

Evans, D.J. *et al*. (1994) Earth from the sky. *Scientific American*, December, 44–49.

Fairbrother, N. (1970) *New lives, new landscapes*. ??: The Architectural Press.

Fortey, R. (1993) *The hidden landscape: a journey into the geological past*. London: Cape.

Fussell, G. (1978) *The old English farming books from Fitzherbert to Tull* (reprinted as one volume 1978) Aberdeen: Aberdeen Rare Books.

Haines-Young, R. *et al*. (1993) *Landscape, ecology and geographical information systems*. London: Taylor and Francis.

Hartley, M. and Ingilby, J. (1988) *Yorkshire album: photographs of every day life 1900–1950*. London: Dent.

Haskell, T. (1993) (ed.) *Caring for our built heritage*. London: E & F N Spon.

Hoskins, W.G. (1992) *Making of the English Landscape*. London: Hodder.

Hoskins, W.G. (1957) *The Midland peasant: the economic and social history of a Leicestershire village*. London and Basingstoke: Macmillan.

Hoskins, W.G. and Stamp, L.D. (1963) *The common lands of England and Wales*. London: Collins New Naturalist Series.

Howells, R. (1965) *Farming in Wales*. London: David Rendell.

Hywel-Davies, J. and Thom, V. (1986) *The Macmillan guide to British nature reserves*. London: Macmillan.

Joint Nature Conservation Committee (1995) *Coasts and seas of the United Kingdom* (17 volumes, various dates). Peterborough: JNCC.

Kerridge, J. (1967) *The agricultural revolution*. London: George, Allen & Unwin.

Lasden, S. (1991) *The English park: royal, private and public*. London: Andre Deutsch.

McTaggart, M. (1996) *Rounding up the squares Times education supplement extra* 29 March 1996 p VI.

MAFF (1994) Information Park: Environmentally Sensitive areas [Our Living Heritage: Environmentally Sensitive areas plus 22 leaflets] available from MAFF helpline 0645 33 5577.

Marren, P. (1994) *English national nature reserves* Peterborough: English Nature/ T & A D Poyser..

Marren, P. (1995) *The new naturalist*. London: Harper-Collins.

Mather, A.S. (1986) *Land use*. Harlow: Longman.

Maunder, W.F. Reviews of United Kingdom Statistical Sources. Oxford: Pergamon. Vol IV Lewis, F.M.M. and Parker, S.R. *Leisure* and Lickorish, L.J. *Tourism* Vol VIII Coppoch, J.T. *Land Use* and Gebbett, L.F. *Town and Country Planning* [note 2 accounts in ech volume]

Mellor, D., Saunders, G. and Wright, P. (1990) *Recording Britain: a pictorial Domesday of prewar Britain.* Newton Abbot: David & Charles.

Morris, A.E. (1994) *History of urban form: before the industrial revolution.* Harlow: Longman.

Muir, R. (1993) *Reading the landuse: a Shell book.* London: Michael Joseph.

Pevsner, N. (and others) (various dates) The Buildings of England [separate volume for each county or part of county] Harmondsworth: Penguin.

Pollard, E., Saunders, G. and Moore, N.W. (1974) *Hedges.* London: Collins New Naturalist Series.

Rackham, O. (1976) *Trees and woodlands in the British landscape.* London: Dent.

Rackham, O. (1986) *The history of the countryside.* London: Dent.

Sheffield, C. (1981) *Earth watch.* London: Sidgwick and Jackson.

Spedding, C.R.W. (1992) *Principles of food and agriculture.* Oxford: Blackwell Scientific, [Fream's].

SSRC/RSS. *Reviews of United Kingdom statistical sources* (various dates) Oxford: Pergamon Press.

Stamp, L.D. (1967) *Britain's structure and scenery* 6th edn. London: Collins New Naturalist Series.

Taylor, J. (1994) *A dream of England: landscape, photography and the tourist's imagination.* Manchester: Manchester University Press.

Timms, D. (1974) The Stirling Region. Stirling: Stirling University for the British Association.

Wainwright, A. (1984) *Fell walking with Wainwright.* London: Michael Joseph.

Warren, C.H. (1938) *West country.* London: Batsford.

Whittow, J. (1993) *Geology and scenery in Britain.* London; Chapman & Hall.

Wild, A. (1988) *Soil conditions and plant growth* 11th edn. Harlow: Longman.

Young, J. (1967) *Farming in East Anglia.* London: David Rendall.

CHAPTER ELEVEN

Economics and environmental management

HELEN WOOLSTON

Introduction

The number of interested parties and the range of topics that has to be considered when dealing with economic aspects of managing the environment are very large indeed. It is generally not practicable to take a narrow view and factors involved will include broad economic policies, sustainability, social questions, risk ratings, legal requirements, insurance cover and sources of finance, to name but a few. Much that is dealt with in the other chapters of this book is also of major concern.

The range of information sources which can be used to research this topic is similarly broad. This chapter looks at some of the most commonly requested environmental economics topics and at a range of sources which can help to find further information.

Sustainable development – the bigger picture

To many environmentalists, researchers and academics, the scope of environmental economics includes international conferences, development funds and major efforts to promote sustainable development. Sustainable economic development means producing an enduring flow of resources, or balancing resource use with resource availability.

Considering the bigger picture is not an easy task – it means measuring the people's preferences for an 'environmental good' against an 'environmental bad'. To a large extent, the whole issue of sustainable development includes questions of population growth, employment and the development and promotion of industry and agriculture – greater affluence.

Anyone who needs to know more about the general policies and future plans associated with sustainable development should obtain a copy of the proceedings of the Rio Conference (UN, 1992) *Report of the United Nations Conference on Environment and Development* (Rio de Janeiro, 3–14 June 1992). This Report gives the proceedings and conclusions of the Earth Summit, including the Rio Declaration on Environment and Development, Agenda 21 (the action plan for sustainable development and environmental protection) the Convention on Climate Change and the Biodiversity Treaty.

One of the best sources for anyone needing an introduction to sustainable development is the Blueprint series of books from David Pearce. *Blueprint for a green economy* (1989) caused something of a stir in the environmental and business world. While academics had been considering these questions for some time, this seemed to be the first time that such information was available in a paperback on sale in popular bookshops. Theories are presented such as: 'What is being valued is not the environment, but people's preferences for change in the state of it.' The Blueprint series has broken important ground in presenting theories on solving environmental problems and the link with solving economic problems. The first book discussed (Pearce, 1989) the UK economy, but was actually read and considered worldwide. The second, *Blueprint 2: valuing the Environment* (Pearce, 1991) considered international and global issues. The third title *Blueprint 3: measuring sustainable development* (Pearce, 1993a) looks again at the UK, but focuses on sustainable development. All three books contain comprehensive reference listings.

Environmental economics: an elementary introduction (Turner et al., 1993) and *The Earthscan reader in environmental economics* (Markandya, 1992) are also good starting-points. They contain references to introductory texts on environmental economics and review developments in classical economics to take account of environmental issues.

One of the most influential and prolific organizations in the terms of environmental economics publications is the World Bank, which administers government funds to run development projects and now has a vice president for environmentally sustainable development. The organization has given due recognition that environmental 'abuse' is constraining world economic development and its positive response to this dilemma has led to a series of major institutional, procedural and policy reforms, which are provided as examples and suggestions to other financial bodies that need or desire to improve their environmental stance. One of its most powerful policies is on the use of environmental impact assessment. The World Bank administers the

Global Development Facility (GDF) which was established by UN member nations through voluntary contributions as a means of providing for the incremental costs of financing sustainable development.

The *Index of publications & guide to information products and services* is a comprehensive and informative catalogue of World Bank titles in print. It also contains details of online access to documents through the Internet, access through computerized data files and the range of pamphlets, booklets, videos and customer service phone numbers. Material is arranged by title, author, country of publication and subject and there is a section on foreign language publications.

Environment Bulletin is a quarterly newsletter available free of charge from the World Bank. It contains information on general environmental issues, conference reports and initiatives.

In 1994 the World Bank opened a Public Information Center in Washington DC, offering information about development projects from their start to completion and providing documents which review the potential environmental impacts of projects, environmental data sheets and national environmental action plans. The World Bank publishes an annual *Directory of libraries* in more than 90 countries which are designated as depositories of its publications. *Environmental accounting for sustainable development* (Ahmad *et al.*, 1989) is a useful introduction to national environmental accounting.

The International Chamber of Commerce has published J.-O. Williams (ed.) *From ideas to action: business and sustainable development* (1992) and the *Business Charter for Sustainable Development*, which has signatories from many companies around the world.

The International Institute for Environment and Development (incorporating the London Environmental Economics Centre) is the largest environment and development think tank in Europe. It promotes sustainable development through research, policy studies and information. There is an extensive publications programme, for example, *Resource accounting for sustainable development: a review of basic concepts, recent debate and future needs* (Markandya, 1991).

The Organization for Economic Co-operation and Development (OECD) has published useful titles in this field, including *Environmental policy: how to apply economic instruments* (1991) and J. Opschoor's *Economic instruments for environmental protection* (1989).

The UK Department of Trade and Industry (DTI) has an Advisory Committee on Business and the Environment which publishes regular reports of the financial sector working group. These give a good overview of current policy and future possibilities.

Many excellent articles on sustainable development and economic policy are available and are presented in the bibliographies of the titles included in this chapter. There are also certain journals which regularly publish papers on these topics or report on current developments. These include *Ecological Economics, The Journal of Environmental Management, Ambio,* and *Economic Review. Economic Trends* is produced monthly by the UK Central Statistical Office and gives useful facts and figures. Important current developments are also covered in the *Financial Times* and *The Economist.* The *ENDS Report* and *Environment Business* are useful sources of news on all environmental business issues, particularly developments in legislation.

This information can also be found online, using databases such as TEXTLINE, which covers the *Financial Times* and *The Economist,* ENVIRO-LINE, ACCOUNTING AND TAX DATABASE and PTS NEWSLETTER DATABASE.

Market economy/economic instruments

While environmental law is important in dealing with problems of environment and development, it is more successful when combined with economic and voluntary approaches. The Rio Conference Report suggest that governments should 'encourage research and analysis on effective uses of economic instruments and initiatives for competitiveness and international trade'. Prices, markets, and government fiscal and economic policies all play an important role.

Environmental economics encompasses the costs involved in bringing about improvements in environmental problems such as global warming and the greenhouse effect. The question is – who pays? The 'polluter pays principle' is one which is frequently quoted, not least in the legislation, but there are arguments that a 'user pays principle' may be more appropriate'.

There are some difficult questions to answer, such as how should the growth of industry in the third world be managed and the ensuing crippling carbon dioxide emissions, when at the same time these areas present the best possibilities for new expanding markets. International agreements to limit CO_2 emissions consider economic approaches but also look at stages of development. Market economy is a question of balancing individual demand for better circumstances with an overall demand for a better environment.

The Commission of the European Communities has produced the following documents which outline a possible way forward: *Proposal for a Council Directive introducing a tax on carbon dioxide emissions and energy* (COM(92)226); and *Council Regulation of 21 May 1992 establishing a financial instrument for the environment* (LIFE) 92/1973/EEC. The introduction of EU wide carbon tax seems to depend very much on which country has the six-month presidency. Up-to-date sources of European information include the EC Commission

Information Office, *Europe Environment* or *European Chemical News.*

In J.-O. Williams' book *From ideas to action: business and sustainable development*, he states that many business leaders and others in favour of a free market enterprise economy believe that man's ingenuity will make sustainable growth possible. The business sector controls most of the technology and productive capacity needed to conceive more environmentally benign processes, products and services and to introduce them throughout the world.

The Montreal Protocol aims to stop the production of various ozone depleting chemicals and many countries are signatories to this. But what are the economic consequences involved in phasing out these chemicals, and searching for alternatives? What new equipment is having to be brought in to replace that which is obsolete (e.g. dry cleaning industry equipment and automobile air conditioners)? An interim multilateral fund was established as part of the original 1987 Montreal Protocol to aid developing nations in achieving reductions of controlled CFCs and other ozone/destroying substances required under the Protocol. The fund will have to be at least $500 million for years 1994–6.

Economic instruments, including bilateral and multilateral trade agreements should, in so far as is practicable, be structured to avoid undesirable environmental effects resulting from international trade. Established frameworks of laws and enforced environmental regulations as the basic preconditions for the use of economic instruments (EIs). Use of EIs as incentives for sustainable development has historically required significant government involvement, high administration costs and restrictions to prevent deterioration in receptor areas. But these economic instruments have the potential to serve as sustainable funding sources for a variety of actions and jurisdictions. EIs as funding sources for estuaries can be used to good advantage. Instruments include effluent fees, marine fuel taxes, fertilizer sales taxes, stormwater offsets, impact fees, forestation offsets, tradeable permits and tradeable development rights. A more active use of economic instruments to benefit the environment will require an international harmonization of rules and regulations to avoid distortions of international trade relationships.

Economic values and the natural world by David Pearce (1993b) examines some of the issues in more detail. The purpose of economic valuation is to reveal the true costs of using up scarce environmental resources. The virtues of economic instruments such as taxes, permits and other incentive systems based on altering market signals remains, even if the valuation is not carried out.

Economic values reflect individuals' willingness to pay for benefits or to avoid costs. Future gains and losses tend to be played down in economic decision-making due to the practice of discounting the future. Valuation is fundamental to the notion of sustainable development.

The UK Department of the Environment publishes an Environmental Economic Research Series, an example of which is *The potential role of market mechanisms in the control of acid rain*. It has also published information on BATNEEC (Best available techniques not entailing excessive cost) and BPEO (Best practicable environmental option).

Again, the *ENDS Report* and *Environment Business* prove useful, as they both report on the latest developments in the use of economic instruments, particularly the carbon tax.

Risks and liabilities

The financial world recognizes environmental matters, when faced with issues such as due diligence in acquisitions, mergers and sales, liability of staff and products, fines for non-compliance, civil claims for environmental damage, clean-up costs and increased costs of waste disposal and investments. The costs of dealing with environmental liability risks are potentially enormous, even to larger companies. Lack of awareness of possible liabilities and their consequences may even result in imprisonment for directors and officers found responsible.

The UK's Hundred Group of Finance Directors have published *Managing environmental risk: a guide to the questions every business should ask* (Pritchard, 1994) which is an excellent summary of the important issues. Another recently published title on this subject is *Managing environmental risks and liabilities* (Pritchard, 1994) which gives a review of current methods. The *Financial Times* has reported on the Centre for Financial Innovation's suggestions for a risk rating system to compare the environmental standing of various companies.

Investors have been exercising their right to choose companies with 'green credentials' for some time. The Ethical Investment Research and Information Service provides prospective investors with details and assistance. The annual *Directory of environmental investing* (Silverstein) which is published in the USA looks at annual publicly traded companies plus *Fortune 500* firms involved in environmental services.

Environmental Liability Report, a journal from the *Financial Times*, covers key issues such as how the US regime will be reproduced in Europe. Under the American model, virtually all major companies either will be or are already caught in an environmental damage action typically costing several million dollars. Liability is strict, joint and several and retroactive and defences almost non-existent. Legal costs can exceed 50 per cent of the settlement. Increasingly the trend is towards criminal prosecution and imprisonment. Conviction can thus cause heavy damage to company prospects, beyond the immediate costs involved.

Environmental audits and reporting

The internal management of environmental risks requires the implementation of systematic management systems. For example, in the UK the British Standards Institute have produced a *British Standard for Environmental Management Systems*, BS 7750, with an international equivalent on its way. An integral part of such a management system is the initial environmental review, to gauge the state of affairs and the environmental audit to compare activities against set legislation, policy or standards.

Environmental auditing: a guide to best practice in the UK and Europe (Grayson *et al.*, 1993) provides a comprehensive bibliography. *Environmental auditing: an introduction and practical guide* (Woolston, 1993) gives an introductory overview to the benefits of audits, legislative background, voluntary schemes and the carrying out audits. Articles are published regularly on these subjects in the *ENDS Report, Environment Business* and *Environmental Protection Bulletin*. There are also specialist journals such as *Eco Management and Auditing*.

A wide range of companies now produce environmental reports which give details of their performance. *Business and environmental accountability* (Grayson *et al.*, 1993) provides a bibliography and analysis on company environmental performance reporting.

There are several sources of information on how the accountancy profession is thinking about environmental issues. *Green reporting: accountancy and the challenge of the nineties* (Owen, 1992) looks at the impact of environmental awareness on the accounting function, the views of industry and commerce, trade unions, the accounting profession and the future of green reporting. *Accounting for the environment* (Gray *et al.*, 1993) looks at what accountants can do in response to the developing environmental agenda.

The journal *Company Reporting* regularly covers environmental reporting issues, as do the various accountancy journals such as *Accounting, Auditing and Accountability Journal*.

Waste minimization/pollution prevention

A number of successful projects over the last few years have shown how waste minimization techniques can bring significant cost paybacks for industry, while having an environmental benefit. One of the earlier projects was Project Prisma in the Netherlands. Project Catalyst and the Aire and Calder Project in the UK both involved regional groups of companies looking at waste minimization options and finding many money-saving opportunities. Information on these projects is available from the DTI (see also Centre for Exploitation of Science and Technology, 1994). There are many articles in the waste management journals which review the success stories, for example *Industrial Waste Management* and *Waste and Environment Today*.

Pollution prevention involves the sensible theory that prevention is better than cure. Various sources are available which will help with manufacturing redesign and which offer waste minimization methods. These include the US Environmental Protection Agency's *Facility pollution prevention guide*.

As recycling programmes are expanded, the need for public and private co-operation in the development of recycling facilities increases. The USA leads the way with sophisticated kerbside collections of material for recycling in many regions. The UK is still struggling with its pledge to recycle 25 per cent of household waste by the end of the century. The WARMER Campaign, Waste Watch and the Waste Management Information Bureau can all help with information on recycling policy and experiences. ISWA and the National Association of Waste Disposal Contractors are good sources of information on waste management and disposal methods and services.

Organizations

Association of Environmental and Resource Economists
1616 P St. NW
Washington DC 20036
USA
Tel: +1 202 328 5000

Centre for Social and Economic Research on the Global
   Environment
University College
Gower Street
London WC1

University of East Anglia
Norwich
NR4 7TS

Tel: +44 1603 56161
Coalition for Environmentally Responsible Economics
711 Atlantic Avenue
Boston, Mass. 02111
USA
Tel: +1 617 451 0927

Commission of the European Communities Information Office
8 Storeys Gate
London
Tel: +44 171 973 1992

Department of the Environment (DoE)
2 Marsham Street
London SW1P 3EB
Tel: +44 171 276 3000
Fax: +44 171 276 0818

Department of Trade and Industry (DTI)
151 Buckingham Palace Road
London SW1W 3EB
Tel: +44 171 215 1016
Environment Helpline 0800 585794

International Chamber of Commerce
38 cours Albert 1er
75008 Paris
France
Tel: +33 1 45 62 34 56

International Institute For Environment and Development
  (Incorporating the London Environmental Economics Centre)
3 Endsleigh Street
London WC1H 0DD
Tel: +44 171 388 2117

ISWA (International Solid Wastes and Public Cleansing
  Association)
Bremerholm 1
DK-1069 Copenhagen K
Denmark
Tel: +44 33 91 44 91

National Association of Waste Disposal Contractors

6–20 Elizabeth Street
London SW1A 2HH
Tel: +44 171 824 8882

Organisation for Economic Co-operation and Development
94 rue Chandon-lagache
F-75016 Paris
France
Tel: +33 1 45 24 82 90

Overseas Development Institute
Regents College
Inner Circle
Regents Park
London NW1 4NS
Tel: +44 171 487 7413

UK Centre for Economic and Environmental Development
3E Kings Parade
Cambridge CB2 1SJ
Tel: +44 1223 67799

The WARMER Campaign
83 Mount Ephraim
Tunbridge Wells
Kent TN4 8BS
Tel: +44 1892 24626

Waste Management Information Bureau
Culham
Oxon
Tel: +44 1235 433442

Waste Watch
68 Grafton Way
London W1P 5LE
Tel: +44 171 383 3320

World Bank
1818 H Street NW
Washington DC 20433
USA
Tel: +1 202 477 1234
Fax: +1 202 477 6391

66 avenue d'lena

75116 Paris
France
Tel: +33 1 40 69 30 00
Fax: +33 1 40 69 30 66

Journals

Accounting, Auditing and Accountability Journal. Bradford: MCB University Press.
Ambio: A Journal of the Human Environment, Research and Management. Oslo: Univeritesforlaget.
Company Reporting. Edinburgh: Company Reporting Ltd.
Eco Management and Auditing. Shipley: ERP Environment.
Ecological Economics. Amsterdam: Elsevier.
Economic Review. Helsinki: Kansallis-Osake-Pannki.
Economic Trends. London: HMSO.
ENDS Report. London: Environmental Data Services.
Environment and Planning. London: Pion.
Environment Bulletin. Washington DC: World Bank.
Environmental Liability Report. London: *Financial Times.*
Environmental Resource Economics. Amsterdam: Kluwer.
Green Marketing Report. London: Business Publishers Inc.
Financial Times. London.
Industrial Waste Management. Croydon: Faversham House Group.
Journal of Environmental Economics and Management. London: Academic Press.
Journal of Environmental Management. London: Academic Press.
Journal of International Economics. Amsterdam: North Holland.
UK CEED Bulletin. Cambridge: UK CEED.
Waste and Environment Today. Culham: AEA Technology Waste Management Information Bureau.

References

Adams, R., Carruthers, J. and Hamil, S. (1991) *Changing corporate values: a guide to social and environmental policy and practice in Britain's top companies.* London: Kogan Page.
Ahmad, Y.J., El Sarafy, S. and Lutz, E. (1989) (eds) *Environmental accounting for sustainable development.* Washington DC: The World Bank.
Barde, J. and Pearce, D.W. (1991) *Valuing the Environment.* London; Earthscan.
British Standards Institute (1994) *BS 7750 standard for environmental management systems.* BS 7750. BSI: Milton Keynes.
Centre for Exploitation of Science and Technology (1994) *Waste minimisation: a route to profit and cleaner production* (an interim report on the Aire and Calder Project). London: HMSO.

Commission of the European Communities COM (90) 3 594/91 *Regulation on substances that deplete the ozone layer.*

Commission of the European Communities COM (92) 226 *Proposal for a Council Directive introducing a tax on carbon dioxide emissions and energy.*

Commission of the European Communities *Council Regulation of 21 May 1992 establishing a financial instrument for the environment (LIFE)* 92/1973/EEC.

Department of Trade and Industry (1994) *Project Catalyst, report to the DEMOS project event, 1994.* London: DTI.

Goodland, R.J.A. (1992) Environmental priorities for financing institutions. *Environ. Conserv*, 19, 1, 9–21.

Gray, R. *et al.* (1993) *Accounting for the environment.* London: ACCA.

Grayson, L. (1993) *Environmental auditing: a guide to best practice in the UK and Europe.* London: The British Library.

Grayson, L., Woolston, H. and Tanega, J. (1993) *Business and environmental accountability.* London: The British Library.

Markandya, A. (1991) *Resource accounting for sustainable development: a review of basic concepts, recent debate and future needs.* London: London Environmental Economics Centre.

Markandya, A. (1992) *The Earthscan reader in environmental economics.* London: Earthscan.

Organization for Economic Co-operation and Development (1991) *Environmental policy: how to apply economic instruments.* Paris: OECD.

Opschoor, J. (1989) *Economic instruments for environmental protection.* Paris: OECD.

Owen, D. (ed.) (1992) *Green reporting: accountancy and the challenge of the nineties.* London: Chapman and Hall.

Pearce, D. (1989) *Blueprint for a green economy* (The Pearce Report). London: Earthscan.

Pearce, D. (1990) *Sustainable development: economics and environment in the third world.* London: Earthscan.

Pearce, D. (1991) *Blueprint 2: valuing the environment.* London: Earthscan.

Pearce, D. and Turner, R. Kerry (1990) *Economics of natural resources and the environment.* New York: Harvester Wheatsheaf.

Pearce, D. (1993a) *Blueprint 3: measuring sustainable development.* London: Earthscan.

Pearce, D. (1993b) *Economic values and the natural world.* London: Earthscan.

Pearce, D. and Turner, R. Kerry (1990) *Economics of natural resources and the environment.* New York: Harvester Wheatsheaf.

Pritchard, P. (1994) *Managing environmental risks: a guide to the questions every business should ask in the Business and the environment practitioner series,* Technical Communications.

Pritchard, P. (1994) *Managing environment risks and liabilities,* Stanley Thomas Publishers, Ltd. in the Business and the environment practitioner series.

Schram, G. and Warford, J.J. (1989) *Environmental management and economic development,* Baltimore, MD: Johns Hopkins University Press.

Silverstein, M. *Directory of environmental investing.* Philadelphia: Environmental Economics, 1026 Irving St. Philadelphia, Pa. 19107. Tel: +1 215 925 7168. (Annual publicly traded companies plus *Fortune 500* firms involved in environmental services.)

Turner, R. Kerry, Pearce, D. and Bateman, I. (1993) *Environmental economics: an elementary introduction.* London: Harvester-Wheatsheaf.

United Nations (1992) *Report of the United Nations Conference on Environment and Development: Rio de Janeiro, 3–14 June 1992.* New York: United Nations (available London: HMSO).

US Environmental Protection Agency (1992) *Facility pollution prevention guide.* Washington DC: EPA.

Willums, J.-O. (1992) (ed.) *From ideas to action: business and sustainable development – the greening of enterprise: business leaders speak out.* London: ICC Publications.

Winpenny, J. (1991) *Values for the environment – a guide to the economic appraisal.* London: HMSO.

Woolston, H. (ed.) (1993) *Environmental auditing: an introduction and practical guide.* London: The British Library.

World Bank *Index of publications & guide to information products and services.* Washington DC: World Bank. (Every six months.)

CHAPTER TWELVE

Environmental technology and technology and the environment

JOHN GOODIER

Introduction

Technology is often accused of damaging the environment. In the first
part of this chapter the use of technology to protect, monitor and
improve the environment will be considered. In the second part the
problem of identifying land damaged in some way by industrial
processes will be discussed. Both these section can be little more than
brief introductions and guides to the literature of chemistry, engineering and local history should be consulted if more detail is needed. The
aim of this chapter is to introduce the reader to wide range of literature
and information sources that will help to solve problems about the
historical and the current effects of technology on the environment.

Current industrial technology and the protection and remediation of the environment

A brief introduction to this topic has been produced by the European
Communities Chemistry Council. Much of the information in this area
can be found in the industrial technology literature rather than the
biological or environmental. The underlying sciences are mainly
chemical, but biochemical and biotechnological solutions will become
increasingly important. The general thrust is practical and technical
magazines, trade literature and newspaper articles are important
sources of information. The Department of the Environment (DoE) is
a major publisher in this area. Some of their publications are sold
through HMSO, but many more are sold from the Publications Sales
Unit. DoE produce a monthly publications list. Currently DoE also

publish the report literature of Her Majesty's Inspectorate of Pollution (HMIP), but this organization, together with the National Rivers Authority and some functions currently the responsibility of local authorities are being reformed as a new Environment Agency. The agency will be a valuable source of publications. All DoE items are included in the *DoE catalogue*, and much of the report literature is included in SIGLE, an EU-wide database on grey literature. The UK input is provided by the British Library.

Background information can be found in Kirk and Othmer's *Encyclopedia of chemical technology* and *Ulmann's Encyclopedia of the chemical industry*. These are both multi-volume works containing authoritative descriptions of chemical processes and describing the uses of chemical products. They contain limited information on environmental matters but are useful starting points. More environmental information can be found in Pfaffin and Zeigler *Encyclopedia of environmental science and engineering*. Croner's *Environmental management*, a looseleaf handbook, includes technology as well as legal and managerial aspects.

The underlying philosophy is integrated pollution control; the production process is considered as a whole and the polluting effects on air, water and the general environment are considered and controlled as an integrated system. Earlier approaches addressed individual pollutants and individual media and were often restricted to the most serious or most obvious effects. Pollution control technologies are be built into the production system. The philosophy behind this used to be Best Practical Means (BPM). Recently this has been replaced by Best Available Technology Not Entailing Excessive Costs (BATNEEC). BATNEEC guidance is published in the UK as HMIP *Chief inspectors guidance to inspectors*. For details see the current HMIP bibliography. An interesting innovation is the development of clean technologies. These avoid the use of pollutants like metal catalysts and volatile organic solvents by using biotechnological processes and non-polluting solvents like superheated water and liquid carbon dioxide. A review of these technologies can be found in the journal *Science* (6 August 1993). The guidance tends to concentrate on what should be achieved. The solutions to the problems will be found in trade literature and in patents.

Environmental concerns are now part of the operating philosophy of industry. A large number of newsletters are aimed at process and environmental managers, executives, lawyers, marketing managers and middle managers. They vary in quality and viability but often contain information not published elsewhere. Those currently in print are listed in *Willings press guide,* which also indicates the readership. The DoE and Department of Trade and Industry have set up an Advisory Committee on Business and the Environment which produces progress reports, available from DoE.

Specific problems

Land that has been used for industrial purposes in the past can be derelict or contaminated. The term derelict mainly applies to land left after an industrial enterprise has been abandoned; this includes old factory and dock sites, mining wastes tips and undermined land. Contaminated land is where the residues left behind are dangerous. Wickens' *Survey of derelict land in England* has been produced by DoE together with reports on the management of land reclamation. A good introduction to derelict land is Fleming's (1990) *Recycling derelict land* produced for the Institution of Civil Engineers. Interest in contaminated land developed in the 1960s among ecological geneticists interested in how plants were able to grow on such sites. Their accounts often include a description of the site and contain more details of the chemical problems than those done by industrial historians. The work of both groups of experts are often the earliest good descriptions of contaminated land or, as they were called in those days, derelict areas. They predate the current concerns about pollution and environmental protection by thirty to forty years. Both literatures present problems for the information scientist. The botanical data predate the online versions of most databases and the industrial history literature is often published in local history or specialist publications which are often not well represented in secondary sources either online or as hard copy.

Warren Springs Laboratory have produced a *Review of innovative contaminated soil clean-up processes* (Report LR819(MR) 1992) and CIRIA (1995) publish *A guide to safe working practices for contaminated land.* One particularly polluting process was gas production and a separate literature on the clean-up of gasworks sites exists. The Inter-Departmental Committee on the Redevelopment of Contaminated Land (ICRCL) have produced a series of guidance notes which are regularly updated. These are available from DoE.

In the USA the special effort made to clean up contaminated land is called the Superfund Program. Documents produced by the US government on those topic are included in the NTIS database. The US Environment Protection Agency has produced a *Compendium of Superfund Program publications* that is well indexed; which is updated periodically.

Another problem affecting land is that mining will have left voids which may lead to sudden and sometimes spectacular collapse. This has been a particular problem in the limestone areas of the East Midlands, although similar problems are caused by Bath stone mines. In sandstone regions such as Nottingham the construction of cellars can give rise to complexes of voids.

Treatment of oil spills is a controversial area. *Oceanic Abstracts* covers the technical aspects of this topic and the more commercial aspects are included in *Petroleum/Energy News*. A recent technical account of bioremediation has been provided by J.R. Bragg (1994).

Pollution control technologies are covered in the industrial and process chemical literature; a guide to this literature is provided by Bottle and Rowland (1993). As well as producing regulations and recommendations, HMIP commission research in the field of pollution control. These reports continue the series on radioactive waste management produced by the former Radioactive Waste Inspectorate and are available from the DoE. The Radioactive Waste Inspectorate reports and some of the HMIP reports address the various problems of the management of radioactive wastes, such as storage, containment geology and nuclear chemistry. The Inspectorate also used to produce an inventory of radioactive waste, which is now produced by the DoE. The commissioning of nuclear power stations are the subject of extensive planning enquiries which contain some technical information that is of environmental (in the narrow sense) interest.

The Noyes Data Corporation produce technical books in several series including Pollution Technology Reviews and Chemical Technology Reviews but it should be borne in mind that standards may have been raised since the books were published.

Sources of information

Company information can be found in the Kompass directories (published by Reed Information Services), where the services provided by major companies are set out in section 84-52.0 'Environmental, anti-pollution and public health engineering services'. There are Kompass directories for most major countries. Information on the providers of pollution control technology, as well as other services such as consultancy and legal advice, can be found in *Environment industry yearbook: the directory of environmental products, services and contacts* (Macmillan).

The problem with information in this area is that it is not usually found in the refereed primary literature and so does not get included in the major academic databases. SIGLE is the European grey literature database. UK, German and Dutch information predominate the data set and the coverage of technical information is good. Similar information produced by the US government is included in the database NTIS.

Databases worth considering in this area are those which bridge the gap between technology and business: CHEMICAL BUSINESS NEWS DATABASE, CHEM-INTELL, COMPENDEX*PLUS™ and BIOBUSINESS. It should be remembered that industry-based databases are likely to include news on clean technologies. For example, a list of chemicals being substituted for PCBs can be found by searching INSPEC (the electrical engineering database) with the keywords 'PCB and Substitutes'.

As this area overlaps with health and safety, the magazines covering the subject are often useful sources of information. The general industrial and controlled circulation magazines are also useful sources of information. The *ENDS Report* often contains information on new pollution control and clean-up technologies. Newspapers and general science magazines such as *New Scientist* often contain information on pollution control initiatives. There are several databases covering this sort of literature, for example, TRADE & INDUSTRY INDEX. There are also full text databases such as TRADE & INDUSTRY ASAP and MCGRAW-HILL PUBLICATIONS ONLINE. UK newspapers are included in the database PROFILE.

Both H&S and pollution control are served by a number of exhibitions and conferences. These can be a useful source of information. A collection of trade literature can provide other sources of information, as well as being useful in its own right.

Patents are covered by several databases; UK and European patents are included in DERWENTS database and US patents are found in CLAIMS™. Patents are a specialized form of literature and if one is going to make a lot of use of this material then one of the guides should be consulted (e.g. Auger). Where the interest is more general the abstract produced by the database is probably sufficient. It should not be assumed that just because a patent exists the product is available.

There are a number of newsletters which contain information on control technologies, clean-up and pollution control. examples include: *Air and Water Pollution Report, Environment Business Briefing, Environment Business* and *Environment Report.* The chemical industry magazines such as *Chemistry and Industry, European Chemical News* and *Chemical Week (international edition)* are another good source. New Civil Engineering contains news of major clean-up and reclamation projects which are often an integral part of any major civil engineering project.

Identification of land affected by industrial processes

Urban land use

This section concentrates on British sources, but should act as an outline of the types of information sources which are likely to be available in other countries. The *Guide to the history of technology in Europe* (Carding, *et al.* 1992) provides details of researchers and research institutions in Europe. The focus here is on industrially used land, more general information is provided in Chapter 10.

The historical uses of urban and industrial land can have significant environment effects. Concern over this lead to the idea that a register of potentially contaminated land should be produced. This was included in the Environment Protection Act (1992) but the idea has since been dropped by the government. Originally industry was carrying out the investigation of the sites on a voluntary basis but this has now been formalized as a requirement in the redevelopment of sites. The Department of the Environment is producing a series of reports on the management of contaminated land, one of which deals with documentary research (DoE, 1994). It covers much of the information in this chapter, but is particularly useful for its analysis of the publication history of the 25-inch Ordnance Survey plans.

In the context of this chapter it is important to note use of the word 'potential'; most sites are likely to be free of serious contamination. Those that are contaminated can usually be cleaned up or made safe, though the cost may be very high, especially now that there is a tax on dumping contaminated soil.

The investigation of the physical history of industry became a distinct discipline in the 1960s. A good introduction to industrial archaeology which also has references on major industries and a brief regional account with references is provided by Buchanan (1982). Another readable introduction is provided by Kenneth Hudson in *Exploring our industrial past* (1975). This concentrates on the methods of industrial archaeology and explains how the basic observations can be developed into a more complete history. It also contains useful references to museums, journals and societies. Another useful introduction is provided by Parnell (1966). For current purposes the problem can be expressed as two questions: what industry took place on a site and what processes were involved in this.

Many of the better general books date from the 1960s, in particular the regional industrial archaeology surveys and the regional industrial surveys published by David & Charles.

Location

The UK has been mapped by the Ordnance Survey (OS) since 1791. There have been a number of complete surveys which can be used as a time series. Unfortunately there is no good guide to the many editions but some useful information is found in Harley (1975). The base mapping scale is 6 inches to the mile for rural areas and 25 inches to the mile for urban areas. At this scale the layout of factory buildings is clear and the maps will often indicate the type of industry carried out on a site. There are a number of maps, such as the Geological Survey and Soil Survey Maps, derived from the OS series. These may give detail of military installations omitted from the published OS maps. The Soil Survey maps indicate made land, that is infill and disturbed land. In addition to the OS maps there is a wide range of local maps of varying quality. Most towns and cities were mapped at 1:500 scale between 1863 and 1893. Some towns are covered by insurance plans produced by Chas. E. Goad Ltd. between 1885 and 1940 on a scale of 1:148.

Aerial photographs are another source of information on location. Of particular value in the present context are low-level oblique photographs which show considerable detail. The NAPLIB *Directory of aerial photographic collections* is the main guide to the material.

Archival photographs can also provide some information, together with photographs taken for other purposes such as postcards. However, it should be borne in mind that landmarks such as churches, houses and railway stations can change their names. There has been a number of official surveys of contaminated land which have been summarized by the Parliamentary Office of Science and Technology (POST). Information to help to identify the whereabouts of specific trades can be found by consulting street directories such as Kelly's. Archival collections of these are held by the Guildhall Library in London and by *Kelly's Directories* Archive Section in Sutton.

Transport systems

Transport systems present a range of problems. While they are being built waste materials are used to fill in voids and to make embankments, including mineral working spoil and pottery moulds and wasters. Once such transport systems are abandoned they can become filled with waste; the range of materials dumped is considerably less well controlled than in the construction stage. A particular problem with railways was the ash from steam trains which had high concentrations of heavy metals. With canals a major problem is that they were used for the disposal of liquid wastes and the mud at the bottom can be highly polluted. The cargoes transported may have also left problems, which is especially important for major docks. Fortunately, as a result of the nature of the industry in the catchment area of the docks and the requirements of Customs and Excise the use of a particular wharf can generally be identified.

There are less problems involved in obtaining information concerning transport systems than for other topics. Such systems are major undertakings and usually well documented. They also feature reliably on maps. Transport systems have their enthusiasts and as a result have an extensive literature, often with detailed maps. Railway systems have been mapped by Jowett and there are many books containing historic photographs of canal and railway systems.

Mines

Mines present special problems. The location of shafts can be identified from maps but the extent of the underground workings are not so easily determined. The British Geological Survey has an extensive collection of coal mine plans. The archives of British Coal are being transferred to Newtongrange near Edinburgh and next to the Lady Victoria mining Museum. Mineral mines are less well documented. In the case of very old mines and miscellaneous man-made holes, the help of local potholers or members of the National Association of Mining History Organisations (NAMHO) may be necessary.

Archives

Local history collections and archives often contain plans, company records and special maps with details of industrial sites. They may also hold collections of artefacts which will indicate what was made locally and allow some interpretation of how items were made. Two Aslib directories *Museums and special collections* (Dale, 1993) and *Literary and historical collections* (Reynard, 1993) will be of use in identifying main sources. Information on record repositories has been provided by Church and Cole (1992). Although their interests are in family history the book could provide useful clues. Company records are recorded by the Business Archives Council.

What happened on the site

Having identified the site and the industry it may be necessary to identify the processes that went on there. The DoE produces a series of Industry Profiles. These describe the main potential contaminants on sites, with some details of the processes involved where they may have affected the distribution of contaminants. About forty titles are planned.

The processes in the past were not necessarily the same as today. For example, early plastics were made of phenols and were bulked with a variety of materials including asbestos; mercury was used in hat-making and gilding metal; carbon tetrachloride was used for dry-cleaning. There have been less environmentally significant changes in the heavy industries, which have been dealt with more frequently by historians. The Industrial Archaeology Series, edited by L.T.C. Rolt and published under the Allen Lane imprint of Penguin Books Ltd., includes several useful titles.

In addition to industrial histories there are company histories which contain less technical and more economic data but are useful in dealing with specific sites. The Shire Album and Discovering series published by Shire Publications of Princes Risborough give some information, often including references to more complete texts and the location of collections, which could also mean locations of expertise. But for full details of processes it is necessary to go back to contemporary books aimed at company staff. Unfortunately such books are not included in the stock of SRIS or BLDSC. They should be included in the Humanities Collection and can be ordered from there via SRIS. Detail of the material can be found in the BRITISH LIBRARY CATALOGUE and HUMANITIES AND SOCIAL SCIENCES databases which are accessible on BLAISE-LINE. Company records and company archives may also contain some clues.

For both location and industrial processes oral history can be of great value. The decline of UK heavy industry started in the 1960s and is not yet complete; many workers and managers are still alive. In some areas there are oral history projects and even if what has been collected is not relevant to the problem of land use the participants can be sources of contacts. A lot of amateur work of high standard is done on local history and there is a range of journals and indexing systems. An introduction to local history for librarians has been produced by Reed.

References

Auger, C.P. (1994) *Information sources in grey literature*, 3rd edn. East Grinstead: Bowker Saur.

Battersby, S. (regularly updated) *Croners environmental management*. Kingston upon Thames: Croner Publications.

Bottle, R.T. and Rowland, J.F.B. (1993) *Information Sources in Chemistry*. East Grinstead: Bowker Saur.

Bragg, J.R. (1994) Effectiveness of bioremediation for the *Exxon Valdez* oil spill. *Nature*, 31, March, 413–418.

Buchanan, R.A. (1982) *Industrial archaeology in Britain*. Penguin: Harmondsworth.

Carding, J. (1992) *et al. Guide to the history of technology in Europe*. London: Science Museum.

Construction Industry Research and Information Association (CIRIA) (1995) *A guide to safe working practices for contaminated sites*. London: CIRIA.

Church, R. and Cole, J. (1992) *In and around record repositories in Great Britain and Ireland*. Huntingdon: Family Tree Magazine.

Dale, P. (1993) *Directory of museums and special collections in the UK*. London: Aslib.

Department of the Environment (DoE) (1990) *Contaminated land Cm 1161*. London: HMSO.

Department of the Environment (DoE) (1994) *Documentary research on industrial sites*. London: HMSO. (CLR Report no. 3).

Environment industry yearbook (annual). Basingstoke: Macmillan.

European Communities Chemistry Council (1993) *Chemistry for a clean world*. London: Royal Society of Chemistry (or national equivalents in EC).

Fleming, G. (1990) (ed.) *Recycling contaminated land*. London: Thomas Telford.

Friends of the Earth (FoE) (1993) *'Buyer beware' A guide to finding out about contaminated land*. London: FoE.

Harley, J.B. (1975) *Ordnance survey maps: a descriptive manual*. Southampton: Ordnance Survey.

HMIP (1990 –) *Chief inspectors guidance to inspectors*. London: HMSO.

Hudson, K. (1975) Exploring our industrial past. London: Teach Yourself Books.

Jowett, A. (1993 –) *Jowett's atlas of railway centres of Great Britain showing their development from the earliest times up to and including the 1990s* (several vols; vol. 1 1993). Sparkford: Patrick Stephens.

Kirk, R.E. and Othmer, D.F. (1991) *Encyclopedia of Chemical Technology*, 4th edn. Chichester: Wiley.

Kompass: The authority on British industry (annual). East Grinstead: Reed Information.

NAPLIB (1994) *Directory of aerial photographic collections*. London: Aslib.

Parnell, J.P.M. (1966) *Techniques in industrial archaeology*. Newton Abbot: David & Charles.

Pfaffin, J.R. and Ziegler, E.N. (1992) *Encyclopedia of environmental science and engineering*. 3rd edn. Reading, PA: Gordon & Breach.

POST (1993) *Contaminated land*. London: Parliamentary Office of Science & Technology.

Reed, M. (1975) *Local history today. Curren themes and problems for the local history library. Journal of Librarianship*, 7, 3, 161–181.

Reynard, K. (1993) *Directory of literary and historical collections in the United Kingdom*. London: Aslib.

Wickens, D. (1995) *Survey of derelict land in England*. London: HMSO.

Willings Press Guide (annual). East Grinstead: Reed Information.

PART FOUR

Controls and Public Awareness

CHAPTER THIRTEEN

Environmental law

JOHN P. O'HARA

Note

The author acknowledges the assistance of his colleague Sue Fuller.

Introduction

Environmental law in industrial society dates back at least to 1863 when Britain's Alkali etc Works Act sought to control emissions from the sodium carbonate industry, though in the modern era environmental law is often said to have started in the 1970s. However, one can perhaps see the late 1980s and early 1990s as representing the latest phase both in environmentalism and in environmental law. The expansion which began in the late 1980s has been accompanied by a corresponding expansion in sources of information on this topic. Many established publishers have developed their coverage of environmental law and are continuing to do so and new information providers are entering the market. Consequently some of the best sources of information on environmental law are also among the newest. Whatever the source used, access to up-to-date information is essential in the legal field. Lawyers cannot risk giving advice based on old information if the state of the law has since changed.

An important distinction to bear in mind is that between law and legislation. Legislation is a country's written law. In the UK the term is often used to refer only to Acts of Parliament (also known as the statutes) though in its broadest sense it includes 'delegated legislation' (i.e. orders, regulations, etc. made under the Acts as Statutory Instruments (SIs)). The law, on the other hand, is wider than this. In countries which have an English-style legal system it includes the decisions made by the courts (i.e. case law or judge-made law). In recent years there has been a rise in awareness in industry, partly due to the publicity attached to the so-called 'Cambridge Water' case, that environmental liability may arise not only under statute but also under judge-made law. Researchers should be aware that some information sources deal only with legislation, others cover case law and some cover both.

In many cases, the environmental legislation which is implemented in the UK derives from European Community environmental legislation. To provide comprehensive information on both European environmental law and that of the UK is an ambitious task and one which most publications avoid. In general, the sources of information are different for the two areas so that these are reviewed separately below.

The source of information one uses depends one what one needs to know about the law. One might require a copy of a statute or court transcript, news on the latest (or forthcoming) legislation or cases (in the UK or Europe), or comment on how the law is being, or is likely to be, applied and what effect it will have. As a result, the relevant information source may be a Government publication, an encyclopedia produced by a traditional legal publisher or a journal issued by a trade association.

UK Government publications

Probably the single most important primary source of information on UK environmental law is Her Majesty's Stationery Office (HMSO) since it is through this that the UK Government publishes legislation, parliamentary publications and some Government department publications.

Fortunately, HMSO provides a comprehensive bibliographic service for titles it publishes via daily, monthly and annual lists. The *HMSO daily list* is a particularly useful day-by-day list of all publications issued by HMSO. It lists new parliamentary publications, which include Bills, Acts and Hansard (the official Parliamentary record) the reports of the Royal Commission on Environmental Pollution and the reports of (and evidence given to) the House of Commons Select Committee on the Environment. It also details non-parliamentary publications, including those of government departments (e.g. Department of Environment's series of Pollution Papers and Waste Management Papers). There is also an *HMSO monthly catalogue* and *HMSO annual catalogue* listing all parliamentary publications and non-parliamentary publications published by HMSO and a separate *HMSO agency catalogue* for the publications of foreign organizations, including the EU, for which HMSO is an agent.

In addition to the bibliographic lists and catalogues, there are a number of finding tools which can be used to trace Government publications. All statutes are listed chronologically (with notes on amendments and repeals) in HMSO's *Chronological table of the statutes* (the latest issues is for 1235 – 1991). Similarly, the *Table of Government orders* lists all SIs chronologically whether in force or revoked and also notes all amendments (the latest issue is for 1671 –1990).

Two other useful indexes are the *Index to Government orders in force* (a subject index to statutory instruments in force on a particular date) and the *List of statutory instruments: together with the list of statutory rules of Northern Ireland*, issued monthly with an annual cumulation.

The business of Parliament is well documented by the *House of Commons Weekly Information, Bulletin*, compiled in the House of Commons Public Information Office and published by HMSO. It lists all Bills currently before Parliament and their progress as well as giving details of the current and forthcoming business of Select Committees (including the Environment Select Committee). The *Bulletin* is the official source for the notification of issue of Government consultation papers on proposed legislation including, of course, those from the Department of the Environment.

One should note that many non-parliamentary official publications (including consultation papers) are published directly by the Government departments concerned and not by HMSO – for lists of these one can use the *Catalogue of British official publications not published by HMSO* which is produced by Chadwyck-Healey.

HMSO publications and those official publications not published by HMSO are listed on CD-ROM, for example, JUSTIS SI-CD and UKOP. JUSTIS SI-CD is a database of SIs from 1980, with those from 1987 onwards held in full text. The SIs are comprehensively indexed and search routines enable the user to locate all SIs containing any word or combination of words. UKOP (Catalogue of United Kingdom Official Publications) is compiled from HMSO's bibliographic database and Chadwyck-Healy's *Catalogue of official-publications not published by HMSO* (which is separately available online and on CD-ROM).

Online sources for government information include the PARLIAMENTARY ON-LINE INFORMATION SYSTEM (POLIS) which covers information contained in parliamentary questions, proceedings and papers as well as official publications emanating from Government departments, the European Community bodies and international organizations. It can be accessed through the Public Information Office of the House of Commons.

Legal sources

Environmental law has only recently been recognized as a separate specialism in its own right. A significant step came in 1986 when lawyers founded the UK Environmental Law Association (UKELA), an organization aiming to provide a professional forum in the field of environmental law. Membership of UKELA is open to non-lawyers as well as those in the legal profession and is a useful source of information. The Association publishes a quarterly journal, *Environmental Law*, and organizes evening meetings and an annual conference.

However, the practice of environmental law is still firmly within the domain of the legal profession generally and consequently the sources of information upon which environmental lawyers rely are, in many cases, the standard general law sources. A feature of many of these is that they are published in looseleaf form to allow ease of updating.

One of the most important standard reference works for a lawyer is *Halsbury* published by Butterworths. This includes *Halsbury's Laws of England* (Hobbs *et al.* 4th edn., 1973) which is not a primary source, in that it does not reproduce the statutes themselves, but it does discuss what the law is and refers the reader to the appropriate statute cases. *Halsbury's Statutes of England and Wales* (Davies, 4th edn., 1973) on the other hand, is a standard primary source and reproduces statutes as amended with an annual subject index as well as indexes to the individual volumes. SIs in all fields of law are reproduced in *Halsbury's Statutory Instruments* (Sutherland, 4th edn., 1973).

A source of similar status is the collection of publications under the name Current Law published by Sweet & Maxwell. *Current law yearbook* and *Current law* (which is published monthly) include details of new statutes and SIs. *Current Law* also includes citators which can be used to track down statutes. They list legislation by year and note amendments made to statutes and statutory instruments by later legislation.

Cases in the UK of interest with regard to environmental law are reported in a wide range of different law reports (including the specialist *Environmental Law Reports* which began in October 1992). To trace a case it is best to use one of the various case citators – these give references to the full report of a case and note any mention of a case in later cases. The *Current law case citators* are sister volumes to *Current law yearbook* and *Current Law* (monthly) and cover both statute and case law arranged by subject (so that cases may be found even when the names of the parties are unknown). In *Current law case citators* cases are indexed by the first named party and citations include references to other cases in which a particular case has been applied or considered.

There are other indexes such as the *Law Reports Index*. Particularly worth a mention is the *Daily Law Reports Index* which covers the newspaper law reports and has an excellent subject index.

The most comprehensive online database for both statutes and cases, with which all lawyers should be familiar, is LEXIS. This includes the full text of all statutes and statutory instruments currently in force in England and Wales and of all English cases reported since 1945. It also includes selected transcripts since 1980. There are separate cases files for Scotland and Northern Ireland. Some foreign jurisdictions, notably the USA, are also covered. In practice, the environmental lawyer would not normally use LEXIS for statutes; its main use is as a source of information on cases, especially those which are 'unreported' (i.e. have not been the subject of a published law report). Use of LEXIS is restricted to subscribers and it is not cheap, which means that LEXIS is generally only used by law firms and some large libraries.

EC environmental law

As mentioned above, much environmental law for the UK (as with other member states) derives from the EU. This comprises legislation (usually in the form of Directives and Regulations) and case law (judgments of the European Court of Justice).

The principal source of information on EC law is the Office for Official Publications of the European Communities (OOPEC) in Luxembourg. Its main publication is the *Official Journal of the European Communities*, colloquially known as the *OJ*. This has two main series; series L contains the text of all legislation, and series C contains the text of proposed legislation, Commission communications and notices and notes of Court of Justice judgements (not long after they are delivered, which is useful). There is also a series S which contains details of offers for tenders for public contracts and an annex which contains debates of the European Parliament.

Tracing proposed legislation in the *OJ* is best done using JUSTIS CELEX (the computerized form of the *Official Journal*) or a current awareness tool such as *Butterworths EC brief* (see below). CELEX is the official legal database of the European Community and is essentially the computerized form of the *OJ*. It is available on CD-ROM and online (e.g. via LEXIS). CELEX includes case law and in many cases the full text of a case is included. In others only the title, case number and notes on the case are given. Citations are included to law reports if they exist. This can be a very useful way of searching for cases if you have incomplete information.

Proposed legislation is published by the European Commission in its series of 'COM Docs'. Many of these are eventually published in the *OJ* (C series) but COM Docs are usually the first publicly available source of legislative proposals and these are available on subscription from HMSO.

All EC legislation currently in force is listed in the biannual *Directory of Community legislation in force and other Acts of the Community institutions* (two volumes). References are given to where the full text of legislation can be found in the *OJ* and amendments to legislation are noted.

As well as these official publications, there are a number of other useful sources of information on EC legislation, notably *Butterworths EC Brief*. This is a weekly current awareness service covering new legislation, proposed legislation, recent cases and newspaper articles with bibliographic references and is useful for tracking recent developments.

It is worth noting that *Halsbury's Laws of England* (Hobbs *et al.*) has two volumes (51, 52) on European Communities law. A similar publication is *Law of the European Communities service*, commonly known as 'Vaughan' after its editor. This is a standard reference work on EC law in looseleaf form. Chapter 8 is on Environment and Consumers. Another well-respected work is the *Manual of environmental policy: the EC and Britain* (Haigh). This looseleaf manual, updated twice a year, analyses the development and effect of EC environmental directives and regulations and how they have been implemented in Britain.

As well as legislation, many of the sources already mentioned can be used to trace cases decided before the Court of Justice of the European Communities in Luxembourg. The Court issues transcripts of judgments and opinions not long after they are delivered. The official series of Court of Justice reports is published by OOPEC as *European Court reports* but they are published more quickly in the *Common Market law reports*, which also cover national cases which include a European element.

LEXIS includes the *European court reports* and the *Common Market law reports*. It also includes transcripts of cases before they are fully reported. Given the delay in the publication of full reports this is important. LEXIS can be a very useful way of searching for cases if you have incomplete information.

In the same way as for UK law, cases can be found most effectively using a citator. The *Current law case citators* and *Current law yearbooks* (Sweet & Maxwell) include EC cases reported in the newspapers and also in the *European Court reports* and the *Common Market law reports* but they are very selective. *Butterworths EC case citator* covers far more EC cases than *Current law*. The *Daily Law Reports Index* may also be used.

Many OOPEC publications, including the *OJ*, are available through

HMSO as an agent (these are listed in the *Daily list*). Another source is the network of European Documentation Centres based in major academic libraries throughout the country, which support academic research not only within their own institutions but also within their geographic area. These receive a large number of publications from the European Commission and they also collect transcripts of Court of Justice judgments. In addition there is a network of European Information Centres, established by the European Commission with the information needs of business in mind and based at institutions already serving business in some way such as Chambers of Commerce. The Centres can provide current information on EC legislation, on contracts for public works and EC research and development programmes amongst other things.

Environmental encyclopedias, journals and books

For a practising lawyer, the preferred source of information will frequently be an encyclopedia, typically produced by one of the traditional legal publishers in looseleaf format for ease of updating. Looseleaf encyclopedias gather together legislation, often with annotation, and other materials featuring commentary and narrative. Although the encyclopedias are updated as legislation is amended this may not necessarily be very frequently. There is a number of encyclopedias in this field but probably the best known and most respected is *Garner's environmental law*. Previously titled the *Control of pollution encyclopaedia*, it is often known simply by the name of its original author, Garner. However, this is an area of publishing in which new products which may become standards have appeared in the past couple of years. These include the *Encyclopaedia of environmental law* (Tromans and Grant, 1993 –), *Commercial environmental law and liability* (Payne, 1994 –), and, in the European field, *European environmental law* (Salter, 1994 –). An important compilation, in summary form, of important environmental cases appears in the newly launched (1995) *Croner's environmental management case law* (O'Keeffe, 1995 –).

Useful encyclopedias within defined sectors of the environment include *Water and drainage* law (Bates, 1990 –), which attempts to provide a comprehensive discussion of the water and drainage law of England and Wales and is primarily intended for legal practitioners, *Marine Environment Law* (Bates and Benson, 1993 –), a work aimed at legal practitioners and covering marine pollution and the protection of the marine environment, and *Croner's Waste Management* (Kellard, 1991 –) which is not a specifically legal encyclopedia and does not contain copies of statutes but does include a substantial and informative chapter on 'Legal aspects of waste management', as well as others covering the technical aspects.

Up-to-date news and commentary on environmental laws (both as they are being formed and once passed) can be found in a number of journals. The monthly *ENDS Report* contains all major new environmental statutes and regulatory developments in the UK (and some in the EC) and it has an 'In Court' section which often reports on criminal prosecutions for environmental offences as well as featuring some civil cases. *ENDS* has been around since 1978 and has a very good reputation. It is certainly not written for a legal audience since it appeals to a wide cross-section of those in industry, consultancy, etc. Its coverage is of environmental matters in general, not just the law, but many environmental lawyers find it indispensable. Another newsletter which is widely read and has a similar coverage is *Environment Business* which appears fortnightly and gives concise information on the latest environment developments including new and proposed UK and EC legislation.

Among the journals specifically aimed at a legal readership, the monthly *Journal of Planning and Environment Law* is one of the best respected in this field by legal specialists. It includes articles and news but is particularly strong on reports of recent court cases and planning inquiries. A more academic publication is the *Journal of Environmental Law*. This offers in-depth analysis of environmental law topics and cases. A disadvantage is that it appears only every six months so that cases (and books) can be quite old by the time a review appears. The monthly *Environment Law Brief* is more of a news bulletin and is accessible to non-lawyers. It includes case reports (often culled from the national and local press) and information on new and proposed legislation. Perhaps somewhere between the refereed journal and the newsletter is *Environmental Law and Management* (formerly known as *Land Management and Environmental Law Report*). It reports on new legislation and cases in the fields of pollution control, waste management and conservation but it also tends to include planning law.

There are a number of journals focusing on particular sectors of the environment. These include *Waste Planning*, which covers many of the law and regulatory issues connected with waste, as does *The Waste Manager*, the magazine of the Environmental Services Association (formerly the National Association of Waste Disposal contractors). *Water Guardians*, the newspaper produced by the former National Rivers Authority, is a useful source of information on prosecutions brought for cases of water pollution. Also *Water Bulletin*, the organ of the water industry's Water Services Association, has a very useful information section tracking UK and EC legislation of interest to the water sector.

There are some good journals and newsletters focusing specifically on EC environmental policy and law, some of which have been launched only within recent years. One which has been around for a while and is one of the most useful is the fortnightly newsletter *Europe Environment* which gives strong coverage of the environmental developments in the EC and covers some other European and international organizations. The monthly journal *European Environmental Law Review* was launched in June 1992 specifically to provide news and articles on environmental law in the EC and individual European countries.

As far as books are concerned, although there is an increasing number of books in the field of UK environmental law it seems that few have established themselves as standard works. A major problem is that the law changes constantly and out-of-date information can be worse than useless. One book which is updated yearly is the *Pollution handbook* (Murley, 1995) produced by the National Society for Clean Air and Environmental Protection. It provides an excellent overview of pollution control legislation as well as a reading list of further reference books. Other books to be recommended are *Environmental law* by Ball and Bell (now in its third edition) and, for an accessible introduction, the *Environmental law handbook* (Hellawell, 1995) published by the Law Society.

There are also many books on EC environmental law (or specific aspects of it). A particularly authoritative author on this topic is Ludwig Kramer, formerly Head of Legal Affairs in the European Commission's Directorate-General XI which covers Environment, who has written several books in recent years, including *EEC treaty and environmental protection.*

The rapidly changing content of environmental law in Europe and the UK means that the researcher would always be well advised to contact the major publishers for their current list.

References

Archer, S. *et al.* (1988 –) (ed.) *Daily law reports index.* Hebden Bridge: Legal Information Resources.

Ball, S. and Bell, S. (1995) *Environmental law.* London: Blackstone Press.

Bates, J.B. (1990 –) *Water and drainage law.* London: Sweet & Maxwell.

Bates, J.H. and Beson, C. (1993 –) *Marine environment law.* London: Lloyd's of London Press.

Butterworths European Information Services (ed.) *Butterworths EC case citator.* London: Butterworths.

Butterworths European Information Services (ed.) *Butterworths EC brief.* London: Butterworths.

Callow, P.M. (monthly) (ed) *European environmental law review.* London: Graham & Trotman.

Chadwyck-Healey, *Catalogue of official publications not published by HMSO*. Cambridge: Chadwyck-Healey Ltd.
Common Market Law Reports, (weekly). London: European Law Centre/Sweet and Maxwell.
Current law. London: Sweet & Maxwell.
Current law case citator (1947 –). London: Sweet & Maxwell.
Current law yearbook (1947 –). London: Sweet & Maxwell.
Davies, A. (1990) (ed.) *Halsbury's statutes of England and Wales*. 4th edn. London: Butterworths.
ENDS Report, (monthly). London: Environmental Data Service Ltd.
Environmental Law, (quarterly). London: UK Environmental Law Association.
Environmental Law and management, (six per year). Chichester: John Wiley & Sons, Ltd.
Environmental Law Brief, (monthly). London: Legal Studies Publishing Unit.
Environmental Law Reports, (quarterly). London: Sweet & Maxwell.
OOPEC. *European Court Reports*. Luxembourg: OOPEC.
Europe Environment, (fortnightly). Brussels: Europe Information Services.
European Environmental Law Review, (monthly). London: Graham & Trotman.
Garner, J.F. (1976 –) (consultant ed.). *Garner's environmental law*. London: Butterworths.
Haigh, N. (1992 –). *Manual of environmental policy: the EC and Britain*. London: Longman.
Hellawell, T. (1995). *Environmental law handbook*. London: The Law Society.
HMSO. *HMSO agency catalogue*. London: HMSO.
HMSO. *HMSO annual catalogue*. London: HMSO.
HMSO. *Chronological table of the statutes*. London: HMSO.
HMSO. *Daily list*. London: HMSO.
HMSO. *Monthly catalogue*. London: HMSO.
HMSO. *Table of Government orders*. London: HMSO.
Hobbs, G. *et al.* (ed.) *Halsbury's laws of England*. 4th edn. London: Butterworths.
HMSO. *House of Commons weekly information bulletin*. London: HMSO.
HMSO. *Index to Government orders in force*. London: HMSO.
Journal of Environmental Law, (six per year). Oxford: Oxford University Press.
Journal of Planning and Environment Law, (monthly). London: Sweet & Maxwell.
JUSTIS CELEX. London: Context Limited.
JUSTIS SI-CD. London: Context Limited.
Kellard, B. (1991 –) (ed.). *Croner's waste management*. Kingston upon Thames: Croner Publications.
Kramer, L. (1990) *EEC treaty and environmental protection*. London: Sweet & Maxwell.
Law reports index. London: Incorporated Council of Law Reporting of England and Wales.
LEXIS/NEXIS. London: Butterworths.
HMSO. *List of statutory instruments together with the list of statutory rules of Northern Ireland*. London: HMSO.
Murley, L. (1995) *Pollution handbook*. Brighton: National Society for Clean Air and Environmental Protection.
O'Keeffe, J. (1995 –) (ed.) *Croner's environmental management: case law*. Kingston upon Thames: Croner Publications.
Official Journal of the European Communities. *Directory of Community legislation in force and other acts of the Community institutions*. Luxembourg: OOPEC.
Official Journal of the European Communities. Luxembourg: OOPEC.
Parliamentary On-line Information System (POLIS). London: House of Commons.
Payne, S. (1994) (general ed.) *Commercial environmental law and liability*. London: Longman.
Salter, J.R. (1994 –) *European environmental law*. London: Graham & Trotman.
Sutherland, L. (ed.) *Halsbury's statutory instruments*. London: Butterworths.
Tromans, S. and Grant, M. (1993 –) (eds.) *Encyclopaedia of environmental law*. London: Sweet & Maxwell.

UKOP, Cambridge: Chadwyck-Healey Ltd.
Vaughan, D. *Law of the European Communities service*. London: Butterworths.
The Waste Manager, (monthly). London: Environmental Services Association.
Waste Planning, (quarterly). Northallerton: Mineral Planning.
Water Bulletin, (weekly). London: Water Services Association.
Water Guardian, (monthly). Bristol: National Rivers Authority.

CHAPTER FOURTEEN

Statutory provision of environmental information in the UK

TIM TREUHERZ

Introduction

If citizens want to improve their environment, first they have to find out exactly what is wrong with it. Access to environmental information is central to a well-informed public debate about environmental quality. Basic information about who is polluting, what is being discharged or emitted, what is being polluted and how much damage is being caused can enable the citizen to make use of legal and administrative remedies to clean up the environment.

Recent changes in the law in the UK and Europe mean that large sections of the work of the environmental policy-makers and the pollution control agencies are – or should be – open to close public inspection. There is, in effect, a 'right-to-know' regime for environmentalists. The various laws which make up this right to know must be distinguished from other right-to-know provisions such as the *Local Government (Access to Information) Act.* A good account of these provisions is given in Birkinshaw[1]. An important recent development is the non-statutory *Code of Practice on Government Information*[2], which covers government information other than environmental information.

The information available is, or could be, of use to a wide cross-section of the community: academic researchers, environmental campaigners, naturalists, commercial interests and the ordinary, concerned citizen. The significance of the various regulations cannot be overlooked.

The data which are available will be at least as important to the researcher as any conventionally published work. It is therefore important that information professionals should understand something of the new laws.

The right to know – some history

The origins of the debate on environmental secrecy go back at least as far as the first environmental regulatory body in England, the Alkali Inspectorate, until 1996, part of Her Majesty's Inspectorate of Pollution (HMIP now part of EPA). The Inspectorate was established by the *Alkali Act* 1863 to deal with atmospheric emissions from the burgeoning caustic soda industry. In its first report[3], the Inspectorate set out its terms: 'all information regarding any work must be considered private unless publication is demanded by the Act or permitted by the owner'. A number of statutes subsequently followed the spirit of the Report.

The Official Secrets Act 1911 made the unauthorized disclosure of any government information an offence.

The Rivers (Prevention of Pollution) Act 1961 made it an offence to disclose any information relating to 'discharge consents' (applications to the authorities to obtain permission to discharge polluting matter into rivers). *The Health and Safety at Work, etc, Act* 1974 outlawed any disclosure of information collected in the course of official monitoring of atmospheric pollution.

Curiously, the first intimation of a change in the law also came in 1974. *The Control of Pollution Act* (COPA) provided unprecedented public access to environmental information held by the pollution control authorities. In particular, it provided for public registers to be held by waste disposal and water authorities containing details of licences and consents which they had issued. It was to be eleven years before the provisions in COPA relating to public access were implemented. Similar provisions are still currently in force under the *Environmental Protection Act* and the *Water Acts*.

The Official Secrets Act 1989 limited the very strict regime introduced in 1911. The release of environmental information is governed by a range of statutory provisions all of which serve to limit the Official Secrets Act to some extent.

The Royal Commission

The Royal Commission on Environmental Pollution considered the question of secrecy on several occasions. Despite some serious lobbying from, among others, the Confederation of British Industry who were concerned to protect commercial confidentiality, the Commission, in its *Tenth report*[4], said that there should be: 'a presumption in favour of unrestricted access for the public to information which the pollution control authorities obtain or receive by virtue of their statutory powers, with protection for secrecy only in those circumstances where a genuine case can be substantiated'.

The case for secrecy

Industry and officialdom lobbied hard against the moves towards reform. Concern centred on the issue of commercial confidentiality – on the need to protect trade secrets. There was also a general fear that such information would be misinterpreted and that its release would lead to a variety of problems from various groups. Of course, information professionals only have to furnish information; the use to which it is put is not something over which they have any control.

The somewhat immoderate remarks made at a conference of Environmental Health Officers in 1977, provide a good example of this fear[5].

> Action groups, civic societies and pseudo environmental organisations persistently petitioned and pressured local authorities to implement those provisions (relating to information) . . . action groups, frequently composed of university research workers, lecturers, people who had failed to gain election through the ballot box, and including many cranks, persisted in twisting the truth concerning emissions to atmosphere, and their predictions of doom were made to the delight of an ever-waiting national press.
>
> (Wilson, 1984)

The law may have changed, but the culture of secrecy certainly survives. The experience of environmentalists during the first two years of the *Environmental Information Regulations* 1992 suggests that there still exists a reluctance to give them their legal rights.

Categories of information

There are two broad categories of information available. The first category consists of twenty-three public registers which provide access to information collected by the various pollution control authorities under their statutory powers. The second and much wider category consists of information which can be obtained under the Environmental Information Regulations 1992[6].

Public registers

To understand how public registers work, it is necessary to understand the rudiments of environmental law and regulation. Briefly, various statutes require people who are carrying out processes or activities which the law deems environmentally hazardous to obtain prior permission from the authorities. A company that wishes to emit certain substances to air, or discharge other substances into a river or a stream, must obtain a licence of some kind (also known as an authorization, consent or permit). The process of applying for permission is in the public domain – the body applying for the licence has to advertise the application publicly and the citizen is given the opportunity to object. The licence, together with any supporting documents (such as conditions imposed by the authorities, or appeals by the company against their decisions) are also in the public domain.

The term 'public register' means more than a particular book or file. It encompasses the paperwork available as part of the regulatory process and in addition monitoring data about, for example, air or water quality may be available.

Different public register regimes exist for what the law terms 'major industrial processes', for air pollution, water pollution, waste management, hazardous substances and radioactive substances. The different registers have varying provisions about exactly what information is available to the public. It has to be pointed out that there are a number of anomalies and inconsistencies. A summary of these registers and of the various statutes under which the information is made public, is produced by the law firm Denton Hall[7].

Water pollution

A good example of the value – and the pitfalls – in the regime are the various registers for water pollution.

WHERE TO GO?

The active citizen wanting information on his or her local water quality may need to go to several institutions. See Table 14.1 which lists eight of the fifteen registers recorded by the Department of the Environment.

Specific provisions about the information which is and is not on registers vary between the various statutes and regulations. There is no common standard, but there are publications aimed at the lay reader and the lawyer which can assist[8,9,10].

WHAT IS AVAILABLE?

The data which are available can be quite technical and detailed, but with a little perseverance and questioning the concerned citizen should be able to make sense of the public registers. Registers may consist of printed documents, printed maps or information held on a computer file capable of being viewed on a screen or printed out.

The consents obtained by the company and the data obtained by the authorities can be used as benchmarks to check whether they are complying with the standards they have set themselves or the standards set by the authorities – or if they are breaking the law.

Environmental information of this kind has been used by campaigners to expose environmental crimes by major polluters. Friends of the Earth in particular have mounted a number of successful campaigns.

Industrial groups lobbied hard to resist the proposals for registers. A local authority environmental health officer in North East England who had responsibility for a number of different registers pointed out to the author of this chapter that most inspections originated from the private sector. Manufacturers of pollution control equipment will glean information about the performance of their competitors' equipment – and about potential customers. Companies who want to build a new factory might be able to judge the quality of the local water before deciding how much effluent to discharge into it.

Table 14.1 Local water quality information sources

Register	Subject	Holder
Register of Bathing Water Quality	Bathing Water	National Rivers Authority (NRA now EPA) regional offices
Register of Drinking Water Quality	Drinking Water	Water supply companies
Maps of nitrate-sensitive areas	Areas where nitrates may leach into aquifers	London offices, Ministry of Agriculture, Fisheries & Food (MAFF)
Director General of Water Services Register	Sewerage and waterworks	HQ Library of the Office of Water Services (OFWAT)
Trade Effluent Register	Industrial Effluent	Local sewerage undertakings
Water Quality Register	Discharge consents, classification of rivers and results of sampling	National Rivers Authority (NRA now EPA) regional offices
Licence Register	Abstraction of river water and impounding (i.e. construction of dams or weirs)	National Rivers Authority (NRA now EPA) regional offices

Environmental Information Regulations 1992

A useful guide to the *Environmental Information Regulations* 1992 and the EC Directive is produced by Friends of the Earth (FoE)[11]. They argue that the Regulations are deficient in that the British government has not fully implemented the Directive and they have complained to the European Commission. A key element of their complaint is that the Regulations do not provide an adequate remedy for people who have been denied information.

Anyone can make a request for information under the Regulations. It is not necessary to state that the Regulations are being invoked. There will be times when it will be useful to mention them and times when it may be prudent not to do so. No one needs a lawyer to invoke the Regulations, but if information is not forthcoming, it might be wise to take legal advice.

The Regulations cover government departments and agencies, local authorities and other bodies with public responsibilities for the environment (Reg. 2(3)). There is some uncertainty about exactly who is and is not covered. Instead of issuing a circular to accompany the regulations, which would need to be addressed to the various bodies who were covered, the government issued a guidance note which included a list of recipients. This suggested a reluctance to provide a definitive list of those who are covered. Private companies are clearly not covered – but privatized utilities probably are. Anyone intending to use the Regulations is advised to obtain a copy of the Guidance[12] and to use it in conjunction with the Friends of the Earth Briefing.

What is environmental information?

Environmental information is defined as information which relates to 'the state of any water or air, the state of any flora or fauna, the state of any soil or the state of any natural site or other land' (Reg. 2(2) (a)); or any activities or measures which adversely protect water, air and so on (Reg. 2(2) (b)) or any activities or measures designed to protect water, air etc. (Reg. 2(2) (c)).

Charging

One of the many grey areas in the Regulations is that charges must be 'reasonable' and must be linked to the supply of the information requested (Reg. 3(4) (b)). One way to get round the problem is for information seekers to inspect the documents concerned in the relevant office rather than run the risk of being charged for the time taken by staff to go through the material. But there have been some stories of high charges.

Response time

The Regulations specify that a response, or a substantive explanation more than an acknowledgement, must be given by the body concerned within two months (Reg. 3(2) (b)).

Grounds for refusal

A request for information may be refused under Regulation 4(2) if it affects or involves:

- international relations;
- national defence;
- public security;
- legal proceedings;
- confidential deliberations and internal communications;
- commercial or industrial confidentiality.

Requests will be refused under Regulation 4(3) if the information is:

- personal information;
- surrendered voluntarily by someone who has not consented to its disclosure;
- likely to increase environmental damage if made public.

Clearly, there are many grey areas, but these should not put people off. It is important to try to use the Regulations first and to consider what to do if disclosure is not forthcoming later.

Case study: contaminated land

The legacy of years of industrial activity is an estimated 100 000 contaminated sites in the UK. Certain industrial activities (for example gas works, waste tips, chemical production, tanneries, metal plating) leave the soil in a condition hazardous to human and animal health and a threat to water quality. Organic matter left in landfill sites for many years can generate highly explosive methane. The property and insurance sectors are only too well aware of such problems. Indeed they have successfully lobbied against a public register of contaminated sites.

The Environmental Protection Act contains provisions enabling a Minister to make regulations to instruct local authorities to draw up a public register of potentially contaminated sites. The property industry lobbied against this proposal and plans for comprehensive public registers have been shelved. A much weaker register regime appears in the *Environment Act 1995.*

One or two local authorities (for example, Warrington Borough Council) are aware of the problems, have investigated sites in their areas and have compiled public registers. To do this they have used the DoE paper on conducting investigations of documentary information about potentially contaminated sites[13].

An investigation into the history of a site to see if there have been any potentially contaminative activities there might be carried out by a proposed purchaser, concerned to see that there were not any serious liabilities hidden beneath the soil. Such a search might accompany a qualitative analysis of the site. If any toxins were discovered, chemical processes known generally as soil remediation could be used to clean up the site.

The sources of information used in a search to see if a site is contaminated – a search for contaminative uses – provide a fascinating insight into the commercial value of information. Whatever the state of the law, archival research into contaminated land will continue to be important to estate agents, surveyors and lenders.

Such a search requires investigations into both statutory sources of the kind discussed above and also local historical material. Old works of reference such as *Kelly's Directory* and papers in the depths of County Record Offices – sources which might previously have been thought to have little or no contemporary commercial value – have become immensely significant to the property industry. Friends of the Earth also provide another useful self-help guide[14]. (See Table 14.2.)

Case study: the Environmental Information Regulations and Thorp[15]

Thorp, the Thermal Oxide Reprocessing Plant, in Cumbria, is one of the recent controversial environmental issues. The processing of spent nuclear fuel to separate plutonium and uranium is, say environmentalists, extremely hazardous. The debate over whether to allow British Nuclear Fuels to operate the plant was one of considerable environmental significance. Although a good deal of information was already in the public domain, there was also a considerable amount which remained confidential during the debate.

The Campaign For Freedom of Information, conducted a study of the regulations which involved making requests from sixteen bodies concerned with Thorp. The Campaign requested documents which it knew existed:

- eight supplied some or all of the information requested;
- six failed to supply anything;

Table 14.2 Sources used in a contaminative use report

Ordnance Survey maps
First edition 1868 – 25″ to the mile
Revised edition 1902 – 25″ to the mile
Revised edition 1915 – 25″ to the mile
Revised edition 1937 – 25″ to the mile
National Grid Plan 1970 1:1250 scale
National Grid Plan 1983 1:1250 scale

Commercial aerial photographs
Aerial photographs can be obtained from a number of companies and are based on Ordnance Survey sheets.

Local and street trade directories
Such directories are sources well known to local studies librarians and can be used to ascertain previous occupiers sites and their trades. Old Registers of Electors and Rateable Valuation lists are also relevant.

Local planning department
local environmental health department
A search for information about contaminated land will involve the examination of public records held by the local authority.

- Who has applied for planning permission for the site in the past?
- Have they any knowledge of contamination or remedial work?
- Have there been any applications under pollution control legislation or any enforcement notices served?

Such information will be a matter of public record.

Water
The local water supply company, the former National Rivers Authority (NRA now EPA) and the former water boards may all have relevant information about local boreholes, groundwater contamination or discharges to rivers which might affect the site. Details may also be available about discharges of industrial or trade effluent to sewers. This information will be held either by the Agency or the water service company but the Water Industry Act places some restrictions on disclosure. The NRA also keeps a record of convictions for pollution offences.

The Agency keeps records of authorizations to carry out polluting activities, enforcement orders issued and information about convictions. All of this may be relevant.

Other sources
Other sources include:

- Waste Disposal Site Licences held by the Environment Agency.
- Results of the survey of derelict and despoiled land in England 1974 (summary tables) (DoE, 1975). Separate reports for derelict land and waste (refuse) tipping, and mineral workings were also published.
- Information kept by the Health and Safety Executive.

- one failed to respond within two months;
- one said it did not hold the information requested.

Four organizations said that they were not subject to the Regulations and had no duty to supply information. These public bodies – which, in the language of the Regulations, claimed not to have responsibility for managing or protecting the environment – were British Nuclear Fuels, the Health and Safety Executive's Nuclear Installations Inspectorate, the Radioactive Waste Management Advisory Committee and the National Audit Office.

The Department of Trade and Industry (DTI) and Cumbria County Council said that the requested information on Thorp did not relate to the environment.

The Regulations also allow bodies to refuse to supply information on the grounds that it is confidential. No organization found it necessary to invoke this provision.

Case study: Glossop Friends of the Earth

Glossop Friends of the Earth applied to the Highways Agency for information about the effect of proposals to widen the M62 motorway. The Agency did not reply within the time limit set down in the Regulations. Only when the group wrote to their MP did the Agency reply.

Case study: unfinished material

A local authority declined to release a document about a local chemical waste facility. They argued that the document did not have to be released because it was not finished. Authorities are permitted not to release unfinished material under the Regulations.

Lawyers acting for the group seeking the document successfully argued that the refusal was entirely unreasonable under the circumstances. The document was subsequently released.

What to do if things go wrong

Anyone who wants information can consult the registers or invoke the Regulations. But there are two organizations in particular who might be able to provide advice if disclosure is not forthcoming or if information is only available for a prohibitive fee.

Earthrights: The environmental law and resource centre
Battle Bridge Centre
Battle Bridge Road,
London NW1 2TL
Tel: +44 171 278 1005

The Campaign for Freedom of Information
88 Old Street
London EC1V 9AR
Tel: +44 171 253 2445

References

1. Birkinshaw, P. (1990) *Government and information: the law relating to access, disclosure and regulation.* London: Butterworths.
2. Cabinet Office (1994) *Open government code of practice on access to government information.* London: HMSO.
3. HM Alkali Inspectorate (1864) *First Report.* London: HMSO. Quoted in D. Wilson (ed.), *The secrets file* (1984) London: Heinemann.
4. Royal Commission on Environmental Pollution (1984) *Tenth Report CMND 9149.* London: HMSO.
5. Wilson, D. (1984) ed.) *The secrets file.* London: Heinemann.
6. *The environmental information regulations* (1992). SI 1992, no. 3240. London: HMSO. (The Regulations implement EC Directive 90/313/EEC on freedom of access to information on the environment OJ L158, 23/6/90, 156.)
7. *A guide to environmental registers* (1993) Denton Hall. Available from Glenn McLeod, 5 Chancery Lane, Cliffords Inn, London EC4A 1BU. Tel: +44 171 320 6115).
8. Murdie, A. (1993) *Environmental law and citizen action.* London: Earthscan.
9. Friends of the Earth (1992) *River pollution: a sleuth's guide.* London: FoE. Friends of the Earth (1993) *Water pollution: finding the facts.* London: FoE.
10. Department of the Environment (1995) *Environment facts: a guide to using public registers of environmental information.* London: HMSO.
11. Friends of the Earth (1994) *Using the right to know.* London: FoE.
12. *Freedom of access to information on the environment: guidance on the implementation of the Environmental Information Regulations 1992 in Great Britain.* London: HMSO.
13. Department of the Environment/Welsh Office (1991) *Public registers of land which may be contaminated: a consultation paper.* London: HMSO.
14. Friends of the Earth (1993) *Buyer beware.* London: FoE.
15. Frankel, M. and Ecclestone E. (1993). *The Environmental Information Regulations and Thorp.* London: Campaign for Freedom of Information.

CHAPTER FIFTEEN

Education, training and research

MONICA BARLOW

Aldo Leopold, in the classic *A Sand County almanac*, (1949: p.18) asked: 'Is education possibly a process of trading awareness for things of lesser worth?' As a scientist and conservationist passionately concerned to save America's wilderness, he was referring to an education which awards university degrees, but whose recipients never saw the magnificent skeins of migrating geese 'that twice a year proclaim the revolving seasons'. His question is echoed today by proponents of a broad-based environmental education which goes far beyond schooling. The role of scientific research is similarly questioned. Lewis Mumford (1970) describes the growth of modern science as a process which lost sight of both the significance of nature and the nature of significance'. The (replacement of an organic world view by a mechanical one has traded 'the totality of human experience . . . for that minute portion which can be observed within a limited time span and interpreted in terms of mass and motion'.

New approaches to environmental education aim to rectify this balance. The benefits gained through science and research need not be outweighed by the destruction of land, life and uniqueness wreaked in the name of progress.

> We abuse land because we regard it as a commodity belonging to us. When we see land as a community to which we belong; we may begin to use it with love and respect. There is no other way for land to survive the impact of mechanised man. . . . That land is a community is the basic concept of ecology, but that land is to be loved and respected is an extension of the ethics. That land yields a cultural harvest is a fact long known, but latterly often forgotten.
>
> (Leopold, 1949: Foreword, p. viii)

The links between community and environmental wellbeing have been drawn as clearly as Juvenal's requisite of a 'healthy mind in a healthy body' and demand a radical new and integrative approach to education, research and training.

The Brundtland Report recommended multi-disciplinary studies:

> to foster a sense of responsibility for the state of the environment and to teach students how to monitor, protect, and improve it. These objectives cannot be achieved without the involvement of students in the movement for a better environment, through such things as nature clubs and special interest groups. Adult education, on-the-job training, television, and other less formal methods must be used to reach out to as wide a group of individuals as possible
>
> (World Commission on Environment and Development, 1987: p.113)

The recognition of informal learning reflected the growing strength of pressure groups and the media in creating environmental awareness.

The Earth Summit in 1992 further encouraged the principle of indivisibility of people and environment. The Conference was hailed as a 'milestone event'. It brought together more heads of government than any other meeting in world history, as well as representatives of international and non-governmental organizations from all over the world:

> We can no longer think of environment and economic and social development as isolated fields. The Declaration of Rio contains fundamental principles on which States must base their future decisions and policies, considering the environmental implications of socio-economic development.
>
> (Keating 1993: Foreword p.vi)

The principle of a global community facing common crises of poverty and environmental degradation was accepted, and an action plan for worldwide sustainable development was created in Agenda 21, 'the most comprehensive and far-reaching programme of action ever approved by world community'. (UNCED, 1992: p.9)

Agenda 21 adopts the model of a broad-based and integrative lifelong education. This was not created as a policy document signed by national governments, but it has been used in governmental and non-governmental sectors to formulate new approaches to the implementation of sustainable development. Education, the raising of public awareness, and training are 'critical for promoting sustainable development'. Agenda 21 creates four principal objectives in its chapter on education:

> to ensure universal access to basic education; to achieve environmental and development awareness in all sectors of society on a world-wide scale as soon as possible; to strive to achieve accessibility of this education from

primary school age through adulthood to all groups of people; and to promote integration of environment and development concepts in all educational programmes.

(UNCED, 1992: p.221)

The Agenda urges development of national and regional strategies for implementing these educational objectives, through effective collaboration among educational governmental and voluntary agencies. Throughout the document, education about our local and global environment is considered essential to the creation of a population aware of the environmental implications of all decision-making. Furthermore formal, informal and traditional educations are recognized:

> While basic education provides the underpinning for any environmental and development education, the latter needs to be incorporated as an essential part of learning. . . . To be effective, environment and development education should deal with the dynamics of both the physical biological and socio-economic environment and human (which may include spiritual) development, should be integrated in all disciplines, and should employ formal and non-formal methods and effective means of communication:

(UNCED, 1992: p.221)

The *British Government panel on sustainable development first report* was published in January 1995; environmental education and training was one of the four main issues identified for early consideration (Tickell, 1995). General principles continued the trend towards a lifelong education on environmental issues and values, with particular emphasis on individual responsibility for a healthy environment. Business, commercial and professional communities and the voluntary sector would play 'vital roles': 'sustainable development involves society as a whole'. The Panel recommended that 'the Government should develop a comprehensive strategy for environmental education and training to cover both formal and informal education and to bring in the wide range of related activities by official and voluntary bodies, industry and commerce, and local communities'. It further recommended improving teachers' access to local and national resources.

The term sustainable development holds innumerable interpretations and although 'not so much an idea as a convoy of ideas' (Tickell, 1995) it has become a useful central theme for environmental education (see Fien, 1993a, b). Sustainability promotes prevention rather than cure; an image of positive planetary health replaces an environmentalism which merely listed problems from deforestation to ozone depletion. Moreover, it encourages a development of understanding and interpretation to which both academics and communities can contribute. It is in this broadening of decision-making that Agenda 21 creates opportunities for new departures. Its 500-plus pages summarize problems and discuss ways of solving them, while stressing the interdependence of solutions. One major theme is that all groups in society must be allowed and enabled to participate fully in the processes of decision-making. The World Conservation Strategy (IUCN, 1980, 1991, 1993) had already called for education which would lead to people's more active participation in the management of their own environments. The development of Local Agenda 21 now offers opportunities to create this broad base of decision-making. Groups in local government and the voluntary sector throughout the world are grasping the potential inherent in the process of devising their own strategies for local sustainability, and are drawing on local resources for the education of their own communities (UNEP, 1992; LGMB, 1993, Grundy and McLeish, 1994). The newsletter *New Frontier* covers issues ranging from community development to indicators for sustainability, with case studies and practical examples of community development (UNA, 1994). Much of this is text-based only as a means of documenting and spreading good practice; it is not text-reliant and, indeed, often aims to remove the dominance of text by stressing oral history and unwritten local traditions.

An example from within this broad-based movement for public environmental education is the charity Common Ground, which has pioneered a movement for people to reclaim their 'local distinctiveness' by identifying and charting their own localities through projects ranging from parish maps to apple diversity. Publications such as *Holding your ground*, *Orchards*, *Local distinctiveness* and the *Apple map of Britain* provide resources which draw directly from experience and inspiration. (King and Clifford, 1987; Clifford and King, 1993). In the USA the bioregional movement reflects this need for local identity through mapping. *Boundaries of home: mapping for local empowerment* offers examples of cartography from contemporary western society to aboriginal cultures, as well as ideas about design, discussion of 'life place' boundary definitions, and simple methods for building maps of local bioregions. A wealth of resources abounds in the thousands of non-governmental organizations working for environmental and community benefits throughout the UK (NCVO, 1994). Regional environment networks make essential links between local groups, businesses and local authorities, and provide opportunities for the creation of local and regional environmental strategies (Enstone, 1993; Krishnarayan 1993).

A recent review of environmental education by John Smyth (1995: p.3), a biologist and President of the Scottish Environmental Education Council, 'relates environment and education to the whole system of human-environment relationships and sees environmental education not as a separable package but as a movement for fundamental educational reform, in a rapidly changing world under increasing stress both from human-induced change and from human nature itself. This holistic view has been incorporated into Scotland's national strategy for environmental education: *Learning for life* (SOEnD, 1993) is both a major policy document and a step forward in the development and implementation of a 'single conceptual structure' bringing together both environmental and social systems.

That education is essential to the creation and maintenance of a healthy society living within its environmental means has been central to policy produced at intergovernmental level in the last twenty five years. The UN Conference on the Human Environment in Stockholm in 1972 called for 'an international programme in environmental education, inter-disciplinary in approach, in schools and out of schools, encompassing all levels of education and directed towards the general public'. The content and direction of this education was developed through UNESCO conferences and formulated in their publications (UNESCO, 1977, 1987, 1988). Further history of this development can be found in the National Association for Environmental Education publication *Coming of age* (Sterling, 1992). This education tends to be described in terms of process rather than subject content. The following list of descriptors appears in the Scottish strategy (SOEnD, 1993):

- lifelong;
- interdisciplinary;
- holistic;
- learner-centred;
- locally relevant;
- concentric "from local to global;
- emphasis on quality and value;
- problem formulating;
- normative rather than empirical;
- exemplary (for example with reference to the quality of the learning environment);
- systemic rather than linear thinking;
- affective integrated with cognitive;
- flexible and adaptable;
- forward-looking, anticipatory;
- interpretative, synthetic, broadening;
- operating in open situations;
- issue-base;
- field-based;
- action-oriented.

These processes require educational resources to go far beyond traditional text-based formats and in this regard the voluntary sector has been instrumental in creating opportunities for interactive approaches to environmental issues. City farms have become a central and much valued support for primary and community environmental education. Members of the National Federation of City Farms support principles of organic agriculture and permaculture, introducing concepts of sustainability in a practical way and at a very early age (see also Mollison 1988, 1993). City farms have linked with local authorities to establish wormery compost schemes: helping to achieve waste reduction targets (and landfill costs) as well as making cheap compost for gardeners. Children's Scrapstores are a major resource for schools and playgroups; by 'turning waste things into play things' they provide an outlet for waste materials from local manufacturing and encourage creative use of recycled materials (see also Ekins, 1992). Local wildlife trusts offer 'nature' education through twilight bat walks as much as through documents. Learning Through Landscapes and BTCV help schools to design and create their own nature gardens as permanent resources for environmental education, while BTCV gives training in practical skills from dry stone walling to reed bed reclamation. Resources are action-oriented and education is never confined to school age children: learning is encouraged through participation in practical work and becomes both useful and fun.

The Education Reform Bill 1988 established environment as one of four cross-curricular themes. In practice, the impetus for improving environmental education in schools has come from non-governmental organizations and individual teachers. The Council for Environmental Education (CEE) in England and the Scottish Environmental Education Council increasingly act as fora for co-operative action. Examples of publications providing essential and specific training for teachers in introducing environmental issues into the curriculum include the CEE's *Inset for environmental education 5–16*. This comes in four modules consisting of an introduction, science, geography and English, tested in local Education authorities and designed for use in INSET or statutory training days. (CEE, 1992, 1993; 1994). A series of information sheets on different aspects of environmental education includes *Environmental education within the National Curriculum* (CEE, 1994). The CEE's report, *Environmental education information needs* recommends ways in which information provision and dissemination can be improved and a follow-up report, *Information in action*, details responses to a consultation paper asking CEE members, local authorities and principal youth officers how these recommendations might be implemented (CEE, 1993).

Despite cross-curricular intentions, for many schools environmental education is still part of geography and science; but materials with cross-disciplinary potential are produced. The international Council for Conservation Education (ICCE) specializes in production and distribution of flexible teaching aids; the obligations of the national curriculum are met through cross-curricular resources with special relevance to science and geography programmes. Examples include educational videos designed for secondary schools but of use also in general education, and slide and tape resource packs for primary and secondary use. *Environmental education activities for primary schools*, *Environment resources on CD-ROM*, *EcoSchool teacher's manuals*, guides on integrating environmental education throughout the curriculum and conducting an environmental audit of your school complement the many issue-based resource packs and even a board game called *Third worldopoly*. ICCE also produces the *Green Letter*, a broadsheet promoting dissemination of environmental resources to schools (ICCE, 1993, 1994). Issue-based groups extend these resources and can offer theoretical and practical help. For example, a project from the Bristol Energy Centre's education team proposed class-based measuring of school energy use followed by analysis and implementation of efficiency measures, all of which could be undertaken by pupils within set activities leading to National Curriculum targets, but which would also contribute to considerable reductions in schools' energy bills.

Another schools-focused resource is the magazine *Green Teacher*, which relates current green debates to ideas and practice in education, provides issue-based materials directly usable with teaching groups and offers a vital network for environmental educators. Articles range from international school exchange projects and historical approaches to the environment to 'moral dilemmas' over issues such as the arms trade (ODEC, 1994, CAT, 1994). The magazine provides information on resources as well as reviews of general and practical environmental information resources for all levels: the Worldwatch Institute's *State of the world* Reports (Brown); the *Gaia atlas of planet management* (Myers, 1994); CAT's New Futures series (CAT, 1994); and the *NAFSO directory* (NAFSO, 1994). It also covers teacher manuals and student materials produced by the education departments of pressure groups (Edwards *et al.*, 1993; FoE, 1993 a, b, Hicks, 1994;). With one or two exceptions, materials of this nature have been produced by voluntary organizations – educational and environmental charities and pressure groups, non-profit-making publishers and co-operatives. Groups such as WWFN and FoE receive thousands of requests for information each week and the vast majority of these come from school children (Cade, 1993).

Nor is environmental information exclusively text-based, even in schools' resources. Campaign groups are widely perceived as primary providers of environmental information, but use text only as part of a communications package (Norman, 1991). Friends of the Earth has a strong local groups network, many of which provide school talks relating local and global issues; information is frequently conveyed by word of mouth from group to group or through local actions to members of the public. Many national organizations also run children's networks which specialize in activity-oriented information (WATCH, Earth Action c/o Friends of the Earth). Essential references (statistics, examples, information outline solutions for particular problems) are carried in newsletters and leaflets: material which is quickly and easily prepared, distributed and updated, and (most importantly) a cheap resource for pressure group and pupil. Books, posters and television, even e.mail, supplement these communications and provide detailed background and reference material (FoE, 1993a, b). International computer networks offer opportunities for school children to share experiences and chat on a global level. Examples include a co-operative project involving schools in Spain, Argentina and the USA; teenagers discussing 'education and a better world', and project-based schools links through Northern Europe (I*EARN 1994). These network conferences fill with letters from children expressing their fears for the world and their desires to build a better future, as well as with case studies of worldwide environmental projects.

The use of a variety of media for communication has been central to the growth of environmental awareness and much credit may go to nature programmes on the television – most obviously, anything by David Attenborough (Norman, 1991). But education for sustainability demands more than just awareness, and requires strategies for turning awareness into practical action. As Smyth concludes:

> I hope we are leaving behind the emphasis on environmental awareness, important as it is as the first step, and aiming for the later stages of environmental literacy, responsibility, competence and citizenship. . . . I hope as educators we have come to view knowledge less as prescriptive – lists of topics and more as the necessary means for understanding, wise choices, and effective action.
>
> (Smyth 1995: p. 18)

Alternative approaches are beginning to supply this model. Human Scale Education publishes a series of booklets whose titles indicate the direction of this movement: *Self-discovery within a community* (Hemming, 1993); *Education for resourcefulness* (Ward, 1993); and *Environmental literacy: education as if the earth mattered* (Orr, 1994). In *Ecological literacy* (Orr, 1992) creates a syllabus for ecological literacy which should be experienced from an inner, rather than from an exterior and supposedly objective viewpoint. He states, moreover:

> that education relevant to the transition to all sustainable society demands first an uncompromising commitment to life and its preservation. Anything less is morally indefensible. By commitment to life I mean a commitment, pervading learning and research at all levels, to health, harmony, balance, wholeness, and diversity as these qualities apply to both human and

natural systems. . . . A commitment to life informs priorities in the creation and advancement of knowledge."

(Orr, 1992, p.133)

Within ecophilosophy, deep ecology forms a popular structure in which this new experience of human interaction with nature can be gained. Naess suggests that environmental ethics goes around and beyond duty or narrow self interest:

> Unhappily, the extensive moralising within the ecological movement has given the public the false impression that they are primarily asked to sacrifice, to show more responsibility, more concern, and better morals. As I see it we need the immense variety of sources of joy opened through increased sensitivity toward the richness and diversity of life, through the profound cherishing of free natural landscapes. We can all contribute to this individually. . . . Part of the joy stems from the consciousness of our intimate relation to something bigger than our own ego, something which has endured for millions of years and is worth continued life for millions of years. The requisite care flows naturally if the self is widened and deepened so as protection of free nature is felt and conceived of as protection of our very selves.

(Naess, 1986: p.28–9)

This passionate commitment may be a small but growing component of environmental education and the resources required for its fulfilment, but it is still for the most part absent from research and training. The British Government Panel on Sustainable Development noted that implementation of the recommendations of the Toyne Report in Further and Higher Education had been 'slow and patchy', though added, 'perhaps not surprisingly given current changes in the system of higher education'. (Tickell, 1995). However, the means for establishing some commitment to sustainability (and its interpretation) are present in documents such as Agenda 21. The Panel recommended that institutions subscribe to the Talloires Declaration (UPSF, 1990) and that both government and institutions take early action on implementing the detailed strategies of the Toyne Report.

In the last few years there has been an unprecedented expansion in the number of university courses taught in subjects relating to the environment: ecology and society, environmental management, environmental technology to name just a few (ECTTIS, 1994) This reflects two developments: first, students' requests to study environmental issues and, increasingly, to work in environmental protection; and second, university needs to run courses which are relevant to training and employment. New environmental laws and regulations are requiring specialized skills in administration, monitoring, audits and impact assessments. But new courses also indicate responses to new challenges. Environmental Toxicology, for example, at the University of Central Lancashire, builds on the university's expertise in toxicology and environmental science, and is run as a joint venture with the national Health and Safety Executive. The University of Wales offers specialization in organic farming through the multi-disciplinary Rural Resources Management course. The Department of Agricultural Sciences explains that: 'Organic farming is seen by many European governments as a means of enhancing the environmental impact of agriculture and has this year become a major focus of the EC's agri-environmental package. Students will now be able to get the training they need to allow them to participate in one of the significant growth areas of European agriculture and environmental policy' (*Greening Universities*, March 1994). The European Research and Training Centre on Environmental Education at the University of Bradford is an example of a resource base for policy in this field, with a range of international projects supported by UN agencies, the European Union and the British Council (Filho and Hale, 1992 ERTCEE, 1994).

Training 'is one of the most important tools to develop human resources and facilitate the transition to a more sustainable world', according to Agenda 21, and training curricula should incorporate consideration of environmental and developmental issues. Specific texts on environmental issues in further and higher education stem largely from early works such as *Greening Polytechnics* (Ali Khan, 1990), produced by the Committee of Directors of Polytechnics together with WWF. Three areas identified for action are curriculum development, institutional practice (purchasing, energy efficiency, recycling, sites), and local and global community links. The legislative contexts in which the paper works range from EC Directives (civil liability, access to information), the European Environment Agency and the UK government's White Paper, to submissions from umbrella bodies such as the TUC and CEE. *Greening the Curriculum* (Ali Khan, 1990b) and *Colleges going green* (Ali Khan, 1991) cite examples of changes such as environmental policy statements and green working groups (Khan, 1990, 1991). *Learning for the future* takes the debate into adult education (Fisher, 1993).

The Toyne Report, *Environmental responsibility – an agenda for further and higher education* (Toyne, 1993) outlines specific roles for colleges in responding to the growing demand for developing environmental skills and understanding. These include specialist courses for environmental qualifications, updating courses for those already in work and environmental education for all students in every discipline. The Report focuses on employment opportunities in particular; it recommends the inclusion of occupational environment issues in all National Vocational Qualifications, and support from the Department of Education and the Department of the Environment for COSQUEC's programme for integrated environmental competence standards across all sectors of work (Toyne, 1993). Implementation involves policy statements, consultation, audits, curricular reviews and ongoing training, to ensure, among other things, that the potential environmental relevance of all courses is realised as fully as possible'. One college commented on the need for consensus in the process, but 'we will be aided in this task by the large number of staff and students who are genuinely committed to the principle of institutional Greening. . . . Institutional Greening is an idea whose time has come and for which there is already considerable commitment and enthusiasm.' (Money, 1994). One particular area in which concern has been expressed for the lack of environmental input is that of business studies, a lack caused by 'the challenge of incorporating the interdisciplinarity of the environment into a largely unitary discipline'. Brunel University's Environmental Management Programme has faced this challenge and offers training through qualification-based courses, distance learning supplements and collaborative ventures with commercial and public organizations (*Greening Universities*, March 1994).

In noting that there 'is still a considerable lack of awareness of the interrelatedness of all human activities and the environment, due to insufficient or inaccurate information', Agenda 21 creates a vital role for research into all aspects of environment and development. The International Conference on an Agenda of Science for Environment and Development into the 21st Century (ASCEND 21) was established in Vienna in 1991 by the International Council of Scientific Unions. ASCEND 21 was a major influence in the Earth Summit, and has largely set the scene for research in the natural sciences. The highest priorities were given to issues such as population growth, consumption, resource depletion, inequality, poverty, climate change, loss of biological diversity, industrialization, waste, water and energy. Most recommendations were for further research, but ASCEND also proposed the involvement of wider sections of the population in environmental problem-solving, regular communication with policy-makers, media and public, and a wide review of environmental ethics (*The Globe*, 1992; Pickering and Owen, 1994).

Just as Agenda 21 has given individuals a structure within which to work towards increased participation in decision-making through implementation of Local Agenda 21, so, through its insistence on information availability on all topics and at all levels, it can offer opportunities to improve communications between research and action – whether policy-making or comment from pressure groups. The Rio Declaration concentrates on access to information rather than the provision of education:

Environmental issues are best handled with the participation of all concerned citizens, at the relevant level. At the national level, each individual shall have appropriate access to information concerning the environment that is held by public authorities, including information on hazardous materials and activities in their communities, and the opportunity to participate in decision-making processes. States shall facilitate and encourage public awareness and participation by making information widely available. Effective access to judicial and administrative proceedings, including redress and remedy, shall be provided.

(Rio Declaration, UNCED, 1992: p.11)

Research, in the non-governmental as well as the formal academic sector, is essential to this process.

The UK Research Councils, together with government agencies such as the Meteorological Office, the British National Space Centre and the Department of the Environment, form the Inter-Agency Committee for Global Environmental Change. The secretariat for this is provided by the Global Environmental Research Office (GERO) which publishes *The Globe*, a newsletter of research articles and events relating to global environmental change. *The Globe* also carries calls for research proposals (for example, for the Commission of the European Community Framework on Environment and Climate, which includes research into human dimensions of environmental change and environmental technologies as well as the natural environment, environmental quality and global change). GERO also produces a *National directory of UK GER programmes and contact points*, listing major UK science programmes, and an *International directory of global environmental research*. The Directories provide contacts and information about projects in many universities and UK participation in international research and monitoring programmes (such as the International Geosphere-Biosphere Programme); they are a major resource for academic research (GERO, 1991–95).

The GENIE project has been initiated by the IACGEC to create an infrastructure which would facilitate access to data holdings in the UK and to provide a basis for international data access in the future. The main objectives of the project were to create a Master Directory which would allow GEC researchers to find out about data holdings, and to provide a federal network facility which would link existing UK data centres but allow them to maintain control over access to their data. GENIE also provides a focal point for information on international science and policy developments in GEC data management and lays the groundwork for full future international links through the INTERNATIONAL DIRECTORY NETWORK, sponsored by the Centre for Earth Observation. GENIE and IDN are meta-data directories (providing data about data) accessible through computer networks and dial-in lines. GENIE currently has a casual user service on the Internet, offering a free online environmental metadata service through a World Wide Web server. Through this service access is available to material in the ESRC Data Archive, a major resource for the social sciences and humanities, and to the NERC Corporate Database which contains material from designated data centres such as the Antarctica Environmental Data Centre, the British Oceanographic Data Centre, the Environmental Information Centre, the National Water Archive, the National Geosciences Information Service, and NERC's own Scientific Services (GENIE, 1944).

Systems such as GENIE begin to address the problem of communication between research and environmental information, although it must be noted that most academic data are not interpreted for environmental policy-making, and their use still causes great controversy within academic establishments. However, these resources are increasingly accessible via the Internet and electronic communications can offer an excellent source for educational and research material. 'Quick Look' images from the AVRR sensor aboard NOAA satellites, which we would recognize from the TV weather forecasts, combine data from the University of Dundee and the British Geological Survey and are available on World Wide Web pages. The EARTHRISE database of pictures from Space Shuttle astronauts, and a complete list of Internet GIS and Remote Sensing Sites, are other examples of the resources available (URL resources).

As well as academic research institutes putting their data online, groups such as Friends of the Earth have established World Wide Web pages and the World Conservation Monitoring Centre offers partial data access via the Internet. Although it is not the place here to go into the history and organization of the Internet, it is worth noting that, apart from costs of setting up and telecommunications (which can vary from cheap to very expensive), most information on the Internet is free. Moreover, since these organizations have evolved their own computerized information systems in recent years, it is relatively easy to transfer data from in-house systems to online public access. Unlike some academic sources this information is interpreted: data are used to formulate arguments and to propose solutions which may range from local to global policies. Academics such as Norman Myers and Paul Ekins stand out among researchers who openly espouse environmental causes (Ekins 1992; Myers, 1994).

Commercial data sources are also available, primarily from professional, scientific and technical associations via online and CD-ROM publishing companies. These resources are international and can provide a useful source of material for professional researchers. However, they are usually expensive and frequently lack reference to any environmental indicators unless these have been specifically included through legislative or other regulatory obligations.

The starry-eyed travellers of the superhighway should, nevertheless, cast a gaze over the surrounding (non-digitized) landscape, for vast quantities of information resources are not computerized. A prime example of this might be the knowledge of local sites and species built up over many years (sometimes centuries) in local museums. The *UK directory of ecological information* is a superb reference for local resources collected by ornithological societies, wildlife trusts, local museums, biological record centres, national parks, herpetologists, ecologists and botanists. Formats range from maps and publications such as the 1859 *Flora of Manchester* to computerized RECORDER databases developed by English Nature (Donn and Wade, 1994). The *ECO directory of environmental databases* lists information resources in the voluntary, statutory and commercial sectors which are held in computer format for ease of storage and analysis, but the information which comes out of these databases is often in straightforward print. (Barlow *et al.*, 1992; Barlow and Button, 1995).

Environmental education requires a public involvement in academic debate and can also demand a response from within this research. The processes of learning which create models of environmental citizenship are holistic and integrative and question the reductionism which 'permits context-free abstraction of knowledge, and creates criteria of validity based on alienation and non-participation, which is then projected as "objectivity"' (Mies and Shiva, 1993). The Science Museum has recognized the need for science and technology to be discussed by ordinary people and in the context of real everyday life. The UK National Consensus Conference on Plant Biotechnology enabled for the first time in the UK, a panel of members of the public to be consulted about this rapidly developing area of science and technology, and to make recommendations for its future. Through open sessions, and radio broadcasts, research is made relevant to the people whom it will ultimately affect. It offers, too, a chance to dismantle the 'arbitrary barrier between "knowledge" (the specialist) and "ignorance" (the non-specialist)' and to reconsider 'our understanding of what constitutes knowledge' (Shiva, 1989, 1993). The practice of environmental awareness and responsibility is as great a part of education as any theory.

Organizations

National Federation of City Farms
The Green House, Hereford St., Bedminster, Bristol BS3 4NA

British Trust for Conservation Volunteers (BTCV)
36 St Mary's Street
Wallingford
Oxfordshire OX10 0EU

Learning Through Landscapes
Third Floor, Southside Offices
The Law Courts
Winchester
Hampshire SO23 9DL

Wildlife Trusts/RSNC Watch
The Green
Witham Park
Waterside South
Lincoln LN5 7JR

International Council for Conservation Education (ICCE)
Greenfield House
Guiting Power
Cheltenham
Glos GL54 5TZ

Friends of the Earth
26–28 Underwood Street
London N1 7JQ

Computer conferences, networks and home pages

- I*EARN on: gn.apc.org
- URL:http://www.sat.dundee.ac.uk
- URL:http://deimos.ucst.edu/calspace.html
- URL:ftp://gis.queensu.ca/pub/gis/docs/gissites.html

References

Aberley, D. (1993) (ed.) *Boundaries of home: mapping for local empowerment* The New Catalyst Bioregional Series. Gabriola Island, B.C., Canada: New Society Publishers.
Ali Khan, S. 1990a) *Greening polytechnics*. London: CDP.
Ali Khan, S. (1990b) *Greening the curriculum* London: CDP/WWF.
Ali Khan, S. (1991) *Colleges going green: a guide to environmental action in further education colleges*. London: FEU/CEE.
Barlow, M., Button, J., and Fleming, P. (1992) *ECO directory of environmental databases in the UK 1992*. Bristol: ECO Trust.
Barlow, M. and Button, J. (1995) *ECO directory of environmental databases 1995/6*.

Bristol: ECO Trust.

Brown, Lester R. (ed.) (1994) *State of the world* New York: World Watch Institute.

Cade, A. (1993) *Environmental enquiry services*. Presentation at a seminar on environmental information services. English Nature.

Centre for Alternative Technology (CAT) (1993, 1994) *Green teacher*. Machynlleth: Centre for Alternative Technology.

Clifford, S. and King, A. (1993) *Local distinctiveness: place, particularity and identity*: Common Ground.

Common Ground *Orchards, a guide to local conservation*: Common Ground.

Council for Environmental Education (CEE) (1993) *Information in action*. Reading, U.K.: CEE.

Council for Environmental Education (CEE) (1992, 1993, 1994) *INSET for environmental education 5–16*, Harlow: CEE/Longman.

Council for Environmental Education (CEE) *Annual Review of Environmental Education, Vol. 6 (1992/3) On the fringe of the machine*. London: CEE.

Council for Environmental Education (CEE) (1994) *Taking responsibility*. London: CEE.

Donn, S. and Wade, M. (1994) *UK directory of ecological information*. Loughborough/ Packard.

Edwards, P. *et al.* (1993) *Make the difference: science, technology and the environment*, Godalming: WWF.

Ekins, P. (1992) *Wealth beyond measure*. London: Gaia Books.

Enstone, M. (1993) *The NEST directory of environmental networks*. London: NCVO.

Environment and Development Education and Training Group (EDET) (1992) *Good earthkeeping: education, training and awareness for a sustainable future*. UNEP-UK.

ERTCEE (Autumn 1994) *ERTCEE Newsletter* Bradford: University of Bradford.

Fien, J. (1993a) *Education for the environment: critical curriculum theorising and environmental education*. USA: Deakin UP.

Fien, J. (1993b) *Environmental education: a pathway to sustainability*. USA: Deakin UP.

Filho, W.L. and Hale, M. (1992) *Promoting international environmental education: proceedings of the International Workshop on Environmental Education, Rio de Janeiro*. London: British Ecological Society.

Fisher, H. (1993) *Learning for the future: adult learning and the environment*. Leicester: NIACE.

Friends of the Earth (FoE) (1993a) *Your home – your planet*. London: FoE.

Friends of the Earth (FoE) (1993b) *Green your school*. See also: *Friends of the earth yearbook; Green gang leaflets; Discovering the environment leaflets;* FoE calendars and diaries. London: FoE.

GENIE (1994) *Genie News*. Loughborough: Loughborough University of Technology.

Global Environmental Research Office (GERO) (1991–5) *The Globe*, Newsletter. NERC-Swindon: GERO.

Greening of Higher Education Council (GHECo) (1994) *Greening Universities*. Newsletter. Oxford: GHECo.

Greeves, T. (1987) *Parish maps*. London: Common Ground.

Grundy, L. and McLeish, E. (1994) *Educating for a sustainable local authority*. Luton: Local Government Management Board.

Hemming, J. (1993) *Self-discovery within a community*. Bath: Human Scale Education.

Hicks, D. (1994) *Educating for the future, a practical classroom guide*. Godalming: WWF.

International Centre for Conservation Education (ICCE) (1993a) *Environmental education activities for primary schools*. Guiting Power: Glos.: UNESCO/ICCE.

International Centre for Conservation in Education (ICCE) (1993b) *EcoSchool modules 1, 2, 3*. Guiting Power, Glos.: Greenwatch Ltd.

International Centre for Conservation Education (ICCE) (1993c) *Third worldopoly*. Guiting Power, Glos.: Orcades.

International Centre for Conservation Education (ICCE) (1994a) *Environment resources* on CD-ROM: climate change, dwindling resources, conservation. Guiting Power. Glos.: ICCE/Interactive Learning Productions.

International Centre for Conservation Education (ICCE) (1994b) *Caring for the earth: the background, principles and key action points to the second world conservation strategy*. Guiting Power, Glos.: ICCE.

IUCN, UNEP & WWF (1991) *Caring for the earth: a strategy for sustainable living*. London: IUCN.

IUCN, UNEP & WWF (1980) *World conservation strategy: living resources conservation for sustainable development*. London: IUCN.

IUCN, UNEP & WWF (1993) *Caring for the earth: a strategy for survival*. London: Mitchell Beazley.

Keating, M. (1993) *Agenda for change*. Geneva: Centre for Our Common Future.

Khan, 1991, 1990.

King, A. and Clifford, S. (1987) *Holding your ground*. London: Common Ground.

Krishnarayan, V. (1993) *So you want to start an environmental network?* London: NCVO Environmental Support Team.

Leopold, A. (1949) *A Sand County almanac*. Oxford: Oxford University Press.

Local Government Management Board (LGMB) (1993) *A framework for local sustainability*. Luton: LGMB.

McHarry, J. and Church, C. (1994) *Measuring sustainability*. UNASCP.

Matthews, G. and Stephens, D. (1992) *Environmental education information needs: a report of a survey of environmental education information needs in schools and youth work*, CEE.

Mies, M. and Shiva, V. (1993) *Ecofeminism*. London: Zed Books.

Mollison, B. (1979) *Permaculture two: practical design for town and country in permanent agriculture*. Tyalgum, NSW, Australia: Tagari.

Mollison, B. and Holmgren, d. (1978) *Permaculture one: a perennial agriculture for human settlements*. Tyalgum, NSW, Australia: Tagari.

Mollison, B. (1989) *Permaculture: a designer's manual*, Tyalgum, NSW, Australia: Tagari.

Mollison, B. (1993) *The permaculture book of ferment and human nutrition*. Tyalgum, NSW, Australia: Tagari.

Money, M. (1994) In Toyne's backyard: a green university germinates. *Greening Universities*, 1 (2), March.

Mumford, L. (1970) *The myth of the machine: the pentagon of power*. London: Harcourt Brace.

Myers, N. (1994) *The Gaia atlas of planet management*. London: Gaia Books.

Naess, A. (1986) Self-realisation: an ecological approach to being in the world. In *Thinking like a mountain*, J. Seed *et al.* (1988). London: Heretic/New Society.

National Association of Field Studies Officers (NAFSO) (1994) *NAFSO directory of field studies and environmental education centres and consultants 1994*. Peterborough: NAFSO.

National Council for Voluntary Organisations (NCVO) (1992 – 1995) *NEST, the magazine of NCVO's Environment Support Team*.

Norman, D. (1991) *The green maze: environmental information and the needs of the public*. Bristol: ECO Trust.

Orr, D. (1992) *Ecological literacy: education and the transition to a postmodern world*. State University of New York, Albany, NY: SUNY Press.

Orr, D. (1994) *Environmental literacy: education as if the earth mattered*. Bath: Human Scale Education.

Oxford Development Education Centre (ODEC) (1994) Arming the world: the international trade in arms. *Green Teacher*, 32, November 1994.

Palmer, J. and Neal, P. (1994) *The handbook of environmental education*. London: Routledge.

Pickering, K.T. and Owen, L.O. (1994) *An introduction to global environmental issues*.

London: Routledge.

Randle, D. (1989) *Teaching green: a parent's guide for education for life on Earth.* London: Green Print.

Scottish Office Environment Department (SOEnD) (1993) *Learning for life: a national strategy for environmental education in Scotland.* Edinburgh: HMSO.

Shiva, V. (1989) *Staying alive: women, ecology and development.* London: Zed Books.

Shiva, V. (1993) *Monocultures of the mind.* London: Zed Books.

Smyth, J.C. (1977) The biological frramework of environmental education, *Journal of Biological Education,* 11, 103–108.

Smyth, J.C. (1994) Prospects for a strategy for environmental education in Scotland. *Royal Society of Edinburgh Symposium Proceedings Learning for Life.*

Smyth, J.C. (1995) Environment and education: a view of changing scene. *Environmental Education Research.*

Soil Association (1993) *Food, farms and futures.* Bristol: Soil Association.

Sterling, S. (1992) *Coming of age: a short history of environmental education (to 1989).* Walsall: NAEE.

Thorpe, D. (1994) (ed.) *New Futures.* Machynlleth: Centre for Alternative Technology.

Tickell, C. (1995) *British government panel on sustainable development first report.* London: HMSO.

Tilbury, D. (1994) The international development of environmental education: a basis for a teacher education model? *Environmental Education and Information,* 13, 1–20.

Toyne, P. (1993) *Environmental responsibility: an agenda for higher and further education.* London: HMSO.

UK Government White Paper (1994) *Sustainable development: the UK strategy.* London: HMSO.

UNA Sustainable Communities Project (1994) *New frontier.* London: United Nations Association.

UNEP Environment Development Education and Training Group (1992) *Good earthkeeping: education, training and awareness for a sustainable future.* London: United Nations Environment Programme.

UNESCO (1977) *International workshop on environmental education, Belgrade, October 1975, Final Report.* Paris: UNESCO.

UNESCO/UNEP (1987) *Intergovernmental conference on environmental education, Tbilisi.* Paris: UNESCO.

UNESCO/UNEP (1988) *International strategy for action in the field of environmental education and training for the 1990s.* Paris: UNESCO.

United Nations Conference on Environment and Development (1992) *Earth summit 1992.* London: Regency Press.

UPSF (1990) *University presidents for a sustainable future: the Talloires Declaration.* New York: Tufts University European Centre.

Ward, C. (1993) *Education for resourcefulness.* Bath: Human Scale Edition.

Wheeler, K. (1985) International environmental education: a historical perspective. *Environmental Education and Information,* 4, 144–160.

World Commission on Environment and Development (1987) *Our common future* (Brundtland Report). Oxford: Oxford University Press.

CHAPTER SIXTEEN

The public library and the environment

JOHN SMITH

Visioning, networking and truth telling are useless if they do not lead to action. There are many things to do to bring about a sustainable world . . . children have to be taught and so do adults . . . books published, people counselled, groups led. . . . Each person will find his or her own best role in all this doing . . . use your action whatever it is to learn.

The depths of human ignorance are much more profound than most humans are willing to admit. Especially at a time when the global society is coming together as a more integrated whole than has ever been before . . . when new ways of thinking are called for no one really knows enough . . . no policy can be declared as the Policy to be imposed on the world. . . . Learning means the willingness to go slow to try things out and to collect information. . . . In the quest for a sustainable world it doesn't take long before even the most hard boiled rational and practical persons begin to speak with whatever words they can muster of virtue, morality, wisdom and love.

(Meadows *et al.*, 1992: 231–2)

Introduction

Why should public librarians be concerned with environmental issues? The reason is that these are the most important contemporary issues reflected in the culture and consequent publishing of books, information and research. There is increasing public awareness and concern that action needs to be taken at a local, national and global level. Democracy requires these decisions to be taken at various levels, from the personal to the collective, and to be understood locally, nationally and globally. Therefore, in order to understand and to act, the public and decision-makers need to be informed. This information, however it is presented, needs to be reliable, supported by a larger network and usable at a variety of levels from primary education to erudite scientific research. The public library has an important part to play in ensuring access to relevant published information.

The underlying cultural imperative

Why is this an important issue? Simply put, the American Academy of Sciences advised George Bush that the USA had 5000 days to change its ways. The successors to the Club of Rome (Meadows *et al.*, 1992) advise us globally that we have twenty years to rethink our lifestyles and tell us how. Other experts (Harrison, 1992; Kennedy, 1993) are convinced that we are in the middle of major social changes, where environmental considerations will dominate our in the way that economics does now. To be hopeful, many suggest that we are in the middle of a new renaissance and that the basic paradigms of our society are changing.

There is, therefore, something afoot in the culture and this science is now affecting our lives; our lifestyles are changing both locally and globally (for example, disposal of CFCs locally, unleaded petrol, bottle banks, paper banks reduction of pollutants). The awareness of this generation has been raised on environmental issues and following generations will have to take urgent action.

Given the publishing, journalistic, scientific and legal developments in this part of the culture of our society, there is obviously a media, book and information explosion taking place which should be of concern to the public libraries. There is a need in our society not only for the population at large to understand environmental issues, but also for reliable authors and authorities to have their concerns raised in ways so that the complexity can be understood. The public library is an agency well fitted to bring the various levels and communities into awareness of the problems, challenges and solutions, which must start locally but extend to national and global understanding and action.

To promote understanding of these issues, libraries need specialists on their staff who have some grasp of a variety of environmental problems, as well as a fundamental appreciation of nature and our biodiversity which is an essential part of the National Curriculum. Such specialists do not need to be scientists but should develop a community concern. The more efficient use of resources proposed by much of the science should make positive changes to our society, both now and in the future. Such changes will rely on information of all kinds and will include science, technologies and lifestyles. Knowledge is required to change from environmental degradation to environmental enhancement. How to increase the efficiency of our lifestyles is an information-based question.

Freedom of information

There are constraints in the UK on freedom of information and much research is enclosed in secrecy. This is an issue which is of concern to librarians but little can be done except to recognize the constraints under which some information and science have to operate. Unfortunately, many of these projects relate to local environmental studies (Jeffers, 1993).

Areas of understanding

Study of the environment is a major cross-curricular item of the National Curriculum in both primary and secondary schools, resulting in the pre-emption of many resources by the education service. Education for green issues has become big business. Many agencies, including national parks, outdoor pursuit institutions and school library services, are now geared to meet these educational demands, which in part are proving successful.

Industry is being required to be environmentally conscious, both through regulations and requirements to audit their emissions and environmental impact. There are now environmental lawyers, environmental directives, environmental consultants and specialist areas of environmental information for businesses and industry such as the British Library/CBI initiative, which not only saves them from prosecution but also increases efficiency. Business is increasingly going green and this trend will continue. Business information services are being used for many issues in this area. Environmental science databases to meet these needs are now available.

Television and the media have aroused the interest of the general public. There are many environmental television programmes; regular newspaper items appear in the quality press; and popular science, as expressed in *New Scientist*, delivers between one and four environmental articles every week. Publishers, both minority and mainstream, are issuing material of interest. There is now deep green eco-philosophy (Naess, 1989), eco-psychology (Roszak, 1993), eco-history (Kennedy, 1993), plus eco-economics.

One area of interest is computer programs, where the complexity of the situation can be recreated or anticipated. These need to be experimented with as they are largely sophisticated computer games. There are, however, a valuable learning tool (Sim Earth, 1990).

Bibliographic tools and databases are available, both national and international. *New Scientist, Futures* and *Turning Point 2000* are useful sources of worldwide information. *Turning Point 2000* gives useful coverage of items of minority interest and fugitive publications.

The National Library of Scotland (Nisbet, 1993) has reviewed the need for environmental information in organizations. This report begins to analyse needs beyond those of the general public and is good base for further research.

Practical experience: one county library

Cumbria County Library responded to this cultural challenge. Having evaluated the situation and considered the importance of environmental issues, the library decided to review all the resources available within the county of Cumbria. There were two environmental research stations, one teacher training college which specialized in environmental education, an important collection at Lancaster University, across the county border, and other collections which included an agricultural college, environmental health officers' resources, waste disposal departments. and work in the arts and museums. There was also the County Library's own developing collection in response to considerable public need.

Accordingly, in 1990, an Environmental Information Plan was drawn up covering the county and extending to Lancaster University. This 189-page review not only looked at what was available in the county but also how these resources could be pulled together for the mutual advantage of everybody (Cumbria County Library, 1990). The Plan suggested three ways forward: networking; publicity of the resources; and the provision of a dedicated environmental information service which would co-ordinate and promote the resources and work of the network.

Within a year the Cumbria Environmental Information Network (CEIN) was established, with quarterly meetings to examine the development of services in the area and to increase awareness of the resources available to other agencies. Funding was obtained through sponsorship to develop the work of the Network through the publishing of a directory (CEIN, 1992). The directory was planned to be self-editing; Network members would fill in proformas which would become their entries. The directory was then indexed and published (the second edition became available in 1994). The secretariat of CEIN is the County Library.

Obviously, the provision of a service was the next thing to consider. Both the Network and the County Library supported this proposal but there were no resources available and it was recognized that such a service would have to be self-financing. Accordingly, CEIN, the Lake District National Park Authority and the County Library made a

Public Library Application Development Scheme (1992) for the provision of a service which would be self-financing from income generated through the National Park's sales outlets.

A feasibility study was made (1993) which clearly showed that public libraries are not good sales outlets. The public do not expect to buy things from libraries, but the National Parks could eventually generate sufficient income from the sale of educational material to support the service. No other area of income generation, such as business or the general public, was seen to produce sufficient money to maintain the overall service, which relied heavily on the hundreds of thousands of children who visit Cumbria each year to learn about the environment. Sponsorship would be required to establish the service, as well as the PLDIS grant, to support a developing organization.

The proposal to sell prepackaged material was abandoned because it would have been in direct competition with the National Park's own information service. The study produced many useful lessons which might be applicable to other authorities who wished to develop in this particular way. There is, it appears, a considerable demand for prepackaged environment information in the educational sector and this could generate, within a National Park area, sufficient income to support a wider service.

The School Library Service in Cumbria also recognized that the environment is the major cross-curricular subject in the National Curriculum. An exhibition collection was prepared of material suitable for children which was made available to schools within the county. This collection circulated around the schools and generated considerable interest and enthusiasm. However, one of the main supporters of the environmental project work being undertaken by the schools in the county is, of course, the public library. It was decided that the County Library should set up a special collection of material in one of its least environmentally conscious areas so that it could be available across the county. One of the problems of environmental material is that it appears in various places in the classification and, therefore, needs to be brought together in a special collection. The initiative has been repeated in other counties such as Cleveland and Bedfordshire.

The collection was extremely well used locally and there was considerable was extremely well used locally and there was considerable demand for this material by both the general public and school children. Accordingly, the situation has now been reviewed and four collections at major libraries in the county are now being developed.

The possibilities of community development were another concern and funding was sought from the Countryside Commission to develop the concept of local environmental auditing with State of the Environment Reports (SOERs). From the information standpoint, apart from banks, there is a great deal of information about the environment contained in local authorities, health authorities, planning departments, economic development departments and water boards, as well as the regular monitoring that goes on in such agencies as British Gas, Norweb and British Rail.

In order both to act locally and think globally, a series of environmental auditing projects was embarked upon, involving three communities and three schools, with a published report on the small township of Aspatria (Wood, 1993). The result showed the range of information that is available and how this can be pulled together to give a State of the Environment Report (SOER) for the community. Environmental information sources were examined which covered not only local data such as sunshine, rainfall and air quality but also the natural resources of the area. The larger concerns of CFCs, global warming or world population problems were not excluded. There was, therefore, a relationship between published books and local information. Where local information on an important area was not available it was noted. Where they exist these gaps in understanding may vary from community to community. What has emerged from this exercise is the result of one library service's attempt to show how a local community, using information, can produce their own SOER as a basis for developing environmental awareness.

Blennerhasset primary school (1993), who also developed a project, worked with the County Library and produced an interesting and scientific document about their community with various testing done on pollution and other concerns for the village. This produced a large report which has since received national financial prizes.

The initiative of the Cumbria library service has revealed that there is a local environmental information base which can be developed and has shown one way in which this could be done. Elsewhere local environmental mapping has been undertaken. The final conclusion from this study is that both books and information are of interest. They can support the work of education and they can provide a basis for the increased understanding of the environment through the local library.

The work undertaken by Cumbria County Library showed that there is a growing demand for environmental material. Both the community and the individual need access to resources which provide this information and support in seeking it out. The information may be required by a community undertaking local environmental auditing or by individuals concerned about their environment.

A useful training seminar was organized which brought together staff from the County Library, CEIN and other authorities, together with scientists and information specialists. New ideas on both the importance and dissemination of the information were discussed and developed (Jeffers, 1993).

The Public and School Library Services would appear to be the proper place for these local developments and the local contact for a variety of basic monitoring and information sources.

Lessons

Numerous lessons can be drawn from the experience so far, based on the conclusion that this is an important issue and one relevant to the information and learning services offered by the public library.

Environmental issues produce a large public response, especially in education areas. There is an increasing awareness of the problems and thoughtful readers are looking for appropriate material. At the same time many organizations are also considering these issues, varying from government and international agencies to local interest groups and churches. Supporting this concern is a growing body of science and research, publications and legislation, backed by publicity at a variety of levels.

The public library, therefore, has a duty to respond authoritatively to this open concern among the public it serves and retains the published resources to do so. Environmental education will grow due to curriculum pressures and the availability of grants to encourage children's concern in this area. Again, there is an extensive publishing programme of books and other media which supports this initiative, backed by a developing outdoor and environmental education sector. There are growing groups of teachers who exchange information and practice and network their experiences. One of the advantages of environmental studies is that it is an area of science which can be researched and understood locally and can be geared to primary schools.

Information is now readily available on many points: new legislation; EU regulations; how to buy green; how to assess green policies in the political arena; how to buy non-polluting products; how to think locally and globally at the same time. Books, databases, journals and articles abound and can be assessed as either sound or sensational. Local information is sometimes more difficult to get hold of and there can be resistance to access to publicly available information, for example, in economic development areas.

Material concerning environmental issues varies considerably in quality from the scientific to the sensational and unreliable. The moving nature of scientific truth needs to be understood; it is not fixed and can change rapidly. The complexity of the issues has somehow to be grasped. The library has an important part to play in the provision of relevant materials.

Computer programs

The complexity of environmental problems could perhaps be better understood through maths and computer programs, which should be accessible to the public as part of the learning process or at least be available in schools. Such an approach needs to be explored by educationalists. In relation to this chapter the program *Sim Earth* (Maxis/Ocean) was examined and found to be understandable to young children to some extent. In *Beyond the limits* Meadows *et al.* examine computer analysis of environmental issues.

Much is promoted through video and the press but books have an important role to play in effectively popularizing this global problem and assisting in its understanding. Books should not be abandoned in favour of new technology; they can explain complex issues at the learner's own speed and simplify difficult problems into blocks of lay understanding. Librarians should take note of this.

Bart van Steenbergen's (1994) comprehensive review of published global modelling reports finds them wanting in that they are too much based in the first world and do not examine deeply enough other more radical paradigm changes. Deep green thinkers such as Naess or Roszak add to this body of thought, which can be provided only through books.

Conclusion

An informed society is one that makes the right, democratic decisions and an informed society is one that supports the difficult decisions that must be made by politicians, especially at times of social change, such as at present. Libraries have a part to play in this process. The responsibility of the public library and the school library at a time of change is to inform and educate the readers and to ensure that the changing culture receives its due voice in a media that is suited to the complexity of the issue. Librarians have a very real responsibility to be aware of cultural changes and to raise awareness of them. The more complex the issues, the greater is the need for a variety of media to understand those issues.

At this time of considerable change, the public library has considerable responsibility to raise awareness on environmental issues and to allow the voices of concerned scientists, philosophers, theologians, economists, futurists and historians to be heard. The book is the ideal vehicle by which to broadcast these issues to lay people so that their complexity may be understood.

Journals

New Scientist. Weekly.
Futures. 10 issues per annum.
Turning Point 2000. Quarterly. James Robertson, The Old Bakehouse, Cholsey, Nr. Wallingford, Oxon OX10 9NU.

References

Blennerhasset School (1993) *Quality of the environment*. Blennerhasset, Cumbria. Summer.

Bookchin, M. (1986) *Toward an ecological society*. Montreal/Buffalo, Canada: Black Rose Books.

Carley, M. and Christie, I. (1992) *Managing sustainable development*. London: Earthscan.

Cumbria County Library (1990) *Environmental information plan*. Internal. Carlisle: Cumbria County Library.

Cumbria County Library and Lake District Special Planning Board (1993) *Feasibility study for an environmental information service*.

Cumbria Environmental Information Network (CEIN) (1994) *Directory of information sources* 2nd edn. Carlisle: CEIN.

Harrison, P. (1992) *The third revolution*. London: I.B. Taurus.

Jeffers, J.N.R. (1993) Information and the environment. *New Library World*, 94 (1110), p. 23–25.

Kennedy, P. (1993) *Preparing for the twenty first century*. London: Harper/Collins.

Meadows, D.H., Meadows, D.L. and Randers, J. (1992) *Beyond the limits*. London: Earthscan.

Naess, A. (1989) *Ecology, community and lifestyle*. Cambridge: Cambridge University Press.

Nisbet, M. (1993) *Environmental information questionnaire. Analysis and report*. Edinburgh: National Library of Scotland.

Public Library Development Scheme Application (1992) *En environmental information service for Cumbria*. Cumbria County Library and the Lake District Special Planning Board.

Robertson, J. (1983) *The sane alternative*. Cholsey: James Robertson.

Robertson, J. (1985) *Future Work*. Aldershot: Gower.

Roszak, T. (1993) *Voice of the earth*. London: Transworld.

Sim earth (1990) Maxis/Ocean (computer program).

Steenbergen, B. van (1994) Global modelling in the 1990s. *Futures*, 26 (1), 44–56.

Wood, L. (1993) *Aspatria. State of the Environment*. Countryside Commission. Carlisle: Cumbria County Library, CEIN.

World Conservation Union, United Nations Environment Programme and World Wide Fund for Nature (1991) *Caring for the earth: a strategy for sustainable living*. Gland, Switzerland: IUCN, UNEP, WWF.

CHAPTER SEVENTEEN

Environmental information and decision-making: a UNESCO training package

DOROTHY WILLIAMS

Introduction

Policy and decision-makers across the world are increasingly faced with the challenges of achieving economic development while conserving levels of natural resources, and avoiding environmental damage. Environmental problems and solutions operate over different timescales, from short-term alleviation of immediate disasters to long-term preventative solutions. In addition, because the environment is a local as well as a global issue, environmental decision-making has to take place at different levels – global, regional and local.

To support sound decision-making there is a need for environmental information which is relevant to localized problems and opportunities while at the same time allowing local decisions to be made in relation to global issues and conditions. Potential users of environmental information operate at many different levels. There are pressures on governments and business to keep abreast of environmental legislation of trading partners. For those involved in environmental disaster planning there is a need to learn from the experience of others. For those involved in economic and social planning, the need for long-term sustainable solutions leads inevitably to questions of environmental impact and the need for relevant information. The average citizen is also increasingly being asked to make choices that will affect the environment and will need sufficient information of the right kind to support those decisions.

Informed opinion is often limited by a lack of availability of readily accessible and intelligible information. The need to harness a wide range of environmental information to the decision-making process has already been recognized in many countries. The United Nations

Environment Programme (UNEP), the Environmental Protection Agency (EPA) in the USA, the new European Environment Agency, and Friends of the Earth International are large scale examples of the kind of organizations attempting to improve the flow of information. A growing number of more localized agencies and centres is also being set up in an attempt to increase access to information for those who need it.

The need for information in the right form, in the right place, at the right time, has never been greater but solutions rely on the skills and expertise of those who can search for, evaluate, consolidate and manage information. Experience and technology will vary greatly across regions, especially the less developed. In many regions the complexity of environmental decision-making is compounded by the competing claims on scarce resources, coupled with a lack of sound information in the first place. However, while solutions to information management may vary between the developed and less developed regions, many of the underlying information issues will be similar.

UNESCO has been aware of the importance of these issues for some time and is seeking ways to bring them to the attention of decision-makers and information professionals in developing regions. The approach taken is to encourage the sharing of expertise and knowledge in seeking new solutions to local as well as global needs. Towards this end a new educational package has been developed by the School of Information and Media at The Robert Gordon University in Scotland. The package focuses on issues related not only to the collection, analysis, storage and dissemination of environmental information, but also on issues related to communication between experts and non-experts, a process which lies at the heart of many problems associated with the understanding of environmental issues. The underlying approach is to raise awareness of the issues and to stimulate development of information management solutions suited to localized needs.

This chapter discusses some of the issues and challenges of environmental information support for decision-making and outlines the approach which is being taken in the UNESCO package.

Environmental decision-making

Traditionally environmental policy and decision-making in developed and developing countries has proceeded within established conventional sectors: agriculture, forestry, manufacturing industry, education, etc. These disciplines work within traditional boundaries, their researchers communicate through subject-specific networks and policy is often made within government departments based around these sectoral divisions. Ultimately, however, complex problems require a more holistic view, exemplified in the concept of sustainable development. In recent years there has been a shift in awareness of the delicate nature of the balance between human activities and development, and the availability of resources to maintain that development. The growing concern of politicians, scientists and decision-makers generally over the 1970s and 1980s has been less on preserving the status quo and more on the practicalities of achieving sustainable development: 'a new era of economic growth, one that must be based on policies that sustain and expand the environmental resource base' (World Commission on Environment and Development, 1987). Global acceptance and commitment to the concepts of sustainability and conservation of environmental diversity culminated in the statements and agreements of Agenda 21. This international programme of action for global sustainable development into the 21st century was adopted by 178 governments at the United Nations Conference on Environment and Development (UNCED) in Rio de Janeiro, June 1992.

In order to understand the importance of information to sustainable development we must start, therefore, with the concept of sustainability.

Information for sustainability

Sustainability involves the development of society in such a way as to be able to endow the same resource, or an improved one, to the future and is based on the concept of the earth as a delicately balanced system in which the inputs such as energy and water, must be balanced against the outputs (e.g. waste and pollution) produced by human activities. Such a model emphasizes the need for policy and decision-makers to take a holistic view of the issues. Just as the policy-maker has to take a rounded approach to sustainability, combining scientific information with societal information, the decision-maker at all levels tends to be faced with the need to balance different kinds of information. For example, it is not enough to know about the scientific interactions of toxic chemicals with natural systems (including human systems). Indeed this may be of little significance to a decision-maker. It may be much more important to be able to compare the relative risks of different chemical processes on the health of a community. Environmental information is therefore needed but within the context of the decisions that are being made.

Decisions and policy-making are also coloured by the fact that there are different definitions of sustainability. There have been two main viewpoints (although each with their variants) of how sustainability can be achieved – the economic model and the ecological model. The major differences between the two models lie in the extent to which manmade resources can be substituted for natural ones. (For a readable discussion of sustainability, see Cairncross, 1991.) In reality differences tend to blur as the arguments for conserving a renewable natural resource base are increasingly viewed from an economic perspective. It is not just the cost of clean-up operations when things go wrong, although this is certainly an expensive approach to environmental problem solving, but also the loss of developmental opportunity which is now being recognized. Pearce (1991) gives examples of the cost of natural resource degradation in the 1980s in OECD countries: pollution damage alone is estimated to be causing damage equal to 1 per cent GNP in the Netherlands, and up to 5 per cent GNP in Germany, based on mid-1980s figures. The cost of resource degradation in developing countries is considered to be much higher, given that environmental protection legislation has been less prominent. Thus Pearce quote figures for deforestation damage as equal to 3.6 per cent GNP in Indonesia (1984 figures) and 6–9 per cent GNP for Ethiopia (1983 figures). In Eastern Europe pollution damage in 1987 is estimated at 4.4–7.7 per cent GNP.

With such losses in productive potential, the economic incentives to establish environmental policies are great. It is increasingly being recognized that environmental degradation is damaging to economies and is particularly costly in terms of development opportunity. Thus, the conservation of a natural base is accepted as an important economic aspect of sustainable development.

The economic and ecological models of how sustainability can be achieved also influence the population debate. Economic organizations have tended in the past to regard human numbers as a positive factor in economic development and to have taken a comparatively relaxed view of population growth. The ecological model places greater emphasis on the impact of human numbers on the environment and the need to slow population growth to make sustainable development possible (Royal Society, 1994).

Taking the above broad definition as a starting-point, there are some common information related needs which will arise for policy- and decision-makers. These have been neatly summarized under three broad headings in the OECD's Environmental Indicators Programme:

- pressures on the environment (e.g. population change, economic growth, structural change, public concern, etc.);
- the state of the environment itself (e.g. trends in emissions of air pollutants, amounts and nature of waste disposed of, water extraction rates relative to water regeneration, etc.);
- the response of society in terms of government policies, measures

undertaken by individuals or businesses, social response in terms of environmental activism, etc.

Added to these, is the need for economic information. Information is needed on the relative costs of rehabilitating or policing and regulating environmental change, yet there is very little information available on costs of environmental protection or monetary valuation of depreciation of assets (rate of use less rate of regeneration) (Pearce and Freman, 1992).

However, it is not enough to understand the breadth of information required. To improve information provision, we also need to consider the nature of information users – the decision-makers – and the way in which they use information.

The decision-maker

Within the context of sustainable development, decision-makers operate at different levels from the global to the regional to the local level. This broad and divergent group includes government departments, non-governmental organizations (NGOs) and individuals operating in a very wide range of circumstances such as planners, politicians, legislators, business managers, educators, researchers and, of course, the public.

These decision-makers can be broadly categorized as those who are involved in policy-making and those who are not (i.e. recipients of policy) (Pearce and Freman, 1992). The environmental issues with which they are concerned may be similar but they will vary in the use which they make of the information. Some of these decision-makers are primarily concerned with environmental management or resource management, while for others the environmental concerns may surface as a natural consequence of their role in society. (For further discussion of the classification of environmental information users see, for example, Neufeld's description, 1983). Their 'need to know' may arise for a number of reasons, influencing both the nature of the information needed as well as the speed with which it is required.

Perception of threat

Public health issues, damage to the environment, and long-term global decline can all be perceived as potential threats. The sudden dangers to family and health are often the prime motivators of public concern and the perception of damage to the wellbeing of the community is an important motivator in the formation of localized lobby groups.

Perception of opportunity

The motivation to learn more about environmental issues within the business sector may often stem from the fact that maximizing efficiency in resources is seen as a cost-saving exercise and thus a way of maximizing profits. In the political or business arena, demonstrating environmental concern may be perceived as a way of attracting public support or selling products.

Response to disaster

The sudden need to respond quickly to an oil spillage or to minimize the impact of drought on a region, creates an urgent need for information, often of a very localized nature.

Outside pressures

There are many external pressures which influence the need for environmental information. These factors may operate at local, regional or global level.

INCREASED SCIENTIFIC KNOWLEDGE

It was recently estimated, for example, that there are some 700–800 professional articles per week plus popular literature, relating to the environment (Weiskel, 1991). New technology also allows increased opportunities to monitor and measure environmental change. For the scientist or decision-maker this creates a pressure to keep abreast of new information.

INCREASED PUBLIC AWARENESS

This is exemplified in the increasing number of local lobby groups; the increasing demand for public enquiries; green consumers; the presence of Environmental Charters, and so on. Although some of this is due to increasing levels of environmental education in schools, much is also due to increased coverage of environmental issues in the media. To some extent the two go together: education of the young creates awareness of issues in the population as a whole. The resulting increased demand for more information has tended to push environmental issues higher up the media's news agenda. Unfortunately this can also create problems in terms of accurate interpretation and portrayal of issues.

INCREASED POLITICAL AWARENESS

It is not only 'green' parties who have the environment on their agendas – increasingly the environment is part of mainstream political thought at national and local level.

ECONOMIC PRESSURE

Scarcity of resources means increasingly expensive raw materials. In turn this leads to pressure on industry to avoid waste, and pressure on government to fund research into resource production, waste reduction, etc.

STANDARDS

In many countries national environmental standards are being introduced to provide a measure of quality assurance. In the UK, for example, BS7750 provides a specification for environmental management systems, designed to ensure that an organization's activities are compatible with environmental policy objectives and targets, (e.g. minimizing waste, reducing emissions, etc.) Companies are increasingly encouraged to undertake environmental reviews or environmental audits of their activities, processes which require that they are informed about environmental issues and are able to collect relevant information concerning their own activities.

LEGISLATION AND REGULATION

Many countries have already introduced stringent legislation governing industrial processes, transportation of waste, etc. In relation to pollution and waste management, for example, the UK Environmental Protection Act (1990) has introduced stringent new controls on gaseous emissions from both large-scale and small-scale 'prescribed processes'. The Act also places a legally binding Duty of Care on all waste producers to ensure that the transport of waste is carried out responsibly and with safety. Similar moves towards increasing environmental legislation can be seen across the world (e.g. the Czech and Slovak Republics are attempting to deal with severe pollution problems by introducing new legislation governing Environmental Impact Statements, waste management, etc). Thus, the business sector has a need to keep up-to-date with regulations which will affect not only their own production but also their ability to trade across transnational boundaries. As well as national legislation, many countries are influenced by regional legislation (e.g. the EC's Directive on Access to Environmental Information). Countries may also be signatories to various international conventions such as the United Nations Convention on the Law of the Sea, the Convention on International Trade in Endangered Species of Wild Fauna and Flora (CITES), the African Convention for the Conservation of Nature and Natural heritage, etc.

Information users

The varying motivations and needs of potential users gives rise to the need for different levels of information. As well as the need for action-oriented information – the information upon which decisions can be based and actions taken – there will also be the need for awareness-raising information. Taylor also distinguishes between these two types of information need when he uses the terms 'informing knowledge and productive knowledge' (Taylor, 1986). In fact, policy- and decision-makers will be instrumental in creating a need to make others (i.e. often the public) more aware.

These broadly different information needs have profound implications for the way in which information is packaged and processed to make it useful. The variety of needs and uses also has relevance for the methods chosen to gather, store, analyse and disseminate environmental information. It is not enough to provide access to large quantities of information. The level of the information, the way in which it is presented, the need for it to be consolidated, are important factors which may influence the uptake of information at a local level. Such issues impact not only on the design of local models of information systems and services but also on the evaluation of information sources and their relevance to user needs.

It is also important to understand something of the barriers to understanding which may arise in the communication and understanding of complex issues. The classic model of the decision-making process involves objective analysis of a problem, identification of goals, a weighing up of all alternatives before reaching a decision, and the evaluation of the impact of that decision on the problem. This rather idealistic model implies a systematic processing of all relevant information concerning the issue and its potential solutions. However, in reality decision-makers are likely to be influenced by many factors which alter their receptivity to information. Ingram (1985) lists a number of ways in which decision-makers' levels of education, preconceptions, and so on, will influence the way in which they view a particular issue. On a practical level there is also a tendency to steer away from potentially unpopular or overly risky decisions, to stick with the familiar and to avoid information overload.

These factors are understandable in the light of the difficulties of taking risks, of trying to see things from different viewpoints, and of finding time to evaluate a wide range of information. These influences tend to narrow the information base, and while they may appear to make the process more manageable for the decision-maker, they also artificially narrow the options and alternatives for change.

At a more general public awareness level, the way people react to information about the environment will be affected by three broad factors. These tend to dominate how effectively information is used or acted upon and include: education and awareness; misconception and misunderstanding; and skills and knowledge.

EDUCATION AND AWARENESS

Levels of education about the environment will create greater interest and alertness to issues. A recent study in one public library service in the UK indicated that there were very few 'environmental' enquiries from those over 60 years old compared with the younger people, who would have had more environmental education at school (Hodges, *et al.*, 1993). While in countries like the UK environmental education tends to be integrated within the school curriculum, in many developing countries this is not yet the case, and environmental education is reliant on the work of NGOs. This is likely to affect the readiness to take up information and response to local environmental policies.

MISCONCEPTION AND MISUNDERSTANDING

Incomplete or partial understanding of issues may give rise to misconceptions or biased interpretations. This can be particularly true where there is a need to rely on simplified information and/or the media. Misconceptions of environmental risks can be common. One of the findings of a recent study of business managers in Hungary was that managers' views on pollution risk from different industrial sectors coincided with public opinion much more than with actual emissions data (Kerekes, 1994). Increasingly in the United States lay juries are asked to make judgements in environmental litigation cases where it is quite possible to have experts with differing views. In such circumstances, any public misconceptions, or partial understanding could have serious consequences one way or another.

SKILLS AND KNOWLEDGE

Lack of knowledge of the information sources which exist, and lack of skills to exploit those sources, can be a problem in developed countries as well as in the developing world. For example, health authority planners in any country need to know about health issues related to the presence of toxic chemicals in the environment. There are many databases available commercially, all differing in coverage and scope. Health officials themselves may lack the technical skills to access a range of sources. They may also lack the skills, knowledge or time to evaluate the quality of the data, the local relevance, the breadth and depth, and thus the cost/benefit ratio of subscribing to sources (Fehr, 1993).

Information providers

Many of these issues present challenges to all countries independent of whether there are sufficient technical facilities to provide access to information. These are challenges faced by all information providers, particularly when dealing with need for expert to non-expert communication. The lesson to be learned from studies of environmental risk communication is that there is a need to consider the way information is processed, packaged and disseminated as well as the way information is collected and stored. The methods chosen for disseminating information may have to vary between different sectors and for different purposes and, once again, there is a need for local understanding and local solutions.

It is important to bear in mind, too, that information users may also be information providers, operating at global, regional or local levels. This is true of both governments and NGOs. The scale of their operation is reflected in the scope of their information needs. Their ability to access information will partly determine the quality of the information they provide to others. The range and scope of such organizations varies from those dealing with a wide range of environmental issues on a global scale (e.g. UNEP or Friends of the Earth International) or on a regional scale (e.g. European Environment Agency or African NGOs Environment Network), to those concerned with much more specific issues at a local level. Smaller and more specialized groups and agencies may be more temporary in nature. Local pressure groups often arise in response to a specific local problem, and have an acute need for information of a specific nature over a relatively short period of time. The need, and the group itself, may disappear once a solution has been found or a decision has been taken.

Thus, environmental agencies and groups vary in the scope of their interest, their geographical spread and their size. They also vary greatly in their ability to access information. Large government-funded agencies, such as the EPA or the European Environmental Agency, have highly sophisticated information gathering and dissemination structures compared with small localized groups, with little funding and lack of skills and knowledge to access information. Their ability to access information will, in turn, directly affect the quality of the information they are able to provide to their own members and users.

Thus, environmental information needs may take many forms, from long-term requirements to short-term acute needs which require an immediate response. Effective information management is required at all levels to ensure that such needs are responded to effectively.

The UNESCO educational package seeks to alert decision-makers and information professionals in developing countries to these factors and also to the issues influencing the ultimate reliability and quality of environmental information.

Information issues

While it is important for information professionals to understand the complexity of providing useful information at local and global level, it is also vital for information professionals and decision-makers to understand the information management issues which currently affect the quality of environmental information. These issues relate not only to the storage and dissemination of information but also to the way in which data and information are gathered in the first place. The latter processes are of particular relevance to developing regions where resources and infrastructures may be more limited. These are issues which have to be taken into account if information provision is to be made as effective and efficient as it needs to be.

QUANTITY

Alongside the vast range of print-based sources aimed at everyone from the expert to the lay person, there are growing numbers of relevant databases which vary in scope and coverage. There is now an increasing range of directories and indexes which attempt to control access to this wealth of material. However, the sheer scale can be daunting or bewildering for non-information professionals, and the potential financial risk attached to online or CD-ROM use can be high for the novice user.

INCOMPLETE INFORMATION

Despite the growth in published knowledge about the environment, there can still be inconsistencies and gaps. For example, the scale and quality of environmental monitoring varies between regions creating discrepancies in the nature and scope of information available from different parts of the world. Poor communications infrastructures will affect both the collection of data and access to information. Another information gap is often that of locally relevant information: this is a common complaint of individuals, groups, and local authorities (for example, McCulloch *et al.*, 1995). A third example is the lack of economic information (e.g. import and export data) found in a recent evaluation of environmental chemical-related databases (Voigt *et al.*, 1993).

Incomplete information can also be a problem in the related area of population information. Many developing countries lack the resources

248   *Information sources in environmental protection*

to collect up-to-date population data on a regular basis and obtaining local data can also be difficult unless special surveys are undertaken. There is also the problem of consistency. One study found discrepancies between population data produced by the UN and equivalent data produced by a number of African countries (UNFPA, 1994) and the comparability of demographic data remains a concern because of deviations from standard definitions (Chamie, 1994).

CLASSIFICATION

Lack of standardized schemes for classifying and indexing information can create some problems when searching across a wide range of databases from different countries. For example, toxic chemical information is needed to analyse health risks or pollution risks. There are many different databases to choose from, covering bibliographic, full text, and numeric databanks. However, recent evaluations of several hundred potentially useful environmental chemical-related databases suggests that Chemical Abstract Service (CAS) Registry Number searching, which is preferred to chemical name searches, is only possible in about 35 per cent of online databases and 50 per cent of CD-ROM databases. Bibliographic databases tend not to give the CAS numbers and some countries, for example Russia, use their own numbering scheme. This means that there is no consistent way of searching across these databases for comprehensive information.

BARRIERS

Barriers to the use of existing information can come in many forms. They can be technical: for example the lack of reliable telecommunications infrastructures continues to be a major problem in African countries, although a number of projects have been set up (e.g. by the United Nations Economic Commission for Africa (UNECA), International Development Research Centre (IDRC), and UNESCO) to increase electronic communication. Language barriers can be an issue when dealing with the need to access information on a global scale. Literacy levels may also be an issue when dealing with the need to inform the public and will have an impact on the kind of dissemination methods used.

SCATTER

Useful information may be difficult to get hold of because it is either held in different geographical locations, or in different databases, or through lack of good bibliographic control. Environmental Statements (ES), for example, can be difficult to access in the UK. Unlike the USA, there is no single access point and partial lists are held by different government departments depending on the nature of the ES. Many environmental issues require a multi-disciplinary approach, yet different scientific disciplines publish in different journals and have their own indexing services. In the field of population information the major access points for official population information are well known (the UN-sponsored POPIN network, for example, provides important reference points for population on a worldwide, regional, sub-regional, national and sub-national level in many parts of the developing world). Yet population issues are often dealt with in other disciplines, such as economics, health and social sciences. These sources may not be familiar, even to population information specialists. Having the awareness of a diverse range of sources, the time to access them or the financial resources to do so can be problems for the decision-maker.

LACK OF MAINTENANCE

Maintenance of up-to-date information is critical in the environmental area where long-term monitoring of change is important. This long-term management commitment can be costly in terms of time, although made easier when the information is held in electronic format. An example of the potential loss of valuable information due to closure of manually held databases was discovered by Voigt *et al.* (1993). They found that many potentially useful environmental chemical databases from the former German Democratic Republic had been closed or would not be updated due to reorganization or shut-down of organizations in this area.

DISTORTION

The processing of environmental information for popular consumption can result in a distorted or partial picture. This can arise accidentally from the need to simplify or to appeal to an audience, or can be the result of an attempt to promote a single viewpoint. Such problems arise particularly in the media.

LEVEL

Finding the information required in a form and level of detail at which it can be useful is a particular area of concern with environmental information. The whole concept of sustainable development rests on the assumption that decisions have to be made at many different levels in society. Information is therefore needed at different levels of complexity and detail. The highly scientific and technical information which the expert will require will be quite different from that which will be acceptable and useful to the lay person. Yet both are considered important in achieving a sustainable level of development. The need to provide sound, accurate, consolidated information is increasingly being recognized.

COST

In developing countries in particular cost will be a barrier to widespread access to information. Providing a wide range of expensive computer-based sources of information is always a problem, particularly in countries where priorities may often be much more basic. In the area of environmental monitoring, the cost of buying in high quality satellite data is not cheap, despite subsidies. A recent estimate is that is costs typically US$2000–10 000 for data covering 100–200 sq km, depending on the degree of processing required, although NASA is now making older (more than two-year-old) data available at very low cost (Croze and Vandeweerd, 1992). Developments in information technology are making it increasingly economical to obtain computer software packages for the manipulation of population data, and this is having positive consequences in the developing world. Accessible technology makes it possible for population information to be used in large-scale and local applications.

MEDIA HANDLING OF INFORMATION

In many surveys of public access to environmental information the media are the most common source of information (e.g. studies by McCallum *et al.*, 1991; McCulloch *et al.*, 1995; Norman, 1991). The media treatment of environmental issues can result in a number of information problems. Journalists need to highlight key issues to bring them to the attention of the public. At the same time they often work from the assumption that the public cannot cope with complex issues and difficult terminology. This can result in oversimplification with the danger of creating a distorted picture of an issue. Limits on time and space in newspapers and television can also make these problems worse. All of this can lead to public misunderstanding or partial understanding of environmental issues, even though the journalist may be making a positive attempt to raise public awareness.

Bias or distortion of information can also arise for more negative reasons such as political agendas within the media. For example, media coverage of the Chernobyl disaster in 1987 differed significantly in the former Soviet Union and the West. The Soviet public were presented with less information and much was held back for several days while the West was more fully informed of the extent of the disaster. (Media reporting of Chernobyl has been well documented in articles such as those of Rubin, 1987; Patterson, 1989).

A third source of problems with media coverage can be the way in which journalists process environmental information over a period of time. One study of television news coverage of environmental risk indicated a tendency to take a less than balanced viewpoint for a number of very practical reasons such as lack of time to consult several sources (Greenberg *et al.*, 1989). The authors suggest that television networks should seek out the opinions of at least three different experts, rather than relying on one source as is often the case. However, this also depends on how well sources prepare their information to be attractive and understandable to the public, since there is always competition for air time.

Current research into the local newspaper press in the UK indicates that journalists often use the work of other journalists as their main sources while they develop an issue over a period of time (Campbell, 1995). The use and reuse of existing newspaper cuttings can result in any accidental bias or distortion being perpetuated

It is evident that a range of challenges exists for decision-makers and information professionals in improving the quality of environmental information. The information issues may differ in scale between developed and developing countries but they are in fact worldwide problems. Many of these issues are particularly identified in relation to environmental information needs in developing regions (Environmental Information Forum, 1992). Many of the individual issues are not unique to environmental information, but they are particularly important given the multi-disciplinary and global nature of much environmental decision- and policy-making. These factors present particular challenges for all those who are concerned with improving the quality and efficiency of that decision-making.

There are many attempts currently underway to solve the problems, such as the wider establishment of environmental networks at regional and global level, moves towards establishing reliable communications (for example, the increased use of satellite technology to avoid reliance on poor terrestrial-based telecommunications links) and attempts to create meta-databases which bring together information about the environmental data collections on a global scale, while also supplying data about the way the information has been collected and analysed (e.g. HEMIS; Keune, 1991). It will be important for developing regions to share and examine some of these developments. However, it is also obvious that it will always be important to work on a local level to identify the most appropriate means of providing the information needed to support decision-making.

The UNESCO educational package

What emerges from an analysis of the issues is the need for two kinds of partnerships:

- a partnership between policy- and decision-makers and those with the information skills to design appropriate solutions;
- partnership across transnational boundaries, particularly between developed and developing countries, in examining the options and evaluating the solutions.

These broad aims underlie the nature and approach taken in the UNESCO educational package which will be distributed to regional centres such as Departments of Library and Information Science in Eastern Europe and Africa. The package contains materials for a modular course which can be adapted to meet local needs. It has been designed to be flexible enough to be run at an awareness-raising level with decision-makers; as an indepth programme for information science students, or in continuing education of information professionals. There is also scope to consider integrating elements of the programme in courses for students in other disciplines who are the future producers and consumers of environmental information.

The overall aim is to raise awareness and understanding of issues involved in the provision, dissemination and management of information related to environmental and population issues and to develop a critical and analytical approach to environmental information provision. The package addresses issues of information needs, access and management by organizations and individuals concerned with environmental issues, looks at the kind of information systems and services that exist, and considers the potential role of librarians and information scientists.

The emphasis is on evaluating provision in relation to needs and the impact of information on policy and decision-making.

The package has been loosely based on a model developed for final year students in the School of Information and Media at The Robert Gordon University in Scotland. It has been adapted to meet the needs of a much wider audience and to provide the kind of flexibility that will enable lecturers to select the most relevant parts of the programme to suit their aims, local resources and time available.

The approach taken within the package is to encourage the development of new information solutions based on real needs, rather than simply adopting 'off-the-shelf' solutions. At present there is no evidence to suggest that models of information flow or management in industrialized nations will be relevant to developing countries. While formal information sources may be useful it cannot be assumed that simply by making them available they will be used – the complexity of localized uptake of information, dependent on socio-economic factors, on education and literacy, on political considerations, means that it would be unwise to present a narrow picture of information systems and services based on the few existing models which exist.

Rather it is important to use existing models to try to draw out comparisons, rationale, problems and successes, with a view to learning lessons from them.

There is also no real evidence to date of the actual impact of information on development (Menou, 1993). The value and impact of different forms of information may differ between situations and between countries. As far as investment in new information infrastructures and systems is concerned, there is a need for the skills and attitudes which will identify local needs and solutions. Part of this is the need to investigate the likely impact of information on local decision-making. Therefore a 'research' and 'problem-solving' approach is likely to be a more profitable investment than a traditional approach of familiarizing students with existing tools and sources *per se*. Implicit in this approach is the notion that, by becoming involved in localized analysis of needs and development of solutions, countries are likely to be less dependent on buying solutions from others on a long-term basis unless they know that external information and systems are going to be of real value. It is also more likely that by encouraging a more self-sufficient attitude towards information creation, regions will begin to develop their own potentially marketable information.

The UNESCO package also stresses that information technology (IT) alone is not the answer, although in some cases it will be part of the solution. It is likely that there will be great variation in the facilities, infrastructure and systems available. In addition, IT will continue to change at a rapid pace, and a 'training' type approach will do little to contribute to the long-term relevance of the package. Courses developed from the package should integrate IT within modules as examples of sources and solutions (and challenges) but it may be inappropriate to allow IT to be the sole focus of a module. The 'softer' focus on needs, issues, researching local solutions and analysing existing information patterns offers more potential for a sustainable educational approach.

Where possible the approach taken exemplifies the attitude which is needed in environmental management, reinforcing concepts such as sustainability, long-term planning, and networking. For example, suggested activities when the package is used with information scientists include the introduction of local decision-makers as focal speakers (for example, representatives of local business, government, communities). This approach is designed to encourage the kind of multi-disciplinary communication needed in environmental information management.

The nature of the information problems faced by decision-makers at every level, means that there is a need for information professionals to use their skills in a pro-active way. This can start at the student level and the package has a practical problem-solving orientation, allowing for small local projects to be developed, ideally between course participants and local decision-makers (e.g. businesses, local government, community groups, etc).

An initial meeting with representatives from Eastern European countries has already indicated that there is a need for such a package and that it will be adapted and integrated into a number of different teaching and learning situations. The real challenge lies in the ability not only to influence information professionals but also to persuade decision-makers of the importance of investing in the improvement of environmental information provision in developing regions.

Conclusion

This chapter has examined a range of issues associated with the need for information to support decision-makers at all levels; the importance of understanding the nature and origins of information needs; the issues which arise because of the complexity and nature of environmental information. The challenges of providing reliable information where and when it is needed are being recognized on a worldwide basis. The challenges need to be recognized by information professionals with the skills to select, evaluate, package and manage information, and by decision-makers who need to be critically aware of the way information may influence the decision-making process. UNESCO's approach to providing developing regions with a package of materials which can be adapted and targeted at local audiences is one step towards improving the quality of environmental information management.

References

Cairncross, F. (1991) *Costing the earth*. London: Business Books Ltd.

Campbell, F. (1995) An analysis of environmental information with emphasis on the dissemination, mediation, and interpretation of news. PhD thesis, The Robert Gordon University, Scotland.

Chamie, J. (1994) Population databases in development analysis. *Journal of Development Economics*, 44, 131–146.

Croze, H. and Vandeweerd, V. (1992) Monitoring and data management technology for environmental assessment. *Proceedings of the Environmental Information Forum* (Montreal, Canada, 21–24 May 1991). Ottowa: Environmental Information Forum Secretariat.

Environmental Information Forum (1992) *Proceedings of the Environmental Information Forum* (Montreal, Canada, 21–24 May 1991). Ottowa: Environmental Information Forum Secretariat.

Fehr, R. (1993) Environmental health information systems – overview of the current situation. *Toxicological and Environmental Chemistry*, 40, 179–187.

Greenberg, M.R, Sandman, P.M, Sachsman, D.B. and Salomone, K.L. (1989) Network television news coverage of environmental risks. *Environment*, 31 (2), 16–44.

Hodges, S. *et al.* (1993) Public libraries and questions about the environment. *Library Review*, 42 (4), 5–13.

Ingram, H.M. (1985) Information channels and environmental decision making. *Natural Resources Journal*, 86–105.

Kerekes, S. (1994) The environment challenge for Hungarian industry. *European Environment*, 4 (5), 19–22.

Keune, H. (1991) Harmonisation of environmental measurement. *GeoJournal*, 23 (3), 249–255.

McCallum, D.B. *et al.* (1991) Communicating about environmental risks: how the public uses and perceives information sources. *Health Education Quarterly*, 18 (3), 349–361.

McCulloch, A. *et al.* (1995) *Accessing environmental information in Scotland*. Scottish Office Central Research Unit Papers. Edinburgh: HMSO.

Menou M. (ed.) (1993) *Measuring the impact of information on development*. Ottowa: IDRC.

Neufeld, M.L. (1983) Environmental information services: origins, problems and user needs. *International Forum on Information and Documentation*, 8 (3), 29–32.

Norman, D. (1991) *The green maze*. London: ECO Environmental Trust.

Patterson, P. (1989) Reporting Chernobyl: cutting the government fog to cover the nuclear cloud. In *Bad tidings: communication and catastrophe*, M. Walters *et al.* Hillside, N.J.: Lawrence Erlbaum Associates, 131–147.

Pearce, D. (1991) New environmental policies: the recent experience of OECD countries and its relevance to the developing world. In *Environmental management in developing countries*, (ed. D. Erocal) Paris: OECD.

Pearce, D. and Freman, S. (1992) Informational requirements of policy decision-makers. *Proceedings of the Environmental Information Forum* (Montreal, Canada, 21–24 May 1991). Ottawa: Environmental Information Forum Secretariat, 56–101.

Royal Society (1994) *Population: the complex reality*. London: Royal Society.

Rubin, D. (1987) How the news media reported on TMI and Chernobyl. *Journal of Communication*, 37 (3), 42–57.

Taylor, R.S. (1986) *Value-added processes in information systems*. New Jersey: Ablex.

United Nations (1994) *UNFPA Global Population Assistance Report*. United Nations.

Voigt, C., Matthies, M. and Pepping, T. (1993) Information system for environmental chemicals comparison and evaluation of meta-databanks of data-sources. *Toxicological and Environmental Chemistry*, 40 83–92.

Weiskel, T.C. (1991) Environmental information resources and electronic research systems (ERSs): Eco-Link as an example of future tools. *Library Hi Tech*, 9 (2), 7–19.

World Commission on Environment and Development (1987) *Our common future*. Oxford: Oxford University Press.

Appendix

Selected List of Organisations and Associations

This selected list comprises the details of organisations mentioned in the main text supplemented by details of other key bodies. Those seeking further information will also find the following directories of value:

Guide to libraries and information units in government departments and other organisations. British Library. Updated regularly.

Guide to libraries in Western Europe: national, international and government libraries. British Library. Updated regularly.

Who's who in the environment: England, plus companion volumes for Scotland and Wales. The Environment Council. Updated periodically (also available in machine readable format).

Civil Service Year Book. HMSO. Annual (also available on CD-ROM as the Civil Service Directory)

World directory of environmental organizations. Earthscan. Updated periodically.

The environment encyclopaedia and directory. Europa Publications, 1994

International bodies

Food and Agriculture
Organisation
Viale delle Terme di Caracalla
00100 Rome
Italy
Tel 39-6 52251
Fax 39-6 5225-3152

Friends of the Earth Ltd.
26-28 Underwood Street
London N1 7JQ
Tel 44-171-490 1555
Fax 44-171-490 0881

Greenpeace
Cannonbury Villas
London N1 2PN
Tel 44-171-354 5100
Fax 44-171-690 0112/0014

Industry and Environment
United Nations Environment
Programme
39-43 Quai Andre Citroen
73739 Paris Cedex 15
France
Tel 331-40 588850
Fax 331-40 588874

INFOTERRA
United Nations Environment
Programme
PO Box 30552
Nairobi
Kenya
Tel 254-2 230800
Fax 254-2 226949

International Chamber of
Commerce
38 Cours Albert I
5008 Paris
France
Tel 331-49 532828
Fax 331-49 532942

International Institute for
Environment and Development
(IIED)
3 Endsleigh Street
London WC1 0DD
Tel 44-171-388 2117
Fax 44-171-388 2826

International Maritime
Organisation
4 Albert Embankment
London SE1 7SR
Tel 44-171-735 7611
Fax 44-171-587 3236

International Oceanographic
Commission (IOC)
1 rue Miallis
75732 Paris
France
Tel 331-45 683983
Fax 331-40 569316

International Programme on
Chemical Safety (IPCS)
World Health Organisation
1211 Geneva 27
Switzerland

Tel 41-22 7913589
Fax 41-22 7914848

International Register of
Potentially Toxic Chemicals
(IRPTC)
United Nations Environment
Programme
Case Postale 356
1219 Chatelaine
Geneva
Switzerland
Tel 41-22 9799111
Fax 41-22 7973460

International Tanker Owners
Pollution Federation Ltd.
Staple Hall
Stonehouse Court
87-90 Houndsditch
London EC3A 7AX
Tel 44-171-621 1255
Fax 44-171-621 1783

IUCN-The World Conservation
Union
Publications Service Unit
219c Huntingdon Road
Cambridge CB3 0DL
Tel 44-1223 277894
Fax 44-1223 277175

International Solid Wastes and
Public Cleansing Association
(ISWA)
Bremerholm
DK-1069
Copenhagen K
Denmark
Tel 45-33 914491

Organisation for Economic Co-
operation and Development
(OECD)
Environment Directorate

2 rue Andre Pascal
75775 Paris Cedex 16
France
Tel 331-45 247903
Fax 331-45 247876

United Nations Educational,
Scientific and Cultural
Organisation (UNESCO)
7 Place de Fontenoy
75352 Paris Cedex 7
France
Tel 331-45 681000
Fax 331-45 671690

World Bank
1818 H Street NW
Washington DC 20433
USA
Tel 1-202 4771234
Fax 1-202 4776391

World Health Organisation
(WHO)
Ave Appia 1221
Geneva 27
Switzerland
Tel 41-22 7912111
Fax 41-22 7910746

World Meteorological
Organisation (WMO)
Case Postale 2300
CH 1211
Geneva 2
Switzerland
Tel 41-22 7308111
Fax 41-22 7342326

World Wide Fund for Nature
(WWF)
Panda House
Weybridge Park
Godalming
Surrey GU7 1XR

Tel 44-1483 426444
Fax 44-1483 426409

Those concerned with Europe

European Centre for
Ecotoxicology and Toxicology
of Chemicals
Avenue E van Nieuwenhuyse
4, bte 6
B-1160 Brussels
Belgium
Tel 32-2 6753600
Fax 32-2 6753625

European Commission
DGXII-D2
JMO B4-082
L-2920
Luxembourg
Tel 35-2 34981240
Fax 35-2 34981248

European Commission
Information Unit
Jean Monet House
8 Storey's Gate
London SW1P 3AT
Tel 44-171-973 1992
Fax 44-171-973 1900

European Environment Agency
Kongens Nytorv 6
DK 1052
Copenhagen
Denmark
Tel 45-33 145075
Fax 45-33 146599

**Organisations and
Associations concerned with
the United Kingdom**

British Geological Survey
(BGS)
Keyworth Library

Nottingham NG12 5GG
Tel 44-115 9363205
Fax 44-115 9363200

British Library Environmental
Information Service
25 Southampton Buildings
London WC2A 1AW
Tel 44-171-412 7451
Fax 44-171-412 7954

British Trust for Conservation
Volunteers
36 St Mary's Road
Wallingford
Oxfordshire OX10 0EU
Tel 44-1491 839766
Fax 44-1491 839641

Building Research
Establishment Library
Garston
Watford WD2 7JR
Tel 44-1923 894040

Centre for Alternative
Technology (CAT)
Llwyngwern Quarry
Machynileth
Powys SY20 9AZ
Tel 44-1654 702400
Fax 44-1654 702782

Centre for Exploitation of
Science and Technology
(CEST)
5 Berners Road
London N1 0PW
Tel 44-171-354 9942
Fax 44-171-354 4301

Centre for Social and
Economic Research on the
Global Environment
University College

Gower Street
London WC1E 6BT
Tel 44-171-387 7050

Chartered Institution of Water
and Environmental
Management
15 John Street
London WC1N 2EB
Tel 44-171-831 3110
Fax 44-171-405 4967

Civil Aviation Authority
(CAA)
Library and Information
Centre
Aviation House
Gatwick Airport South
West Sussex RH6 0YR
Tel 44-1293 573725
Fax 44-1293 573999

Coal Authority
200 Lichfield Lane
Mansfield
Nottinghamshire NG22 8ND
Tel 44-1623 427162

Construction Industry Research
and Information Association
(CIRIA)
6 Storey's Gate
London SW1 3AU
Tel 44-171-222 8891
Fax 44-171-222 1708

Council for Environmental
Education (CEE)
University of Reading
London Road
Reading
Berkshire RG 5AQ
Tel 44-1734 756061
Fax 44-1734 756264

Countryside Council for Wales
– Cyngor Cefn Gwlad Cymru
Plas Penrhos
Ford Penrhos
Bangor
Gwynedd
Tel 44-1248 370444
Fax 44-1248 355782

Earthrights: The
Environmental Law and
Resource Centre
Canalside House
383 Ladbroke Grove
London W10 5AA
Tel 44-181-960 8369

Earthscan Publications Ltd
120 Pentonville Road
London N1 9JN
Tel 44-171-278 0433

ECO Environmental
Information Trust
10-12 Picton Street
Montpelier
Bristol BS6 5QA
Tel 44-117-942 0162
Fax 44-117-942 0164

English Nature (formerly
Nature Conservancy Council
for England)
Northminster House
Peterborough PE1 1UA
Tel 44-1733 340345
Fax 44-1733 688345

Environment, Department of
the Library Services
2 Marsham Street
London SW1P 3EB
Tel 44-171-276 4401
Fax 44-171-276 5662
Publications Despatch Centre

Blackhorse Road
London SE99 6TT
Publications Sales and
Distribution Unit
Room 1, Spur 2
Block 3
Government Buildings
Lime Grove
Eastcote HA4 8SE

Environment Agency (from
April 1996)
Rivers House
Waterside Drive
AZTEC West
Almondsbury
Bristol
BS12 4UD
Tel 44-1454 624400
Fax 44-1454 624409

Environment Council
21 Elizabeth Street
London SW1W 9RP
Tel 44-171-824 8411
Fax 44-171-730 9941

Environmental Services
Association (formerly National
Association of Waste Disposal
Contractors)
Mountbatten House
6-20 Elizabeth Street
London SW1 9RB
Tel 44-171-824 8882
Fax 44-171-824 8753

Freshwater Biological
Association
The Ferry House
Far Sawney
Ambleside
Cumbria LA22 0LP
Tel 44-15394 42468
Fax 44-15394 46914

Health and Safety Executive
Information Centre
Broad Lane
Sheffield S3 7HQ
Tel 44-114 2892345
Fax 44-114 2892333

Her Majesty's Stationery Office
(HMSO)
St Crispins
Duke Street
Norwich NR
Tel 44-1603 622211
Fax 44-1603 695582

Institute of Terrestrial Ecology
Monkswood
Abbots Ripton
Huntingdon
Cambridgeshire PE17 2LS
Tel 44-1487 77381
Fax 44-1487 77367

Intermediate Technology
Myson House
Railway Terrace
Rugby
Warwickshire CV21 3HT
Tel 44-1788 560631
Fax 44-1788 540270

International Centre for
Conservation Education
Greenfield House
Guiting Power
Cheltenham
Gloucestershire GL54 5TZ
Tel 44-1451 850777
Fax 44-1451 850705

Learning Through Landscapes
Third Floor
Southside Offices
The Law Courts
Winchester

Hampshire SO23 9DL
Tel 44-1962 846258
Fax 44-1962 869099

London Research Centre
Parliament House
81 Black Prince Road
London SE1 7SZ
Tel 44-171-627 9660
Fax 44-171-627 9674

Ministry of Agriculture,
Fisheries and Food
Whitehall Place Library
3 Whitehall Place
London SW1A 2HA
Tel 44-171-270 8961
Fax 44-171-270 8719

National Environmental
Technology Centre (NETCEN)
Culham
Abingdon
Oxfordshire OX14 3DB
Tel 44-1235 521840
Fax 44-1235 463001

National Federation of City
Farms
The Green House
Hereford Street
Bedminster
Bristol BS3 4NA
Tel 44-117 9231800
Fax 44-117 9231900

National Physical Laboratory
(NPL)
Queens Road
Teddington
Middlesex TW11 0LW
Tel 44-181-943 6880
Fax 44-181-943 6458

National Society for Clean Air
and Environmental Protection
(NSCA)
136 North Street
Brighton
West Sussex BN1 1RG
Tel 44-1273 326313
Fax 44-1273 735802

Natural Environment Research
Council (NERC)
Polaris House
North Star Avenue
Swindon
Wiltshire SN2 1EU
Tel 44-1793 411500
Fax 44-1793 411501

Office for National Statistics
(formerly Central Statistical
Office) Library
Government Buildings
Cardiff Road
Newport
Gwent NP9 1XG
Tel 44-1633 812973
Fax 44-1633 812599

Plymouth Marine Laboratory
(formerly Marine Biological
Association of the UK)
Marine Pollution Information
Centre
Citadel Hill
Plymouth
Devon PL1 2PB
Tel 44-1752 222772
Fax 44-1752 226865

Robens Institute of Industrial
and Environmental Health and
Safety
University of Surrey
Guildford

Surrey GU2 5XH
Tel 44-1483 300800
Fax 44-1482 300803

Royal Commission on
Environmental Pollution
(RCEP)
Church House
Great Smith Street
London SW1 3B2
Tel 44-171-276 2080/2189
Fax 44-171-276 2098

Tidy Britain Group
Head Office
The Pier
Wigan
WN3 4GX
Tel 44-1942 824620
Fax 44-1962 824778

Trade and Industry,
Department of
Environment and Energy
Technologies (EET)
1 Victoria Street
London SW1 0ET
Tel 44-171-215 2816
Fax 44-171-215 2832
Advisory Committee on
Business and the Environment
151 Buckingham Palace Road
London SW1W 3EB
Tel 44-171-215 1016
Environment Help Line
Tel 0800 585794

Transport Research Laboratory
Crowthorne
Berkshire RG11 6AU
Tel 44-1344 773131
Fax 44-1344 770356
UK Centre for Economic and

UK Centre for Economic and
Environmental Development
(UK-CEED)
Suite E
3 King's Parade
Cambridge CB2 1SJ
Tel 44-1223 67799
Fax 44-1223 67794

United Kingdom
Meteorological Office (UKMO)
London Road
Bracknell
Berkshire RG12 2SZ
Tel 44-1344 856655
Fax 44-1344 854924

WARMER Campaign
83 Mount Ephraim
Tunbridge Wells
Kent TN4 8BS
Tel 44-1892 24626

Waste Management
Information Bureau (WMIB)
National Environmental
Technology Centre
AEA Technology
F6, Culham
Abingdon
Oxfordshire OX14 3DB
Tel 44-1235 463162
Fax 44-1235 463004

Waste Watch
68 Grafton Way
London W1P 5LE
Tel 44-171-383 3320

Water Research Centre
WRc Medmenham
PO Box 16
Henley Road
Medmenham
Marlow
Buckinghamshire SL7 2HD

Tel 44-1491 571531
Fax 44-1491 579094

Wildlife Trusts Partnerships
(also known as the Royal
Society for Nature
Conservation)
The Green
Witham Park
Waterside South
Lincoln LN5 7JR
Tel 44-1522 544400
Fax 44-1522 511616

**Organisations based in the
United States of America**

American Geophysical Union
2000 Florida Avenue SW
Washington DC 20009
Tel 1-202 462 6900
Fax 1-202 328 0566

American Meteorological
Society (AMS)
45 Beacon Street
Boston MA 02108
Tel 1-617 227 2425
Fax 1-617 742 8718

Association of Environmental
and Resources Economists
1616 P Street NW
Washington DC 20036
Tel 1-202 328 5077
Fax 1-202 939 3460

Environmental Protection
Agency (USEPA)
EPA Library
Office of Administration and
Resources Management
401 M Street 3404
Washington DC 20460
Tel 1-202 260 2080
Fax 1-202 260 6257

National Library of Medicine
8600 Rockville Pike
Bethesda
Maryland 20892
Tel 1-301 496 2447
Fax 1-301 402 0254

National Oceanic and
Atmospheric Administration
(NOAA)
14th Street and Constitution
Avenue NW
Washington DC 20036-1904
Tel 1-202 482 3436
Fax 1-202 482 6203

National Technical Information
Service
US Department of Commerce
Springfield

Virginia 22161
Tel 1-703 487 4650
Fax 1-703 321 8547

United States Geological
Survey (USGS)
Information Service
Box 25286
Denver Federal Center
Denver
Colorado 80225
Tel 1-303 202 4700
Fax 1-303 202 4693

World Watch Institute
1776 Massachusetts Avenue
NW
Washington DC 20036-1904
Tel 1-202 452 1999
Fax 1-202 296 7365

Index

Environmental Protection Agency, 175, 238
Environmental Protection Agency –
  publications, 12, 58
*Environmental protection and water
  statistics. Digest of*, 6, 133
Environmental protection. Costs of, 241
*Environmental responsibility: an agenda
  for higher and further education
  (Toyne report)*, 217-218
*Environmental science and engineering.
  Encyclopaedia of*, 174
Environmental Services Association, 116,
  192
*Environmental technology. ENTEC
  directory of*, 138
*Environmental toxicology and chemistry
  (journal)*, 60
*Environmental toxicology: impacts of
  chemicals upon ecological systems.
  Introduction to*, 56
Environmentally Sensitive Areas, 152
ESA-IRS, file 13, 149
Ethical Investment Research and
  Information Service, 164
Europe environment (journal), 193
European Chemical Industry Ecology and
  Toxicology Centre – publications, 45
European Communities Chemistry Council,
  173
European Community – Directorate for
  Energy, 142
European Environment Agency, 142, 238
European Federation of Waste Management
  (FEAD), 116
European Union, 11
European Water Archive, 85
Europe's environment, 142
Eurostat – publications, 115, 142
EXICHEM, 11
Extension Toxicology Network, 63
Exxon Valdez oil spill, 59

FEAD *see* European Federation of Waste
  Management
Farm chemicals handbook, 58
Federal register (database), 103
Fifth Environmental action programme,
  (EC), 107
*Fishing for information: a listing of
  network and online resources in
  aquaculture and aquatic science*, 66
Freedom of information, 229
Freedom of Information. Campaign for, 207
Freshwater Biological Association current
  awareness service, 83

Friends of the Earth, 24, 26, 238
Friends of the Earth – and education, 215
Friends of the Earth – publications, 26-28
*From ideas to action: business and
  sustainable development*, 163
*Fundamental and applied toxicology
  (journal)*, 61

GDF *see* Global Development Facility
GEMS *see* Global Environment Monitoring
  System
GENIE *see* Global Environmental
  Information Exchange
GERO *see* Global Environmental Research
  Office
GESAMP *see* Joint Group of Experts on the
  Scientific Aspects of Marine Pollution
Gardens, 153
Garner's environmental law, (1976), 93,
  190
Gas works, 175
GEOARCHIVE, 137
GEOBASE, 138
Geological Society of London, 136
Geological Survey *see* British Geological
  Survey
Geophysical Research. Journal of, 99
GEOREF, 138
Geothermal energy, 140
German Chemical Society – publications,
  45
Global change, 97
Global Development Facility, 161
Global Environment Monitoring System, 68
*Global Environment Research
  programmes and contact points.
  National directory of the UK*, 220
*Global environmental change report
  (journal)*, 103
Global Environmental Information
  Exchange, 220-221
Global Environmental Research Office, 220
*Global environmental research,
  International directory of*, 220
Global warming *see* global change.
Global Watering Monitoring Project, 69
Globe. The (journal), 220
Government publications – UK, 3, 99, 114,
  185-186
Government publications – UK
  departmental publications, 4-5
*Green reporting: accountancy and the
  challenge of the nineties*, 165
Green teacher (journal), 215
Grey literature, 19, 77, 134